T0283225

PRAISE FOR *EXVANGELICAL AND BEYOND*

"An insightful exploration of faith, identity, and activism in a nation at the crossroads of religious fervor and social change. *Exvangelical and Beyond* weaves Chastain's personal faith journey with an illuminating examination of evangelical Christianity's extremist trajectory in the US and abroad. At once alarming and hopeful, this is a book that every American must read, regardless of religious affiliation."

—**Reza Aslan**, *New York Times* **bestselling author of** *Zealot*

"Blake Chastain created the #Exvangelical hashtag. In doing so, he created a category in which millions of people now gather, commiserate, heal, and learn. By giving us *Exvangelical and Beyond*, Chastain continues this legacy in a work that is attentive to the beauties and joys of joining with those who have also left, while remaining aware of the dangers such fragile forms of community hold. He shows the causes, the effects, the triumphs, and the setbacks of a decade of learning what it means to walk together as outcasts, and how those 'lost in the wilderness' have provided a potent counter to the most powerful religious bloc in the country. This is more than either a personal history or a scathing polemic. It's a blueprint of a movement—and a call for change."

—**Bradley Onishi**, **author of** *Preparing for War*

"In this insightful book, Blake Chastain takes readers on a journey through and beyond evangelical religion as he tries to understand why many people like himself have left the church. Part history and part disputation, he suggests that American evangelicalism always held the seeds of its own destruction. As a religious movement, it is, somewhat ironically, unredeemable. His is a valuable study of the decline of evangelicalism, especially in the context of the social media rebellion among young adults that hastened its demise."

—**Diana Butler Bass**, **author of** *Christianity After Religion* **and**
Freeing Jesus

"Chastain has been the thoughtful commentator and mindful observer I have turned to in my often desperate searches online for a counternarrative to American evangelical religiosity that . . . told me my Black, queer, and trans body had no place in the body of Christ. . . . Blake stands out as a trustworthy narrator of these times. . . . While the media machine designed to tell one story of what it means to be seeking Jesus in America continues to . . . get the story wrong, Blake continues to give real-time reports of revolutionary thought at a critical juncture in the church and faith life of this republic. . . . This book, this thinker, and this movement's story are worth your time, attention, and heart."

—lenny duncan, author of *Dear Church* and *Dear Revolutionaries*

"Blake Chastain offers an impassioned portrait of his experience as a key voice in the 'exvangelical' movement. This is a powerful survey and analysis of conservative evangelicalism, its faith, politics, history, and dangers. A vital read for this political moment."

—Katherine Stewart, author of *The Power Worshippers*

"In Blake Chastain's impressive *Exvangelical and Beyond*, we finally have, in a well-crafted and compelling single narrative, both a concise history of American evangelicalism and a whip-smart firsthand accounting of the exvangelical movement written from an exvangelical point of view. Chastain's careful attention to context and his well-informed discussion of the key roles played by media and technology in shaping both evangelicalism and the exvangelical counterpublic really make the effort shine. If you only read one book about exvangelicals, make it this one."

—Chrissy Stroop, coeditor of *Empty the Pews*

"In *Exvangelical and Beyond*, Blake Chastain does three really important things. He offers a bracing (counter)history of evangelicalism as a theologically and ethically flexible US cultural movement that has been far more about whiteness, capitalism, and power than about Christian theology. He documents the numerous failed efforts to reform evangelicalism from within—and from within the terms of its purported religious values. And he documents the birth of the exvangelical movement—which he himself helped to pioneer—treating it as a 'counterpublic' that has explicitly repudiated evangelicalism and is now attempting to chart various new paths forward, in online spaces and otherwise. This book is an essential addition to the current conversation about not just evangelicalism but American religion, politics, and culture today."

—David P. Gushee, Distinguished University Professor of
Christian Ethics, Mercer University

EXVANGELICAL
AND
BEYOND

EXVANGELICAL AND BEYOND

HOW AMERICAN CHRISTIANITY WENT RADICAL AND THE MOVEMENT THAT'S FIGHTING BACK

BLAKE CHASTAIN

A TarcherPerigee Book

an imprint of Penguin Random House LLC
penguinrandomhouse.com

Copyright © 2024 by Blake Chastain

Scripture quotations are from New Revised Standard Version Bible, copyright © 1989 National Council of the Churches of Christ in the United States of America. Used by permission. All rights reserved worldwide.

Penguin Random House supports copyright. Copyright fuels creativity, encourages diverse voices, promotes free speech, and creates a vibrant culture. Thank you for buying an authorized edition of this book and for complying with copyright laws by not reproducing, scanning, or distributing any part of it in any form without permission. You are supporting writers and allowing Penguin Random House to continue to publish books for every reader. Please note that no part of this book may be used or reproduced in any manner for the purpose of training artificial intelligence technologies or systems.

TarcherPerigee with tp colophon is a registered trademark of Penguin Random House LLC.

Most TarcherPerigee books are available at special quantity discounts for bulk purchase for sales promotions, premiums, fundraising, and educational needs. Special books or book excerpts also can be created to fit specific needs. For details, write: SpecialMarkets@penguinrandomhouse.com.

Library of Congress Cataloging-in-Publication Data
Names: Chastain, Blake, author.
Title: Exvangelical and beyond: how American Christianity went radical and the movement that's fighting back / Blake Chastain.
Description: New York: TarcherPerigee, [2024]
Includes bibliographical references and index.
Identifiers: LCCN 2024003372 (print) | LCCN 2024003373 (ebook) |
ISBN 9780593717073 (hardcover) | ISBN 9780593717080 (epub)
Subjects: LCSH: Christian conservatism—United States—History—21st century. |
Evangelicalism—United States—History—21st century. |
Right and left (Political science)—United States—History—21st century. |
Opposition (Political science)—United States—History—21st century.
Classification: LCC BR115.C66 C47 2024 (print) | LCC BR115.C66 (ebook) |
DDC 320.5/5—dc23/eng/20240604
LC record available at https://lccn.loc.gov/2024003372
LC ebook record available at https://lccn.loc.gov/2024003373

Printed in the United States of America
1st Printing

Book design by Angie Boutin

While the author has made every effort to provide accurate telephone numbers, internet addresses, and other contact information at the time of publication, neither the publisher nor the author assumes any responsibility for errors, or for changes that occur after publication. Further, the publisher does not have any control over and does not assume any responsibility for author or third-party websites or their content.

To my family, and to every person whose path to wholeness led them away from where they started

The business man puts up the money to build the
church, he puts up the money to keep it going; and the
first rule of a business man is that when he puts up the
money for a thing he "runs" that thing. Of course he sees
that it spreads his own views of life, it helps to maintain
his tradition.

—UPTON SINCLAIR, *THE PROFITS OF RELIGION*

We do not worship God.
We perceive and attend God.
We learn from God.
With forethought and work,
We shape God.

—OCTAVIA BUTLER, *PARABLE OF THE SOWER*

CONTENTS

EXVANGELICAL
AND
BEYOND

INTRODUCTION

Whether you grew up a devout evangelical, have never been to church a day in your life, or fall somewhere on the spectrum in between, if you live in the United States, evangelicalism has affected you. It is woven into our culture, our politics, our media, our metaphors—our everyday lives. And now more than ever, it is not merely a faith of origin but also a force for harm, with the most powerful factions of white evangelicalism seeking to impose upon the country a Christian nationalist belief system that worships whiteness, capitalism, and power above all else. How did we get here, and how do we resist? These pages will try to provide some answers.

Like so many people, I was raised evangelical, but after years of struggling with the faith's pernicious theology and practices, I could no longer keep calling myself an evangelical. In 2016, I came up with the term "exvangelical," a contraction of "ex-evangelical," as both a title for my podcast and a hashtag. The term was and is meant to encompass a wide variety of experiences. People who have left conservative evangelicalism for more progressive forms of Christianity, other forms of faith, agnosticism, atheism, or any other way of life are included under the exvangelical umbrella. If you fit under that umbrella, this book is for you. If you don't fit under that umbrella but want to understand the forces that have hijacked our national politics and derailed our democracy, this book is for you too.

When I first began using the word "exvangelical," I never imagined the ways it would spread. By now, it has far exceeded the bounds of my humble podcast and suffused the broader cultural lexicon. It has appeared in publications from *The New York Times* to *Christianity Today*. It has a Wikipedia entry. At the time of this writing, the hashtag has 1.7 billion impressions on Tik-Tok, a platform I hardly ever post to. I think the term has become so widespread because it's a useful part of crucial conversations about faith, politics, and culture, but its wide reach also means it has accumulated cruft and all manner of unintended associations. I can no longer control the various ways that people interpret "exvangelical," if I ever could, but I can tell you how I understand it and why I think it helps us have much-needed discussions.

First, "exvangelical" denotes someone who was *formerly* evangelical but is not evangelical at present. By definition, this person has a familiarity with evangelical teaching and evangelical culture, which makes their repudiation of evangelicalism more authoritative. They're not mere naysayers; they know what they're talking about.

Second, the term acknowledges personal autonomy because, although it does define past experience, it does not define a singular present theological perspective. Exvangelicals can be atheists, agnostics, or Christians in more progressive denomi-

nations. They can be mystics or Episcopalians, anything in between or nothing at all. In that sense, the word makes space for
people to explore their own convictions and acknowledges that
beliefs change over time. It doesn't try to dictate what people
who leave evangelicalism *should* believe.

Third, the term "exvangelical" does not require you to
commit to it. You can use it as you see fit, or not. If you fully
transition to another belief system that you affirm, then by all
means, you can discard the term once it no longer suits you.
Some people find value in delineating the various terms they
use to understand and express themselves while others find the
use of labels pedantic and exhausting. I embrace the reality that
people will use the subtleties of language, including "exvangelical," to express themselves as they desire.

Finally, and above all else, the very existence of a term with
a self-evident meaning helps exvangelicals know they aren't
alone. Some people will personally identify with it while others
won't, but anyone deconstructing their faith who hears "exvangelical" will at the very least know that there are enough other
people like them out there that someone had to invent a word
for it. I hope this book will continue that project.

But before I explain further what this book is, I want to explain what it isn't. Though it contains some details from my life,
it is not a memoir or an exploration of my personal spiritual
beliefs. Given the nature of the term "exvangelical," people are
often curious to know if I still identify as Christian, but as I've
written elsewhere, I consider "Are you still a Christian?" to be
the least interesting of all the questions people ask those who
leave a high-demand religion like white evangelicalism. If you'll
be distracted by speculating, I can tell you that, at the time of
this writing, I have no particular compulsion to declare Jesus

Christ (or anyone) as Lord; I also do not have a particular desire to declare God dead or nonexistent. To me, a statement of non-belief feels as binding as a statement of belief. If you must put me in a theological box, I find resonance with Paul Tillich's vision of God as the "ground of being" but have very little faith and even less evidence that God can or does work through miraculous means. If this admission makes you sad, it has at times made me sad too. But I would rather be honest with you and with myself.

That being said, my Christian past will always play a role in shaping my view and experience of the world, and I consider my present agnosticism to be an open invitation to potential future faiths. As Wendell Berry once wrote, "There are an enormous number of people—and I am one of them—whose native religion, for better or worse, is Christianity. We were born to it; we began to learn about it before we became conscious; it is, whatever we think of it, an intimate belonging of our being; it informs our consciousness, our language, and our dreams."[1] And like Berry—for better or worse—I can never deny that.

However, while I remain open to broader questions of philosophy, theology, and divinity, I am not bothered if you don't. This book is not meant to advocate for any particular belief system, and I have no agenda to convert you to my view of the world. Over the course of my life, I've had many faith and identity shifts, and while leaving evangelicalism was the largest, it was not the last. I'll keep changing throughout my life, for better or worse, and I imagine you will too. Your spirituality is your own to do with and cultivate with whatever tools edify you and do not harm others, with or without God. The only "spiritual advice" I'd give is to try to understand the past even as you do not let it dictate your present or future and live your life in widening circles that liberate you and others. Whether this advice has resonance with your understanding of Christianity or any other form of belief, that's up to you to affirm or deny.

Additionally, this book does not seek to reform the white evangelical church or convince evangelicals to listen to reason. As I'll show, many people have tried to achieve these goals for many decades (including, in the past, me), and none have succeeded, for reasons that I'll explore in depth. If some open-minded evangelical is inspired to read these words, I welcome them to do so, but that's not who I'm writing for. My primary audience is the people who have been brave enough to leave the church, no matter where they are on their journey, as well as anyone else who wants to understand evangelicalism's outsize role in the current events of the United States.

So, then, what *does* this book aim to do? First, I want to explain, for insiders and outsiders alike, how the evangelical church went radical. My goal is not to comprehensively document every little detail of the evangelical movement—that would be a different book (in fact, several books). Rather, I use history in the same way journalist Nikole Hannah-Jones describes it: "History revealed the building blocks of the world I now inhabited, explaining how communities, institutions, relationships came to be. . . . It provided the key to decode all that I saw around me."[2] With that in mind, my goal is to illustrate how the modern evangelical movement's inextricability from power, capitalism, and whiteness is the result of close to two hundred years of history. I will highlight some of the events and developments that brought us to the crisis point we've reached today in which evangelicalism functions less as a religious movement than as a Christian nationalist one with a dangerous amount of control over American politics.

The episodes of history I draw from are not limited to a singular denomination, because contemporary American evangelicalism crosses and disregards denominational lines, and has for decades. As I hope to illustrate, the commonalities that bind evangelicalism together are not confined to theological beliefs. Evangelicalism can also be understood as a public, an imagined community, a market, and a voting bloc. And while many of these points of conflict and debate may be simplified to a conservative-versus-liberal divide in which the conservative side routinely prevails, that does not mean that liberal groups cannot be criticized for being complicit in systemic issues; misogyny, racism, queerphobia, and other prejudices can flourish in liberal spaces too. However, by highlighting points of attempted reform that have already occurred within the history of American evangelicalism and were rebuffed, I hope to demonstrate that the claim from today's evangelical apologists that "the church just needs reform" is false. People have tried. For a long time. And their reasons for leaving are justified.

This exploration of history may be deeply emotional for some readers who are relatively new to questioning evangelicalism's version of Christianity. Within these pages, I don't shy away from stating plainly when white evangelicalism has played major (and, at times, leading) roles in sustaining racism and patriarchy, utilizing both capitalist forces and the power of the state to influence American social and civic life. This is not always easy to accept when you've been taught that evangelical Christianity is the truest expression of Christian faith, with the best interests of believers and the country in mind. However, taking an honest look at the historical record and speaking plainly about it is one of the most meaningful ways of countering the narratives that seek to recast American history as a religious war where Christian nationalists must be the victors lest the nation fall to ruin. We each must own this emotional work, and if one critique or another shocks or upsets you, that is also information worth interrogating. Evangelicalism may be a place where your spiritual practices and beliefs were cultivated, and that cannot be taken from anyone; at the same time, evangelicalism is also the source of many injustices, which is why so many people are now leaving.

This brings me to my second aim: I want to explain the *ex-*vangelical movement that isn't content to leave quietly and instead chooses to speak back to and oppose the church. How did it arise, and how did it spread? What are its goals, and how does it differ from the progressive activist movements within the church that preceded it? How has the internet helped and hindered this largely online phenomenon? Does it stand a chance against the money and power of the evangelical church? As the originator of the #Exvangelical hashtag and as someone who has interviewed exvangelicals of every stripe on my podcast, I hope to offer some unique insight into these questions.

Lastly, to the extent that it's possible, I want to consider the future. As I write these words, the 2024 US presidential election is approaching. The future is uncertain, but Christian nationalism will continue to play a large role in shaping it. How can we change the ways we talk and think about the evangelical church, as well as its proponents and opponents, in a manner that serves us as individuals and a society? How can we practice democratic, humanist values in a country struggling to resist theocracy?

My work in this arena has largely existed in the digital realm up to this point, but now I intend to take full advantage of the medium of the book, for, as digital humanities scholar Andrew

Piper writes, "Books are totems against ceaseless activity, tools for securing the somatic calm that is the beginning of all careful but also visionary thought."[3] I believe that with a deeper understanding of our country's past and present religious history we can start to hold accountable those who have wielded faith like a cudgel and offer comfort and understanding to those who have been harmed by the powerful and mighty.

1

WHAT IS EVANGELICALISM?

TOWARD A WORKING DEFINITION

With the rise of Trumpism, the American evangelical movement has more power and influence than ever. At the same time, according to numbers from the most recent Pew survey, more people are leaving the church than ever.[1] For millions of Americans, evangelicalism is—or was—a way of life, influencing every aspect of their existence from the sacred to the mundane. Evangelicalism provides a ready-made worldview complete with stances on ethics, the afterlife, politics, and more, in addition to an entire custom consumer marketplace offering "Christian" alternatives for movies, music, books, and schools. Yet for millions of other Americans who exist outside of the evangelical realm, it's a strange, inscrutable subculture about which they might know little and understand even less, except that it's constantly in the news for trying to outlaw reproductive rights and LGBTQ+ rights.

How did we reach a point where a minority group of Christians (albeit a quite large minority) exerts such tremendous sway over our politics and culture? Why and how are people defecting from this movement and becoming "exvangelical"? And where do we go from here?

To start to grapple with these issues, we first need to understand what evangelicalism is. This is a trickier task than it might seem—deciding who "counts" as an evangelical and what the defining features of evangelicalism even *are* is a favorite pastime within evangelical circles. In the most literal sense, "evangelical" simply means "having to do with the gospel"; the English word *gospel* comes from an Old English translation of the Greek term *euangelion*, meaning "good news." But in the practical sense, it means something much more than that. Use of the word "evangelical" dates back to the Protestant Reformation, but over the centuries, its meaning has shifted and shifted again.[2] Even in the present day, "evangelical" is a nebulous term. Scholars disagree on how to classify it, and believers use it however they see fit. Is it a theological perspective, a religious affiliation, a consumer culture, or a political voting bloc? The answer to all these questions is "Yes."

We might say that, at its most basic, evangelicalism is a type of Protestant Christianity. In the United States, it's usually defined in opposition to Catholicism and "mainline Protestantism." What that means is that most American Christians can be categorized as either Catholic or Protestant, and the Protestants can be further subdivided into mainline Protestant, evangelical Protestant, and "historically black" Protestant.* (Yes, the fact

---

* Of course, there are also plenty of American Christians in other denominations like the Church of Jesus Christ of Latter-day Saints (aka Mormonism) or the Eastern Orthodox Church. Further, charismatic traditions like Pentecostalism elude

that "historically black" is its own category is extremely significant, a fact that I'll explore in depth throughout this book.) But unlike, say, "Catholic" or "Presbyterian," the word "evangelical" does not denote a specific denomination, and there is no centralized authority to adjudicate who is and who isn't evangelical. If you identify as evangelical, you likely also identify as a specific denomination like Baptist or Methodist . . . or you might eschew those categories altogether and identify as "nondenominational." If you're in certain denominations, like Baptist, you'd probably be classified as evangelical . . . but then again, you might not.

This is why, for evangelicals and nonevangelicals alike, the definition of "evangelical" is often akin to Supreme Court Justice Potter Stewart's definition of pornography: "I know it when I see it." To that end, in order to let readers "see it," although this book is not a memoir, I want to start by telling you about a pretty typical American evangelical upbringing: mine.

IF EVANGELICALISM IS A SLIDING scale, I grew up somewhere in the middle. I went to church every week, and while my parents grew up in small, independently run churches in rural Indiana, I grew up attending a United Methodist church in slightly less-rural Indiana. Depending on who you ask, the UM church is more mainline than evangelical, but like any denomination, it takes on the local flavor of its region. The UM church in the majority-white small town in central Indiana where I grew up was more conservative than what you would find at a downtown

---

simple definitions and are sometimes counted alongside evangelicals and at other times treated as a distinct tradition.

Chicago UM church—with the significant caveat that, regardless of geography, the denomination ordains women as clergy. The first pastors I remember were women, and I would not learn until much later just how much that differentiated my faith experience from those who grew up in more conservative denominations (even though I did regularly visit my grandparents' churches, where women were not allowed to preach).

But much of the rest of my church life was in keeping with the more conservative experiences I would have later. While my parents did not tightly control my media access, things still defaulted to a sort of conservative, "family-friendly" milieu. *The Simpsons* was bad because Bart mouthed off—that sort of thing. I remember "committing" to not having sex before marriage before I even really knew what sex *was*.

I didn't know it then, but this was the evangelical bubble at work.

I should note that, as a child, I didn't dislike my experience in church. I was a naturally religious kid and had both fond and formative experiences through church activities. The example my parents and others set has always stayed with me. I was curious about God and loved the Bible stories I learned. I read through the *My First Bible Storybook* I received in a single day. I wanted to be a good kid, and by and large, I was.

I could also be a sickly kid. When I was two, my parents began to notice that I would sometimes slur my words as I spoke, and I was soon diagnosed with focal epilepsy—a form of epilepsy that only affects one area or region of the body. I spent the rest of my childhood undergoing varying degrees of medical intervention. In the 1980s and '90s, medical treatment of seizures was not what it is today. It relied heavily on barbiturates, and by my middle school years, I was on a drug cocktail of sixteen pills a day. I lost my coordination and balance and would see double—not a great condition to have while playing outfield in Little League baseball. If my stomach wasn't just right before I went to bed, I would be up much of the night vomiting. I also gained a lot of weight. Since I couldn't play sports anymore, I became more bookish, and with that bookishness came a renewed sense of religiosity and meaning-making. I understood my epilepsy as a "thorn in the flesh" given to me, just as one was given to the Apostle Paul so that he might not boast (2 Corinthians 12:1–10; Ephesians 2:8–10). Evangelicalism gave me the language for a sort of self-talk in which I convinced myself that my condition was meant to "keep me weak" and thus make me more dependent on God.

When I was fourteen, my family moved to the Chicago suburbs and found ourselves at another United Methodist church down the road from our house. My sophomore year, I joined the youth group there. That small decision had a big impact on the trajectory of my life.

Youth groups are powerful things. They offer ready-made friend groups and a sense of acceptance that teenagers crave. The teen years are all about exploring identity, and youth pastors around the nation are ready and willing to help you "explore your identity in Christ" even before your very first sense of self has had a chance to settle. It was in this environment that I got the brilliant idea to start signing my name with a Bible verse, which seemed like a very mature thing for a fifteen-year-old to do at the time. The verse was John 3:30: "He must increase, but I must decrease." In the space of a few weeks, putting that signature on my job applications lost me the chance at a job at

Barnes & Noble—but got me a job at Lemstone Books, a regional Christian bookstore chain in the Midwest that was big at the time, if not as well-known as LifeWay or Family Christian.

From there, I would walk, willfully, further into the bubble. It embraced me, and I embraced it. Even as it hurt me. My entire teenage life was built up in that environment. In my family, we were church people—my father attended Promise Keepers events, my mom led the staff-parish relations committee—but I was a Jesus Freak.

Much of the money I earned from my job was funneled right back into purchasing books and music from the store—I couldn't resist the 35 percent employee discount. I bought nearly every book by Philip Yancey; a six-book box set of C. S. Lewis classics; *Every Prophecy of the Bible* by John F. Walvoord, with its ominous cover featuring a military helicopter and camel in silhouette; at least eight different Bibles; apologetics books like Josh McDowell's *More Than a Carpenter;* devotionals like *My Utmost for His Highest;* and so much Christian rock music. Switchfoot was my favorite band, followed by Third Day, the Insyderz, Sonicflood, and the Normals.

My friends were all within this circle; any who weren't, I invited in. I didn't know any other way. Our youth group attended worship conferences at Moody Bible Institute; when one girl sprained her ankle during a Sonicflood concert, the lead singer came over and prayed for her. It was at youth group that I met both of the girlfriends I had before I met my wife (whom I met at a Christian college, mind you). It was all-encompassing. It was my world.

By the ripe old age of seventeen, I had decided to become a pastor. I applied to a "Christ-centered" college called Indiana

Wesleyan University, got in, and prepared to walk even further into the bubble.

AT THIS POINT, IF YOU were raised evangelical, you're probably nodding along in recognition. You likely had a lot of the same experiences (and if you're really honest with yourself, you might even be a little jealous of Jeff Deyo's attempts at faith-healing my friend's ankle). If you weren't raised evangelical, you might still feel a sense of recognition: "Ah, you were one of *those* kids."

In the '90s and '00s, there were certain things that distinguished "Christian kids" at public schools. There were the clothes—hackneyed, copyright-infringing T-shirts with proselytizing slogans. There were the clubs, whether they were youth groups, See You at the Pole, Fellowship of Christian Athletes, Fellowship of Christian Students, or 30 Hour Famine. There was the music, much of which was cringeworthy and somehow sounded like the artist was faking it even when they were genuine, though some of it was beautiful, wrestled openly with questions of faith, or simply slapped. And, of course, there were the ham-fisted attempts to "witness to" kids at your school, who, depending on where you lived, were *very likely also Christian.*

Because that's the thing about evangelicalism: it presents itself quite simply as *Christianity.* It is not conditioned or modified. Growing up, I knew that, yes, there existed Christians far afield who were Catholic or Coptic or Orthodox, but as far as I could tell, we only nominally considered them a part of our brotherhood. *Our* teachings, on the other hand, were immutable and eternal, as if the Christians of the first century handed their traditions and ways of life directly to us. Evangelical Christianity was *default-setting* Christianity; everything else was lumped into a big vague category of "other."

But evangelicalism is not default-setting Christianity. It is evangelicalism. As we look back into history, what would become identifiable as modern evangelical theology has its roots in the nineteenth century; for a faith that measures its history in millennia, this is not a very long time at all. So we return once again to the slippery question: What is evangelicalism? The pop-culture and media-consumption signifiers I've cataloged previously identify believers as belonging to an in-group, but what does that in-group believe? If evangelicalism is a religious affiliation, what religious beliefs does it espouse?

Since 1989, evangelicals have been able to answer this question by pointing to a neat list of theological concepts known by the oddly quaint-sounding title "the Bebbington quadrilateral." First posited by historian David Bebbington in his book *Evangelicalism in Modern Britain: A History from the 1730s to the 1980s*, it describes evangelicalism as having four defining characteristics, which I'll explain in my own words.

- **Biblicism:** Evangelicals emphasize the importance and authority of the Bible over that of any clergy or church tradition.
- **Crucicentrism:** Evangelicals focus on Jesus's death on the cross as the defining and central feature of Christianity.
- **Conversionism:** Evangelicals believe you must actively choose Christianity and be "born again" in a transformational moment.
- **Activism:** Evangelicals emphasize bringing others into the faith.

This *theological* definition of evangelicalism is true as far as it goes. You don't have to hang around evangelicals very long to hear about all four of these concepts in depth. Whether you've spent time in the evangelical world or not, you've probably heard phrases like "The Bible is the literal and inerrant word of God" (biblicism) or "Christ died for your sins" (crucicentrism), and you're aware that evangelicals proselytize to others (activism), asking people if they're "saved" or if they've "accepted Jesus into their hearts" (conversionism).*

But is this what's *important* about evangelicalism?

Writing about the Bebbington quadrilateral in *The Scandal of the Evangelical Mind*, evangelical historian Mark Noll calls it a "useful general definition" but notes that

> these evangelical impulses have never by themselves yielded cohesive, institutionally compact, easily definable, well-coordinated, or clearly demarcated groups of Christians. Rather, the history of these evangelical impulses has always been marked by shifts in which groups, leaders, institutions, goals, concerns, opponents, and aspirations become more or less visible and more or less influential over time.[3]

In other words, these theological concepts are not the essential and immutable tenets of evangelicalism. They are bent or broken, emphasized or de-emphasized, reinforced or ignored to

---

* These turns of phrase also betray the fundamentalist assumptions inherent to much of evangelicalism. Notably, for many conservative evangelicals, biblicism also assumes biblical inerrancy, and crucicentrism assumes the belief that mankind is inherently sinful and God requires a substitutionary blood sacrifice.

fit the goals of the evangelical project—not the other way around.

In thinking about whether theology is really the most important signifier of evangelicalism, it may be helpful to look at another "general definition" that is as pithy as Justice Stewart's one-line definition of pornography: the adage attributed to evangelical historian George Marsden that an evangelical is "anyone who likes Billy Graham."[4] While that might have been true once, when you're reading this book in 2024 or later, it would be closer to the truth to say an evangelical is "anyone who likes Donald Trump—or, failing that, would still rather vote for a Republican than a Democrat." This is not just my read on the situation; in a 2021 study, the Pew Research Center reported that "there is solid evidence that White Americans who viewed Trump favorably and did *not* identify as evangelicals in 2016 were much more likely than White Trump skeptics to *begin identifying as* born-again or evangelical Protestants by 2020."[5]

Are these newly born-again white evangelical Christians familiar with the tenets of the Bebbington quadrilateral? If it is as inherent to the evangelical experience as some propose, they should be. But, no, the far more likely reason they adopted the evangelical moniker is Trumpism. They were attracted to his cruel and racist politics, and they were happy to be part of an in-group that affirmed and worked to enact those politics.

Although it may be harmless in a vacuum, the putative neutrality of theological definitions of evangelicalism can be used to deflect criticism from the movement's nontheological aspects. A perfect example of this is Tim Keller's December 2017 *New Yorker* article titled "Can Evangelicalism Survive Donald Trump and Roy Moore?" "Understanding the religious landscape," he writes, "requires discerning differences between the smaller, let's call it 'big-E Evangelicalism,' which gets much media attention, and a much larger, little-e evangelicalism, which does not. The larger, lowercase evangelicalism is defined not by a political party, whether conservative, liberal, or populist, but by theological beliefs."[6] (The theological beliefs he cites? The Bebbington quadrilateral.)

As you can tell from its title, the article was published in response to both Donald Trump's election and the candidacy of Roy Moore, who, while running for Senate in Alabama, became embroiled in a national scandal for having sexually targeted teenage girls as an adult.[7] White evangelicals widely supported both politicians, casting legitimate doubt on their moral qualifications; if they claimed to be casting their votes on religious grounds, why were they voting for people who violated the religious tenets they supposedly held? By invoking the Bebbington quadrilateral as a "non-political definition of evangelicalism," Keller both distances evangelicalism from its bad actors and muddies the historical waters.[8] If the popularity of politicians like Trump and Moore indicates a problem, he implies, it isn't with all the *real* evangelicals like Keller, it's with a few fake, politicized evangelicals who unfortunately tend to get all the media attention.

Keller pulls a second, similar rhetorical trick in the same article by shifting focus away from the United States entirely, declaring that "there exists a far larger evangelicalism . . . around the world, which is not politically aligned."[9] He praises "the enormous energy of the churches in the global South and East," writing, "I have seen scores of churches begun over the last fifteen years that are fully evangelical by our definition, only a minority of which are white, and which are not aligned with any political party."[10] Appealing to the existence of a global evangelicalism is a means of distracting from evangelical sins here in the United States by obfuscating the complicity of white evangelicalism in today's sociopolitical landscape. How can evangelicalism be described as a product of or a vehicle for racist politics, Keller implicitly argues, if so many people of color around the world embrace it in an apolitical way?

Christianity is indeed global, but using that fact to try to dissuade people from criticizing American Christianity is at best disingenuous and at worst deceitful. Yes, evangelical Christians exist elsewhere in the world, but they didn't spring up out of nowhere—their lineage can be traced back to the missionary work of prior centuries, which was quite explicitly racialized and political. Not to mention that while evangelical churches in other countries may not be tied to a given political party as closely as the American evangelical church is tied to the Republican Party, they inevitably play a role in their own sociopolitical contexts—even if Tim Keller and I don't have the expertise to fully understand it. Regardless, this is no excuse to utilize a form of international identity politics to deflect from domestic criticism.

I don't mean to imply that evangelicals across the globe aren't "really" evangelical or detract from the spiritual meaning they find in their faith. What I mean to point out is that, in Noll's words, " 'Evangelicalism' is not, and never has been, an '-ism' like other Christian isms—for example, Catholicism, Orthodoxy, Presbyterianism, Anglicanism. . . . Rather, 'evangelicalism' has always been made up of shifting movements, temporary alliances, and the lengthened shadows of individuals."[11] In her book *White Evangelical Racism*, religious studies scholar Anthea Butler goes even further, saying that historians like Noll, Bebbington, and Marsden "have been concerned . . . with defining evangelicalism via theology and history. Their projects are not expressly concerned with racial, nationalistic, and political concerns of conservative white Americans. Evangelicals are, however, concerned with their political alliance with the Republican Party and with maintaining the cultural and racial whiteness they have transmitted to the public."[12]

The story of white evangelicalism in the United States is more complicated—and less flattering—than the Bebbington quadrilateral suggests. The shadow sides of biblicism, crucicentrism, conversionism, and activism are fundamentalist literalism, the sacralizing of violence, social coercion, and the thirst for political power.

SO, WE MUST ASK OURSELVES again: What is evangelicalism?

Yes, sure, to some extent it is a religious designation indicating a cluster of theological tendencies. And, yes, each individual believer who has ever identified with the label may have their own feelings about what that term means for them and feel a rush to defend their own experience or their own tradition. ("Not all evangelicals!") It is true that there is a wealth of expressions of evangelical faith, and any single book would be hard-pressed to adequately represent them all.

But evangelicalism's greater significance today is as an American cultural and sociopolitical movement based in power, capitalism, and whiteness, and shored up by theologies and systems that support those causes. That is the definition I will use as I explore, analyze, and criticize evangelicalism throughout this book, using the record left behind in evangelical media. As we will see, "proper" beliefs are not the sole determining factor of who remains "in good standing" in evangelical in-groups— and who can transgress the moral obligations of those beliefs and still retain positions of power says volumes more than any theological checklist. What "counts" as evangelical is usually dictated by those with the most power inside evangelicalism, and when power struggles for the soul and direction of evangelicalism have been fought, it is the conservative faction that has routinely won. This movement is much bigger and stranger than a quaintly named polygon, and as we'll see in the next chapter, its roots in the United States go back centuries.

2

THE SLAVE BIBLE

EVANGELICALISM'S ROOTS IN ANTEBELLUM AMERICA

I n some ways, the roots of evangelicalism in the United States go back to some of the earliest European colonists. Per theologian and religious historian Douglas M. Strong, the term " 'evangelical' . . . had been used since the sixteenth century to refer to Lutherans in Germany and since the eighteenth century to describe the pietistic religious renewal that occurred among English-speaking Protestants."[1] But by 1844, it had started to take on a new, uniquely American expression. We know this because that's when Robert Baird published his landmark survey of the country's religious landscape, titled *Religion in America.**

---

*   Well, technically, it was originally titled *Religion in America; or, An Account of the Origin, Progress, Relation to the State, and Present Condition of the Evangelical*

Born in Pennsylvania and educated at the Princeton Theological Seminary, Baird was a clergyman and author who contributed to the founding of organizations as diverse as the Chi Phi
Society, the Swedish Temperance Society, and the New Jersey
public school system. In his work as an agent, first for the American Bible Society then for the American Sunday School Union,
he traveled widely and saw firsthand the many incarnations of
American Christianity.

Strong writes that, according to Baird, by the mid-nineteenth
century, "evangelicalism had become the normative faith expression in the United States. . . . It was evangelicals, he suggested, who were the true paragons of Christianity in the United
States." Who did Baird deem evangelical? In Strong's words, a
"wide range of churches," including "various kinds of Presbyteri-
ans, various kinds of Methodists (including both predominantly
white and African American Methodist denominations), various
kinds of Baptists (white and black), Congregationalists, Lutherans, two-thirds of the Episcopalians, some Friends (Quakers),
various Anabaptists, and many of those from ethnically based
Reformed churches."[2] Any Christians who didn't fall into those
categories he considered " 'unevangelical' . . . a catchall designation for such unlikely bedfellows as Catholics, Unitarians, Uni-
versalists, Shakers, and Mormons."[3]

What criteria did Baird use to join Mormons and Catholics
under one umbrella but divide one third of Episcopalians away
from the rest of their denomination? There was one major hall-
mark: evangelicals participated in religious revivals while une-
vangelicals did not.[4] Broadly defined, a revival is any movement

---

Churches in the United States, with Notices of the Unevangelical Denominations, which
already gives you an idea of evangelicalism's dominance, at least in Baird's view.

in which a trend of increased religious excitement sweeps an area.* It might convert new churchgoers, or it might inspire the already devout to become more passionate about their faith, or both—the specific practices or tenets of the revival are less important than the enthusiastic emotions it sparks.

The revival movement known as the First Great Awakening was, in the words of political scientist James A. Morone, "an early burst of American populism" that rebelled against the "extraordinary dullness" of the day's establishment churches.[5] Its first wave was led by Jonathan Edwards, who whipped up emotional fervor in the "Little Awakening" of Northampton, Massachusetts, in 1734 and 1735. That local manifestation of the revival died out when Edwards's uncle tragically took his own life "in despair over his own failure to feel God's grace," but Edwards kept preaching, and the larger First Great Awakening picked up steam again in 1740 when itinerant English preacher George Whitefield drew massive crowds across New England.[6] Whitefield was dismissive of the established Christian sects that held power. He "disparaged the clergy's work, their organizations, the 'forms' that 'shackled' them" and "offered a simple alternative to the established churches: the itinerant, preaching in the fields. Who qualified to preach? Anyone who could draw and hold a crowd."[7] This emphasis on both the individual preacher and the individual response to the gospel would have an incredible impact on the trajectory of American Protantism.

The First Great Awakening ended around 1755, but a few decades later, around 1790, the Second Great Awakening

---

* The word "revival" can also refer to an individual revival meeting in which church services are held, often in a tent or other temporary structure.

began. Led by figures such as Luther Rice, Charles Finney, and Lyman and Henry Ward Beecher, this revival movement lasted fifty years and lit such a spiritual fire in certain areas that they earned nicknames like the "burned-over district." This era was drawing to a close as Baird was writing *Religion in America* and thus shaped his definition of evangelicalism.

Even at this early stage—*especially* at this early stage— evangelicalism wasn't centered around a particular set of beliefs so much as a particular posture or orientation—what we might call today a "vibe." This was a period of great spiritual activity and excitement, but there was no widely accepted consensus as to what "evangelical" meant or what the goals of evangelicalism should be. Because the definition was so loose, the considerable energy of the still-inchoate movement could be put to almost any cultural or political purpose—and it was. Morone sees this as a distinctly American consequence of the country's Puritan heritage, which mixed religion and politics from the start: "In Europe, the old faiths bucked up the established order. In America, a kind of religious kaleidoscope inspired every political side. Rebels invoked God when they pushed for change. Reactionaries prayed with equal fervor as they pushed back."[8]

Over the course of the nineteenth century, we see evangelicalism used in the following developments and events: the Second Great Awakening; John Wesley's Holiness movement; the origins of the Seventh-day Adventists, with their unconventional behavioral rules; the formation of the abolitionist Anti-Slavery Society but also the formation of the Southern Baptists in order to theologically justify slavery; the temperance movement's attempts to curb alcohol consumption on religious and moral grounds; the emergence of D. L. Moody and other fundamentalist preachers; premillennialism's emphasis on the apocalypse; and the rise of charismatic sects like Pentecostalism. And those are only a few examples.

With aims as diverse as these, it's hard to make broad generalizations about evangelicalism during this period. Evangelicals of varying denominations rallied to various causes, which history has judged very differently. Yet, if we take a bird's-eye view of American evangelicalism, especially as we approach the antebellum period and the denominational splits I'll discuss momentarily, we can clearly see that its nineteenth-century roots laid the foundation for a movement based on power, capitalism, and whiteness. And it did so not by advancing a cohesive set of religious beliefs but by harnessing and directing the energy and emotions of its adherents.

RACISM IS AMERICA'S FOUNDING SIN. Metaphorically, it is not the root, branch, or fruit of the nation; it is the *soil* in which the nation was cultivated. It informs everything else, first and foremost the genocide of Indigenous people and the enslavement of Black people. No American institution exists outside of it, certainly not evangelicalism. Understanding the historical context of whiteness and white supremacy is therefore essential to understanding today's white evangelical Christianity.

This is perhaps nowhere more obvious than in the establishment of the Southern Baptist Convention. Before 1845, Baptists in the United States were just Baptists, though tensions had already arisen. Northern or Southern, they were all part of the same denomination, which was distinguished from other Protestant denominations by certain doctrinal differences, such as "believer's baptism" (reserving baptism for professed believers rather than baptizing infants) and the autonomy of local churches. But as tensions about slavery rose between Northern and Southern states, American Baptists began to fracture along the same geographical lines.

Many Baptists in Southern states were in favor of slavery—some were even slaveholders themselves—and they used their faith to justify their position. But this stance required some mental gymnastics.

It is true that many passages in scripture can be interpreted to support the practice of slavery, which is mentioned close to two hundred times throughout the Bible. The Old Testament lays out numerous laws about owning slaves, while the New Testament contains verses like "Slaves, obey your earthly masters with respect and fear, and with sincerity of heart, just as you would obey Christ" (Ephesians 6:5). However, it is also true that many passages in the Bible can be interpreted to be against slavery, at least the brutal race-based chattel slavery that was practiced in the American South. For example, a few lines after that verse in Ephesians is this one: "And masters, treat your slaves in the same way. Do not threaten them, since you know that he who is both their Master and yours is in heaven, and there is no favoritism with him" (Ephesians 6:9). Baptist and other Christian slaveholders were happy to point to verses like the first one while waving away those like the second.

Perhaps the most egregious example of this kind of selective use of scripture is *Select Parts of the Holy Bible, for the Use of the Negro Slaves, in the British West-India Islands,* which was published in 1807. Commonly referred to as "the Slave Bible," it "was used by British missionaries to convert and educate slaves," and "excludes any portion of text that might inspire rebellion or liberation. . . . Put in another way, there are 1,189 chapters in a standard protestant Bible. This Bible contains only 232."[9] Christian slavers knew their religion could inspire liberation just as readily as obedience, and they took the extreme action of censoring their own holy book to oppress and enslave.

They were also happy to reach for any interpretation of the Bible that would rationalize slavery. One extremely popular rationalization was the idea of the "curse of Ham." In the book of Genesis, Noah (of ark fame) has three sons named Shem, Ham, and Japheth. After the flood ends and they're back on dry land, Ham sees Noah drunk and naked, while Shem and Japheth avert their eyes, causing Noah to curse Ham's descendants to be the slaves of his brothers' descendants (Genesis 9:20–27). In 1578, with the African slave trade fully in swing, English travel writer George Best popularized a strange reading of the story. Ibram X. Kendi writes,

> In Best's whimsical interpretation of Genesis, Noah orders his White and 'Angelike' sons to abstain from sex with their wives on the Ark, and then tells them that the first child born after the flood would inherit the earth. When the evil, tyrannical, and hypersexual Ham has sex on the Ark, God wills that Ham's descendants shall be 'so blacke and loathsome,' in Best's telling, 'that it might remain a spectacle of disobedience to all the worlde.'[10]

There is absolutely nothing in the Bible itself about skin color or about sexual activity on Noah's ark, but that didn't stop the story from gaining widespread purchase among white Southerners.

I could keep going with examples like this, but the point is that proslavery Baptists didn't predicate their support for slavery on universal Christian principles as they pretended they did; rather, they valued a culture of white supremacy that put them at the top of a racial hierarchy, and they invented a particular theological heritage to justify it, selectively interpreting scripture and doctrine as needed. Preservation of this extrabiblical hierarchy was paramount. This is a pattern we'll see in evangelicalism into the present day.

Slave-owning Baptists were adamant that their ownership of other humans did not impugn their good Christian standing. In 1845, Rev. Basil Manly Sr., president of the University of Alabama, pressed the matter, insisting that slaveholders should have the same access "to all the privileges and immunities of their several unions" as Baptists without slaves.[11] When the board of the 1845 Triennial Convention disagreed, ruling that "if any one [sic] should offer himself as a missionary, having slaves, and should insist on retaining them as his property, we could not appoint him," Manly and his allies had their answer.[12] Six months later, they founded the Southern Baptist Convention—not because of differences in their belief about the nature of God but in order to continue enslaving people. Today the SBC is the largest evangelical denomination in the country—in fact, the largest Protestant denomination in the country, evangelical or not—and as we'll see in later chapters, it has done little to reckon with the fact that it was founded explicitly and unambiguously on slavery. In fact, the legacy of white supremacy has been a strong influence on the SBC's actions up into the twenty-first century.

At the same time, however, many evangelical figures were at the forefront of the abolitionist movement. One such figure was

Jonathan Blanchard, the first president of Wheaton College.* Blanchard worked for the American Anti-Slavery Society and, throughout his professional career as a pastor and educator, maintained abolitionist positions based in his evangelical faith. Evangelical historian Donald Dayton writes of Blanchard: "He argued that slavery was a sin to be immediately abolished and suggested that church discipline be brought to bear upon those who held slaves or supported the institution of slavery. He did not view the question of slavery as an individual matter of personal purity, but insisted that 'slave-holding is not a solitary, but a social sin,' deserving attack on all fronts."[13] Blanchard drew on the same revivalist enthusiasm as the SBC but used it to diametrically opposed ends, fighting against slavery instead of for it.

A similar figure was Charles Finney, the president of Oberlin College.** Finney, whom Dayton calls the "father of modern revivalism," also considered slavery a sin, but that conviction was not at the center of his faith.[14] He "was never willing to substitute reform for revival, but he did make the reforms an 'appendage' to revival. . . . For example, the evangelist wished to make 'abolition an appendage, just as we made temperance an appendage of the revival in Rochester.'"[15] Thus, he "preserved the centrality of revivals while still promoting reforms and propelling his converts into new positions on social issues."[16] Finney's use of the word "appendage" is a perfect illustration of evangelicalism's ideological flexibility during this time period; at the movement's core was a group identity based on revivalist

---

* Wheaton, an Illinois liberal arts college nicknamed (by its alumni and no one else) the "Harvard of Christian schools," remains prominent in evangelicalism to this day.

** Oberlin, an Ohio liberal arts college, retains a somewhat less pious reputation today.

fervor, onto which any sort of ideological appendage could be fastened, from a staunch proslavery position to abolitionist activism to anything in between.

Unsurprisingly, white evangelical abolitionism tended to have its limits. Finney, for example, may have inveighed against slavery, but he nonetheless defended segregation and race-based prejudice. He made this distinction in a letter reprimanding a close friend who was supporting integrated seating in their church.

> You err in supposing the principle of abolition and
> amalgamation are identical. Abolition is a question of
> flagrant and unblushing wrong. A direct and outrageous
> violation of fundamental right. The other is a question
> of prejudice that does not necessarily deprive any man of
> any positive right.[17]

Today's white evangelical apologists are often quick to bring up the role nineteenth-century evangelicals had in abolition. Evangelical participation in the abolition movement is valuable and commendable, and it's an understandable source of pride. But today's white evangelicals—and the white people who leave white evangelicalism—can't rest on the laurels of Charles Finney or Jonathan Blanchard as if the work of examining racist belief, practice, and institutional bias were somehow completed in 1865. Evangelicalism has both racist and anti-racist roots because it has roots in countless different social, political, and spiritual causes. What matters today is which roots were fertilized and tended to, and what they eventually grew into. As we'll see in later chapters, it was the racist roots that predominated over the decades and motivated the rightward political turn evangelicalism would eventually be known for, leading us to a modern church that valorizes and upholds whiteness above any theological tenet.*

This is why, for the purposes of this book, "evangelicalism" generally means "white evangelicalism," even though not 100 percent of people within the American evangelical movement are white. As Anthea Butler puts it, bluntly, "Racism is a feature, not a bug, of American evangelicalism."[18]

But before we trace those historical developments, we must stay a little longer in the nineteenth century and examine the roots of other developments that would proliferate alongside whiteness—particularly American capitalism.

---

* Note that when I use the term "whiteness" in this context, I'm talking not about genetic heritage originating in Europe per se but about the ideological category of whiteness that was created as part of a racial hierarchy to justify the depredations of colonialism, slavery, and genocide. The former is, like all ethnicities, completely value-neutral on its own; the latter is the basis of white supremacy.

3

THE BUSINESSMEN'S REVIVAL

EVANGELICALISM AND CAPITALISM IN THE LATE 1800S

In today's world of prosperity-gospel preachers in private jets and multimillion-dollar Christian blockbuster films, evangelicalism is big business. And while it may be hard to imagine it in a world before cars, credit cards, and computers, its history of capitalistic consumerism reaches back further than we might expect, just as with other aspects of evangelical culture.

I don't have room to comprehensively chart that history, which could fill—and has filled—many books on its own. Instead, I'll start by taking a close look at one influential figure who exemplifies the foundations of evangelical consumerism that were laid in the nineteenth century: D. L. Moody. In his story, we see the beginnings of patterns that will repeat over and over in the story of white evangelicalism—patterns of conflict between conservative and liberal factions, with the conservative factions aligning themselves with monied interests in order to accomplish their goals. In his book *Guaranteed Pure*, historian of religion Timothy Gloege calls this the beginning of a "corporate evangelical framework," which had significant long-term consequences for white evangelicalism and American society writ large.[1]

Dwight Lyman Moody was not born into evangelicalism; his mother raised him as a Unitarian after his father passed away when Moody was four. Moody's childhood in western Massachusetts was unstable, and he was a poor student. Headstrong and proud, he initially rejected the offer of a job at his uncle's shoe store, but when he couldn't make it on his own, he went to Boston and became a clerk there.

This was the mid-1800s, and as Robert Baird had noticed (albeit in slightly different terms), by this time, there had begun to emerge differences in American Christianity between a "churchly orientation" (marked by theological tradition, institutional authority, and an emphasis on community) and an "evangelical orientation" (which emphasized a personal relationship to God, individual notions of authority, and personal expression of faith through individual actions like Bible reading or worship).[2] Moody had trouble fitting into "churchly" social circles. He converted to evangelical Protestantism following conversations with Sunday school teacher Edward Kimball. The Mount Vernon Congregational Church in Boston, where he attended services, was not so quickly convinced; his first application for church membership was rejected after he failed "a rudimentary theological exam."[3] He spent ten months preparing for another test, but he was accepted more on the strength of his convictions than on his knowledge of scripture or theology. In fact, Gloege says that this experience "did little more than solidify a lifelong dislike of theology" for Moody.[4]

In 1856, Moody moved to the boomtown of Chicago, where he found success in the shoe business he had learned in Boston. In an experience familiar to many Christians who move to a new town or city, Moody had trouble finding a church home at first, but eventually he found a spiritual community within the city's business community. Two influential businessmen, John V. Farwell and Cyrus Bentley, had begun organizing noon-hour prayer meetings, a novel idea at the time. In keeping with the theme of emotion over substance, "they avoided theological and political issues and focused instead on heartfelt prayer, singing, and Bible reading."[5] But very little is truly apolitical, least of all evangelicalism, and these seemingly neutral lunchtime gatherings were in reality expressions of the participants' values, namely commerce and masculinity. Gloege writes:

> In an age of feminine and domestic-oriented religion, participants depicted the movement as explicitly male, literally erasing women from published illustrations and relegating their bodies to balconies and other peripheral spaces. They conducted meetings in business-district theatres, symbolically centering the movement in public economic life, removed from home and church. Devoid of ministerial oversight, the meetings thus became open space in which these men could reimagine faith in terms of their workaday lives.[6]

These noon-hour meetings, which were collectively nick-named the "businessmen's revival," would eventually evolve into the Chicago YMCA, and by 1860, Moody would decide to "work for Jesus Christ" full-time there.[7] The city's religious establishment initially looked at him askance, but he'd earn what Gloege calls their "grudging respect" during the post–Civil War population boom in Chicago, when concerns about "vice," poverty, and labor unrest loomed large.[8]

This was the time of both the Gilded Age and the Progressive Era: two eras that overlapped, two sides of the same coin, with two contradictory visions of the social order. It was, in other words, an era not unlike our own—a time of technological progress, labor unrest, and considerable social upheaval. Various groups arose to meet these challenges with various perspectives and methods. Proponents of the Social Gospel, for example, advocated for measures like labor reform and public services as a way to end socioeconomic inequality and make earth more like they imagined heaven to be. Per historian Kevin Kruse, they "significantly reframed Christianity as a faith concerned less with personal salvation and more with the public good."[9]

Moody and others, in contrast, saw a different path toward alleviating suffering, one grounded in the capitalist framework called "Christian work." This approach "presented individuals as the source of social ill and the primary means of potential change" and "cultivated the idea that a business sensibility could strengthen both individual piety and Christian society by wedding robust emotions to strict self-control, in the name of an optimized relationship with God."[10] Essentially, the external markers of being a "good Christian" were individualism and self-reliance—the same traits that would supposedly let a person succeed within capitalism.

Initially, for Moody at least, this concept of Christian work was focused on elevating the status of poor workers to the more "respectable" classes in the city. But he soon

grabbed hold of another, even more radical, idea to solve
the problem of the masses: perhaps what was really
needed were Christian workers from a particular
class. . . . Taking a strikingly literal turn, he concluded
that he needed to train Christian workers from the
working classes. Reversing the traditional assumptions
of respectable Protestants, he argued that the most
effective urban missionaries would come from the same
uneducated, working-class backgrounds as those they
were seeking to convert.[11]

Moody and his allies in both the evangelical clergy and the
corporate sphere sought to instill in the working class a combination of Christian piety and adherence to developing capitalist
tendencies. They wanted to convert working-class people but
also held them in low regard and paid them low wages. In
Gloege's analysis, Moody, a salesman-turned-evangelist who
held several revivals with attendees in the thousands, slowly
ingratiated himself with the city's elite, eventually aligning himself directly with the business interests of Chicago. Notably, he
gave a sermon in Chicago on the same day as the Haymarket
Riot, a labor protest that turned violent when a bomb detonated,
killing seven policemen and at least four civilians. Moody had
been trying and failing to raise $250,000 to found a college; the
civil unrest of the Haymarket Riot led the business elites to
pony up.[12] That college would become the Moody Bible Institute, and it would leave a permanent mark on American evangelicalism.

To give you an idea of how closely intertwined the Moody
Bible Institute was with capitalism, consider Henry Crowell,
who was head of the board of trustees there for forty years.[13]

Crowell purchased the bankrupt Quaker Mill Company primarily for its trademark, founded the Quaker Oats Company, and set about pioneering various innovations in packaging, marketing, and intellectual property. Instead of selling his oats to a wholesaler, who would distribute them to retailers to be sold out of open barrels by weight, Crowell sold "Quaker Oats exclusively in two-pound [sealed] packages," which were advertised as cleaner and safer than the bulk-barrel alternative, a matter that hadn't previously been a large cause for concern among consumers.[14] "Relentless promotion . . . proclaimed [the product's] purity, and samples allowed consumers to experience it firsthand."[15] (It is from this advertising innovation that Gloege takes the title of his book, *Guaranteed Pure*.)

With free-market prodigies like these at the helm of the evangelical movement, it is not surprising that a particular brand of evangelical capitalism would also take root. It would eventually grow into one of evangelicalism's defining features.

SO FAR, I HAVE RESISTED the typical compulsion to define the evangelical movement by its broad theological tenets and then "disprove" it on those grounds. Instead, I've focused on the cultivation of whiteness and capitalism and their central role in the development of modern evangelical culture. But that doesn't mean theology was irrelevant to the course of the movement. Several new theological ideas bubbled up during the spiritual ferment of the nineteenth century, and some of them would have long-lasting effects.

This was, for instance, the period in which the teaching of "dispensational premillennialism" became widespread. Dispensational premillennialism is a very boring-sounding name for what was actually quite a dramatic, even frightening theological framework popularized by Anglo-Irish minister John Nelson Darby. The "dispensational" part indicates a belief that history is broken into discrete time periods—or "dispensations"—of revelation from and relationship to God. There was one dispensation extending from creation until Adam and Eve were expelled from Eden, another dispensation between then and Noah's flood, and so on and so forth. The final dispensation, according to this view, will take place in the future, when Jesus will return to earth and reign for a thousand years; because we're living in a dispensation before those thousand years, we are "premillennial."*

If you weren't raised evangelical (or even if you were), you might never have heard the term "dispensational premillennialism," but you are almost certainly familiar with its teaching of the Rapture, which holds that before Jesus returns to earth, he'll perform some version of essentially teleporting all true believers to heaven. This trope has become so ubiquitous today that it's easy for anyone, regardless of religious background, to assume it was spelled out clearly in the Bible two thousand years ago, but really, it's based on a specific interpretation of the book of Revelation and other biblical passages that dates back only to the mid-1800s.**

The apocalyptic fervor that this belief unleashed at the time

---

* Specific theological terms like "dispensational premillennialism" are necessary because Christianity does not have one single eschatology, or set of beliefs about the end times. Over millennia, Christians have interpreted prophetic texts like the biblical book of Revelation differently and come to different conclusions. There are also postmillennialists, amillennialists, etc.

** The idea has penetrated public consciousness so much that it has even been secularized. The HBO show *The Leftovers* (based on the Tom Perrotta novel) focuses on the stories of people left behind after 2 percent of the human population disappears without explanation, upending society.

is hard to overstate. Shortly before Darby, Baptist minister William Miller had built a following by claiming the Bible predicted the world would end on October 22, 1844. The disillusion that occurred among his followers (known as Millerites) was so deep that historians dubbed this apocalypse-that-wasn't the Great Disappointment.[16] Darby and others moved away from *precise* predictions, instead relying on vaguer signs that—as time went on—could find resonance with biblical phrases like "wars and rumors of wars" (Matthew 24:6).

The expectation that the end of days was nigh conditioned believers to expect the world to get worse before the inevitable return of Jesus, which bred both apathy about their present earthly condition and a longing for an unrealized heavenly future. It also renewed the question of Christian involvement in society, as the premillennial perspective assumed societal decline. Historian Matthew Avery Sutton writes:

Millions of Americans and Europeans, most often working through their churches and religious organizations, hoped, prayed, and labored to make the brutal warfare of the nineteenth century a thing of the past. According to many mainstream Protestants, such work could help usher in the kingdom of God. Premillennialists knew better. Minister R. A. Torrey remained skeptical of what he saw in the peace movements. "All our present peace plans," he noted in 1913, "will end in the most awful wars and conflicts this old world ever saw."[17]

Premillennialism has had such a profound effect that it also bred in many believers incredible anxiety, which continues to this day, as evidenced by the #RaptureAnxiety hashtag that has been used on social media since 2017.

So we can see that it's not as if theology is purely incidental to the history of evangelicalism. As a religious movement, it filters its developments through theology even when those developments don't seem closely related to religion. Yet, at the same time, that theology can twist back on itself in an almost paradoxical way. Take Cyrus Scofield, one of the key figures who helped popularize dispensational premillennialism. His annotated Scofield Reference Bible became a popular seller and fed into this apocalyptic view of the world and the sense that Christ would imminently return to earth. But there was another idea, more subtle but no less revolutionary, embedded within his theology: a belief that Jesus's teachings were not the ones most applicable to "the present age," but rather *the Apostle Paul's*.

For readers who may have forgotten their Sunday school lessons, Paul (or Saint Paul to Catholics and Episcopalians) was an apostle in the early Christian church, but he was not one of Jesus's twelve disciples and never met Jesus in person. In fact, according to the book of Acts, he helped persecute early Christians until he was blinded by a vision of Jesus on the road to Damascus; by the time the scales fell off his eyes, he was a true believer and dedicated the rest of his life to spreading the gospel around the Mediterranean. Many of the books in the New Testament are letters Paul wrote to the small Christian churches he and his allies founded throughout the region—the book of Romans is his letter to the church in Rome, the book of Ephesians is his letter to the church in Ephesus, and so on. Of course, it's difficult to know much about the real life of any person in the Bible, but scholarly consensus is that Paul did exist and did write at least some of the letters attributed to him.

In these epistles, Paul gives instructions and lays out doctrinal strictures that aren't always closely connected with the teachings and life of Jesus as they're portrayed in the gospels.*
For example, Paul writes extensively about his belief that Christians don't need to follow traditional Jewish dietary restrictions or circumcision laws, issues that the Jesus of the gospels doesn't seem to have been particularly concerned with. More significantly, the Pauline epistles advance views on sexual relations, the role of women in the church, and the need to convert Gentiles in addition to Jews—again, all matters that either aren't mentioned or aren't emphasized in the gospels.

So for dispensationalists like Scofield and the similar William R. Newell to elevate Paul's teachings above Jesus's was truly radical. Let's return to Gloege's analysis.

> Scofield and Newell . . . emphasized that although "all the Bible is *for* us . . . it is not all *about* us." They limited the parts of the Bible *about* the present dispensation to "Paul's letters." Incredibly, they argued that the gospels . . . were not intended for present-day believers. Jesus is "the Great Teacher . . . in a sense," Newell grudgingly acknowledged, but he was trumped by "those statements of Christian doctrine uttered by the apostle Paul." Scofield similarly argued that the Sermon on the Mount was "the law of the *kingdom*," the final, future dispensation, "not of the *church*." Neither Jesus's teachings nor his miraculous power were directly applicable to the present age.[18]

---

* For those who've never been to Sunday school at all, the gospels are the first four books of the New Testament (Matthew, Mark, Luke, and John), which all tell the story of Jesus's life with differing details.

With these "breathtaking departures from traditional Protestantism," nineteenth-century evangelicals began the process of redefining Christianity to fit their social vision.[19] The combination of a pessimistic outlook that assumed the apocalypse was imminent and a faith that emphasized the Pauline epistles rather than the gospels had a significant effect on determining evangelical concerns. Viewed from this perspective, we can begin to understand why the cultural and theological battles that have taken place within evangelical communities over the ensuing decades have been primarily concerned with matters that were discussed in the letters attributed to Paul: women's rights, restriction of sexual activity to heterosexual marriage, and matters of power and authority in the church and society.* If Christianity is defined not by Christ but by what professing Christians value, it can be defined by whatever you want—capitalism, individualism, racism, sexism, or whatever other ism might keep you and people like you in positions of power and privilege.

Now, it is true that using religion to justify nonreligious aims is not unique to evangelicalism. To a greater or lesser extent, most religious traditions do some version of this. But that's part of the point I'm making: white evangelicalism presents itself as immutable, incontrovertible, and eternal when really it is a religious tradition like any other—and a relatively recent one at that, rooted in historical developments like the ones I've chronicled here. It is not the one true version of Christianity it claims to be, and thinking of it as such is part of what has led to

---

* While the Bible does feature teachings and narratives about sex and sexuality, it is nowhere near as consistent as modern evangelicals often present it and does not uniformly confine celebrations of sex to married heterosexual couples. For instance, Paul would have preferred all believers to be celibate and single, and the marital status of the lovers in Song of Songs is not mentioned.

our current condition, with individual lives unraveled and democracy itself at risk.

BY NOW, I HOPE I'VE given you a solid idea of modern American
evangelicalism's origins in the nineteenth century. It was a time
of a wild proliferation of ideas, some of which would evolve into
the movement we know today. But there's a part of this era that
I haven't addressed yet: *how* these ideas proliferated. By what
means did people learn about, debate, refine, promote, or de-
nounce all these new developments in thought? To answer this,
let's consider how early evangelicals used the media of their
time to change the culture, politics, and religion of the world
around them.

I would go so far as to say that an inherent understanding of
the power of media and a highly cultivated sense of media savvy
is one of the central facets of evangelicalism that goes as far back
as Martin Luther himself. The Protestant Reformation happened due in no small part to a broader *media* revolution that
had begun with the advent of movable type and Johannes
Gutenberg's printing press. Through the power of the printing
press, Luther and other Reformation thinkers were able to
spread their messages farther and faster than anyone could have
anticipated, seeding antipapist propaganda and providing legit-
imacy to a then-heterodox form of faith. In her book *The Printing Press as an Agent of Change*, historian Elizabeth Eisenstein
writes that in addition to dividing Catholic regions from Protestant ones,

the communications shift had a divisive effect;
permanently fragmenting Western Christendom along

both geographic and sociological lines. . . . Loss of
confidence in God's words among cosmopolitan élites
was coupled with enhanced opportunities for evangelists
and priests to spread glad tidings and rekindle faith.
Enlightened deists . . . were thus placed at a distance
from enthusiasts who were caught up in successive waves
of religious revivals.[20]

Crucially, it was not only Reformation leaders who radically
changed their relationship to religion because of media; it was
also masses of ordinary people. When Bibles and other religious
writings became cheaper to produce, more people could buy
them, which meant more people could read and interpret scripture for themselves instead of relying solely on what they were
told in church. And the influence of printed material on lay-
people during the Reformation was as much emotional as it was
spiritual. In Eisenstein's words, "Bible-reading householders
acquired an enhanced sense of spiritual dignity and individual
worth. An 'inner light' kindled by the printed word became the
basis for the shared mystical experiences of separate sects."[21]
Along the same lines, historian Diana Butler Bass writes, "Having read the Word of God in newly translated scriptures and
listened to sermons from reformed pulpits, [laypeople] added
their voices to the devotional cacophony of the day. Speaking
out for Christ became a measure of one's devotion."[22]
    Printed material functioned much the same way in early
American evangelicalism. Evangelical publishers pioneered many
new printing techniques in the first half of the nineteenth century, and by midcentury, they were responsible for "16 percent
of all books published in the United States."[23] Just as the words
of Martin Luther spread far and fast during the Reformation, so

did the words of evangelical leaders; Moody's son-in-law helped cement his father-in-law's influence by publishing his works, while the Scofield Reference Bible became so popular that versions of it remain in print today.[24] And as the nineteenth century drew to a close, there was a new kind of environment in which these ideas could take hold: Christian colleges like the Moody Bible Institute. Between 1882 and 1920, thirty-nine Bible colleges were founded in the United States, which would become institutional stalwarts and keepers of evangelical orthodoxy over time.[25]

The conjunction of the burgeoning evangelical publishing industry and the expanding ecosystem of evangelical colleges helped create what scholar Daniel Vaca calls an "evangelical public," which still exists today.[26] The existence of the media helped create the public, which in turn demanded more media, which was both consumed and generated in Christian schools. (This is why, although education is not strictly "the media" in the way we usually think of it, I will loosely group Christian schools in with the rest of the evangelical media network throughout this book.)

To summarize: white American unease around social and technological change in post–Civil War America helped premillennialist teachings about the end of the world to find purchase in the religious imagination, which was cultivated by preachers like D. L. Moody, who, like a protoinfluencer expanding into merch and coaching, sold books of his sermons and eventually founded the Bible institute that still bears his name. Meanwhile, long-standing racist assumptions went unchallenged even as "corporate evangelicals" utilized capitalist markets to expand their religious endeavors. Moody and his contemporaries built the foundations of the modern evangelical public and the related marketplace that served its separatist needs and desires, creating a network where ideas could flourish. By drawing such distinct boundaries between themselves and everyone else, even other practicing Christians, these late-nineteenth-century evangelicals sought to differentiate themselves, privileging and preferring their interpretations in competition with that of "liberal" Christians, creating in-groups and out-groups.

But the more concrete a network like this becomes, the more intense the feedback loop becomes: a given idea can be disseminated quickly among a large group of people, who adopt it readily not because of the idea itself but because they are a part of the group. Eventually, the network is defined less by a set of beliefs than by membership in the network. And that is exactly what we'll see in the twentieth century as the disparate streams of evangelicalism begin to converge and less prominent versions fall away, leaving a dominant version increasingly based on an in-group cultural identity dependent upon white capitalism.

4

FUNDAMENTAL

EVANGELICALISM IN THE EARLY TWENTIETH CENTURY

I n many ways, the evangelicalism of the 1800s was defined by
its wildness. As we saw in the previous chapter, it encom-
passed an enormous range of practices and beliefs, all grouped
together loosely under a revivalist umbrella and a populist
"evangelical orientation." But as the nineteenth century gave
way to the twentieth, evangelicalism began to become more
narrowly defined—and more oppositional to other branches of
Christianity. Adherents began to cluster around certain aspects
of the movement such as premillennialism and biblical inerrancy, letting other aspects wither away. No longer could the
label "evangelical" be applied to any Protestant under the sun.
Now it began to mean something more specific, something increasingly more socially and politically conservative. That trajectory would continue throughout the twentieth century as

evangelicals used evolving forms of media to create an in-group identity and enforce adherence to that identity in the service of power, capitalism, and whiteness. Again, that's not to say that theology wasn't involved, but rather that a theology that supported a certain conservative ideology was selected, developed, and formalized using the media of the time, while theology that didn't support that ideology was rejected and made taboo.

One of the earliest and most well-known initiatives of this time was *The Fundamentals*, a set of ninety essays published between 1910 and 1915 that laid out what its authors considered to be the most important and unassailable principles of Christianity. *The Fundamentals* is in many respects a culmination of nineteenth-century evangelicalism and a harbinger of what was to come: it was bankrolled by businessmen, published by the evangelical media apparatus, and focused on codifying an evangelical orthodoxy that would include—and exclude—the right people. It is from this publication that we get today's term "fundamentalist."

On the surface, *The Fundamentals* was a purely religious project, making arguments about concepts like the virgin birth and the nature of sin on theological grounds. But from the very start, that theology had a sociopolitical purpose: to resist what its writers, editors, and funders saw as threats to the gospel from their more progressive brethren. Historian Timothy Gloege writes: "The goal of *The Fundamentals* . . . according to the 'resident committee' in Chicago, was to construct a new standard of 'orthodox' belief that would first and foremost rally conservatives from across the denominational spectrum to do battle against modernists."[1] The authors were not subtle about defining themselves as a righteous in-group in opposition to foolish or wicked

EXVANGELICAL AND BEYOND 45

outsiders; essay titles include "Mormonism: Its Origin, Characteristics, and Doctrines" and "Is Romanism [i.e., Catholicism] Christianity?" But it wasn't just non-Protestant denominations they decried; it was any sort of liberalism or modernism, which, after all, blamed society's problems not on the individual but on the capitalist systems that fundamentalist corporate leaders profited from. In Gloege's words, "They wanted this 'orthodox' standard to align with—in fact, to enshrine—their corporate evangelical framework."[2] In the words of Union Oil founder Lyman Stewart, who funded the project, they wanted to send "some kind of warning and testimony to the English-speaking [Christians] of the world . . . which would put them on their guard and bring them into right lines again."[3]

Of course, it wouldn't do to say so in public. So instead of stating that the project was paid for by Stewart and his brother, they stamped COMPLIMENTS OF TWO CHRISTIAN LAYMEN on the title page of each volume, and instead of saying they had a political agenda, they said they just wanted to get back to the titular "fundamentals" of "old-time religion." Inconveniently, their interpretation of Christianity was often only as "old-time" as a few decades, so "they had the additional challenge of creating a patina of historicity, of 'discovering' an evangelical orientation in existing churchly creeds."[4] Lutheran theologian Paul Tillich would later decry this tactic, in which "the theological truth of yesterday is defended as an unchangeable message against the theological truth of today and tomorrow. . . . It elevates something finite and transitory to infinite and eternal validity . . . and it makes [its adherents] fanatical because they are forced to suppress elements of truth of which they are dimly aware."[5] It was quite an effective strategy, however, for harnessing the fear and resentment of those who felt threatened by the rapidity of social change and wanted to curtail it. It laid the groundwork for the role of spite in modern evangelicalism, especially with regard to its capacity to build upon grievances with only tangential connections to issues of faith. By Gloege's reckoning,

> the lasting significance of *The Fundamentals* project laid in its methods, not its contents. It pioneered a means of creating an evangelical "orthodoxy" out of an ever-shifting bricolage of beliefs and practices, each of varying historical significance and some entirely novel. Unencumbered by an overarching logic, the fragments that constituted conservative evangelicalism faded in and out to accommodate contemporaneous circumstances. *The Fundamentals* thus pointed the way forward for modern conservative evangelicalism by modeling the methodology for creating, and constantly recreating, whatever "orthodoxy" the present moment required.[6]

Modeling novel uses of media and marketing techniques, the project was published in quarterly volumes by the Testimony Publishing Company and sent free of charge to as large an audience as possible. At the end of the process, it was republished as a complete set by a key node in the Bible-college network: the Bible Institute of Los Angeles, better known as Biola, which was also founded by Lyman Stewart. If *The Fundamentals* was a test case for the fledgling evangelical media machine, it was an enormous success: the first few volumes were met with more than 300,000 mailed-in responses from readers.[7] And so the evangelical web began to grow.

As it did, it comprised more and more Christian schools similar to Biola and the Moody Bible Institute, including Bob Jones College (now a university), which was founded by its namesake in 1927—the same year he started preaching on the brand-new medium known as the radio. In the book *Fundamentalist U*, Adam Laats describes how the school fit (and continues to fit) the same pattern we will see repeated over and over again: that it is not strict adherence to a set of beliefs that demarcates evangelicalism but a commitment to identity and group affiliation. With its extremely strict rules about everything from sex to clothes to music, "at Bob Jones College, the question of authority was answered repeatedly in unmistakable tones. Fidelity to fundamentalism meant fidelity to the school and its leaders."[8] Students would learn how "to avoid the looming dangers of life in modern America" but with "only tenuous connections to precise theological debates."[9] In short, "at the emerging network of fundamentalist colleges, definitions were shaped by leaders' vague, shifting, and idiosyncratic beliefs about the true meanings of fundamentalism."[10] This was as true in the twentieth century as it was in the nineteenth century—and as it would be in the twenty-first.

THANKS TO UNDERTAKINGS LIKE *The Fundamentals*, the evangelical network of publishing, schools, and eventually radio steadily became larger and more sophisticated during the first decades of the twentieth century. It even made its first forays into harnessing the fame of the day's celebrities, as with professional-baseball-player-turned-evangelist Billy Sunday (incredibly, not a stage name), whose brand of "muscular Christianity" appealed to men who found traditional expressions of piety emasculating.[11] (That audience included the Ku Klux Klan.)[12] Sunday's delivery was brusque and vulgar, to the extent that Wheeling, Virginia, "passed an ordinance aimed squarely at Sunday. It imposed a fine on anyone who 'in a public address should use vile or vulgar language.' "[13] As we will see, Sunday would not be the last evangelist or preacher to use hypermasculinity to sell this particular vision of Christianity.

But fundamentalist attempts to consolidate support were frustrated by a major historical event: the Great Depression of the 1930s. It became more difficult to portray capitalism as a system ordained by God when capitalism had just resulted in a worldwide economic disaster; a gospel rooted in individualism and personal responsibility only goes so far with people who know they weren't personally responsible for the stock market crash. And evangelicals had a formidable opponent in Franklin Roosevelt, a devout Episcopalian who took up the mantle of the previous century's Social Gospel, using Christian rhetoric to advocate for the public good over private profit. Here are just a couple examples of FDR's Bible-based calls to action, collected by historian Kevin Kruse in his book *One Nation Under God*:

> Once, he introduced an otherwise dry speech criticizing
> Republican plans to privatize public utilities by saying,
> "This is a history and a sermon on the subject of water
> power, and I preach from the Old Testament. The text is
> 'Thou shalt not steal.' " . . . [In] his first inaugural
> address . . . Roosevelt reassured the nation that "the
> money changers have fled from their high seats in the
> temple of our civilization. We may now restore the
> temple to the ancient truths."[14]

More liberal-minded Christians arrayed themselves around Roosevelt in a counterbalance to the evangelical ecosystem, accelerating a trend that had begun in previous decades. In a series of events referred to as the "fundamentalist-modernist controversy," the Presbyterian denomination split into fundamentalist and modernist factions that still exist today. Theological and social collaboration between fundamentalists and other Christians became increasingly untenable as evangelicals and nonevangelicals were sorted from each other along increasingly explicit political lines: the Roosevelt "administration's efforts to regulate the economy and address the excesses of corporate America were singled out for praise. Catholic and Protestant leaders hailed . . . New Deal measures, which they said merely 'incorporated into law some of the social ideas and principles for which our religious organizations have stood for many years.' "[15] These policies and their accompanying rhetoric were popular (FDR was elected four times, after all), but fundamentalists and their business partners would not be cowed. During this crucial period from the Great Depression through postwar America, influential white evangelicals began to leverage the institutions they had established over the previous decades.

In 1942, feeling isolated by their exclusion from mainline and ecumenical organizations like the Federal Council of Churches, they formed the National Association of Evangelicals, which brought various fundamentalist denominations together under one umbrella. But some groups were still getting rained on; as Anthea Butler notes, "no Black denominations were represented, even though major Black denominations such as the National Baptist Convention and the Church of God in Christ could have easily signed the statement of belief."[16]

Evangelicals would also find a series of popular champions for their cause, starting with the likes of James W. Fifield Jr. Beginning in 1935, Fifield was a minister in Los Angeles's elite First Congregationalist Church. Though raised in Chicago, he became enamored with the glitz and glamour of LA, and he actively sought out and attracted wealthy congregants from the business and entertainment industries. If Billy Sunday used his social status as a former professional athlete to his advantage while preaching, Fifield used the social status of his parishioners. He was not a fundamentalist and did not agree with theological teachings like biblical literalism. Kruse quotes him saying that "the men who chronicled and canonized the Bible were subject to human error and limitation," and that reading scripture was "like eating fish—we take the bones out to enjoy the meat. All parts are not of equal value."[17]

But his modernist-inflected theology was unimportant in the face of his consistently conservative ethos, which he was able to construct precisely because he read the Bible selectively: "Fifield dismissed the many passages in the New Testament about wealth and poverty and instead worked tirelessly to reconcile Christianity and capitalism. In his view, both systems rested on a basic belief that individuals would succeed or fail on their own merit."[18] His comments from the 1930s are nearly identical to the anti–government spending rhetoric of today's conservatives:

> "The President of the United States and his administration are responsible for the willful or unconscious destruction of thrift, initiative, industriousness and resourcefulness which have been among our best assets since Pilgrim days," he charged. . . . "Every Christian should oppose the

totalitarian trends of the New Deal," he warned in
another tract. . . . "The way out for America is not
ahead but back," he insisted. "How far back? Back as far
as the old Gospel which exalted individuals, which
placed responsibility for thought on individuals, and
which insisted that individuals should be free spirits
under God."[19]

Nicknamed the "Apostle to the Millionaires," Fifield was a
predecessor to today's churches that cater to the rich and famous, like Zoe Church and Hillsong. But he would expand his
influence beyond his own rich congregation by addressing business leaders and ministers directly through the organization he
created as a conservative/libertarian counterpoint to Roosevelt's
New Deal: Spiritual Mobilization. Spiritual Mobilization would
build upon the same tactics used by the publishers of *The Fundamentals*, growing a vast audience of tens of thousands of local
ministers over the course of the 1940s via direct mail, a monthly
magazine, radio, and television. Fifield used this network to
drum up resistance to FDR's social welfare programs among
clergy, emphasize conservative individualism, and portray capitalist thought as compatible with the gospel.

It is important to note that even as we focus on other elements of religious media and capitalism, whiteness still played a
part. Fifield himself repeated an anti-Semitic trope known as
the Franklin Forgery (published in 1934 by William Dudley
Pelley, a pro-Nazi presidential candidate of the Christian Party)
on the air in 1951.[20] In the aftermath, the Anti-Defamation
League demanded a public apology and received a retraction
from Fifield.[21] Such episodes reveal the degree to which the pre-
sumptions of white supremacy were present throughout white

American Christendom, regardless of whether one's theology and politics were identifiably "conservative" or "liberal" by today's standards. As Anthea Butler notes, "While evangelicals and fundamentalists battled each other over theology and scripture, their cultural and social racism held them together."[22]

In 1951, this work culminated in the creation of the Committee to Proclaim Liberty, which sought to codify capitalist sentiment as both pious and patriotic with a campaign it called Freedom Under God. As part of this campaign, they came up with an event they called Independence Sunday, which would take place on the Sunday before the Fourth of July and would see preachers across the country delivering sermons on the holiness of American individualism. The PR campaign for this makeshift holiday swept the nation, enlisting both local church leaders and famous boosters like Walt Disney and Bing Crosby; Jimmy Stewart emceed a special broadcast on CBS's national radio network.

Conservative Christianity, which had so recently considered itself under assault from liberals and modernists, had now found powerful allies in business, entertainment, the clergy, and government. Fifield and his allies had learned to adapt, not by altering their underlying beliefs about capitalism and whiteness but by finding ways to make those beliefs more palatable and moderate sounding through obfuscation or interpretative justification. They laid the groundwork for others to soften the hard edges of fundamentalism and take the gospel of antilabor, pro-business, socially conservative Christianity to broader audiences. With the right aesthetics, they were able to slingshot their message from their already considerable audience into mainstream mass media.

Starting in the late 1940s, a new wave of the movement took

on that mission with enthusiasm. They were called the neo-evangelicals, or New Evangelicals, and their most famous leader was Billy Graham.

BILLY GRAHAM WAS BORN IN North Carolina in 1918 to a Presbyterian family. His family attended church and listened to evangelical radio shows like the *Old Fashioned Revival Hour*, but Graham wasn't particularly drawn to religion at a young age. Historian Frances FitzGerald describes him as "an exuberant, gregarious lad, who dressed spiffily, drag-raced his father's car, and liked kissing girls. . . . He didn't want to stay on the farm, and while he dreamed of becoming a major league baseball player, he was no athlete."[23] In another era, these might not have seemed like the makings of a preacher, but this was a new era, inaugurated by Billy Sunday and expanded by James Fifield.

Graham responded to an altar call* at a local hellfire-and-brimstone revival at sixteen, but his day-to-day life didn't change much, seeing as he already didn't drink or dance. His mother sent him to Bob Jones College, which had been founded in Florida not long before as part of the Bible college boom, but he only lasted a semester there. (He didn't like the draconian rules, an experience millions of Christian college alumni can relate to.) Graham transferred to the nearby Florida Bible Institute, where, after a bad breakup, he recommitted himself to the

---

* An altar call, if you've escaped experiencing one, is when a preacher calls on anyone who wants to make a public commitment to Christ to come to the altar at the front of the church for prayer and blessings. This can be a moment of conversion in which someone is "born again" for the first time or an opportunity for a believer to rededicate themselves to Jesus if they feel they've grown too distant. Many evangelicals experience angst wondering if previous altar calls "counted" or "took" and thus participate over and over. I responded to an altar call at a Carman concert when I was in middle school.

Lord and began evangelizing. He met two local businessmen while working as a golf caddie, and they paid his way to Wheaton College for a year. While at Wheaton, he married Ruth Bell, and after a short stint as a parish pastor, he began working for Youth for Christ in 1945.[24]

Over the next several years, he spent much of his time touring the country, holding revivals he called "crusades," which would often run for days or weeks. The 1949 revivals Graham held in Los Angeles marked a turning point in his career. Two days before they kicked off, President Truman informed the American public that the Soviet Union had successfully tested an atomic bomb. Graham capitalized on the resulting fear and anxiety of the public to advance his cause, mixing nationalism with apocalypticism and denouncing communism as "a religion that is inspired, directed and motivated by the Devil himself who had declared war against Almighty God."[25] At the same revival, Graham followed in Fifield's footsteps by converting celebrities such as country singer Stuart Hamblen. This led newspaper magnate William Randolph Hearst to instruct reporters to "puff Graham"—once again, evangelical messaging had exceeded the bounds of purely evangelical media.[26]

In 1950, in the wake of the previous year's success, Graham founded the Billy Graham Evangelistic Association, which would "assure a reasonable turnout" by preparing local markets for his events via local committees, advertising, and volunteer training.[27] From there, Graham could build upon the cultural and institutional infrastructure of his predecessors, codifying white evangelical power and influence further still. For the rest of the twentieth century, he would leverage his celebrity in order to provide a legitimate, respectable face for conservative white evangelicalism.

While Graham is remembered as a grandfatherly presence among Gen Xers and millennials today, he cut a very different figure when he first entered the public consciousness in the 1940s and '50s. Graham exuded the white masculinity of the "All-American Male" that the era glorified.[28] In fact, this masculinity was part of his conversion story. As historian Kristin Kobes Du Mez writes in her book *Jesus and John Wayne*, "Before his conversion, Graham had 'always thought of religion as more or less "sissy,"' something well suited for 'old people and girls, but not for a real "he man" with red blood in his veins.'"[29] This performative masculinity was as valuable a marketing technique in postwar America as it had been during Billy Sunday's "muscular Christianity" days, and the rigid gender norms it promoted were even more central to its ideology. In Graham's estimation, enforcing a patriarchal family structure wasn't merely the Christian thing to do—it was essential to national security, because "a nation is only as strong as her homes."[30] Du Mez writes that

for Graham, a properly ordered family was a patriarchal one. Because Graham believed that God had cursed women to be under man's rule, he believed that wives must submit to husbands' authority. Graham acknowledged that this would come as a shock to certain "dictatorial wives," and he didn't hesitate to offer Christian housewives helpful tips: . . . "Give him love at any cost. Cultivate modesty and the delicacy of youth. Be attractive." . . . He had advice for men, too. A man was "God's representative"—the spiritual head of household, "the protector" and "provider of the home." Also, husbands should remember to give wives a box of candy from time to time.[31]

Unlike his predecessors who published *The Fundamentals*, Billy Graham was not a scholar; he was an evangelist first and foremost. Yet he evangelized for the same principles: fundamentalist mores, capitalist apologetics, and normative whiteness. These ideas coalesced in a school of thought known as Americanism, which Butler describes as "pride in the nation, in the founders, in the Declaration of Independence and the Constitution—and, most important, in the idea that America was a nation ordained by God to save the world."[32] (It's not hard to see the connection to today's Christian nationalism.)

Graham's Americanist gospel was explicitly anticommunist, antiunion, and procapitalist. He embraced business leaders, offering dedications for airlines and hotel chains, including the infamous benediction he delivered to a convention of hotel owners: "God bless you and thank you, and God bless the Holiday Inns."[33] That blessing presumably did not extend to Holiday Inn workers who might want to organize for better pay or working conditions; during a rally in 1952, Graham described the Garden of Eden as "a paradise with 'no union dues, no labor leaders, no snakes, no disease'" and argued that "a truly Christian worker 'would not stoop to take unfair advantage' of his employer by ganging up against him in a union."[34] Similarly, he said that "the most effective weapon against communism is to be a born-again Christian. . . . You get a man born again, and he will turn from communism."[35] From a theological standpoint, it may seem odd to define Christianity in terms of economic systems that didn't exist during the writing of any part of the Bible (no, not even Paul's epistles), but as we've seen, theology has never been the defining feature of evangelicalism.

Whiteness, however, has been, and Graham did little to break that pattern. As the civil rights era dawned, evangelicals tried to turn back the clock. Following the *Brown v. Board of Education* ruling that desegregated public schools, many evangelicals enrolled their children in "segregation academies" founded by evangelical organizations.[36] Graham preached all over the country, in both segregated and nonsegregated areas, and to his credit, he began leading integrated revivals in the early 1950s. However, despite the issue of civil rights being blatantly political, Graham insisted that the sole solution to racism was spiritual in nature. Historian Jesse Curtis highlights the comments Graham made the day before the March on Washington for Jobs and Freedom to a crusade audience in Los Angeles: " 'I am convinced that some extremists are going too far too fast,' he declared. 'Forced integration will never work.' The racial crisis would 'not be settled in the streets but it could be settled in the hearts of man.' "[37]

Such comments explain why Graham had a contentious relationship with Martin Luther King Jr.; he didn't attend the March on Washington in 1963, and following King's famous "I Have a Dream" speech, he remarked that "it would take the second coming of Christ before we would see white children walk hand in hand with black children."[38] In September 1963, following the bombing of the Sixteenth Street Baptist Church in Birmingham, Alabama, Graham's organization did not respond with support for civil rights legislation—they planned an integrated crusade for Easter 1964 in Birmingham.[39] While this event might have provided many of its attendees real emotional and spiritual healing, this type of response reveals what was permissible and what was not within the moral framework of evangelicalism: individual pain can be ministered to by Christ, but collective action that threatens the social order dictated by white supremacy and capitalism must be resisted. Evangelical elites were happy to encourage change that mimicked capitalist growth—ever-climbing numbers of conversions, rising donations and tithes, record attendance at revivals and crusades, and expanding audiences reached via radio, print, and television—but not change that challenged the racial or economic status quo.

Of course, while people of color were supposed to solve systemic racism on an individual level and women were supposed to defeat communism through their individual marriages, evangelicalism as a movement did not reject political action in the same way when it came to its own agenda. While the previous wave of evangelicals had done ideological battle against FDR, the movement had now accrued enough cachet to take the opposite tack: they tried to ally with politicians in order to enact their agenda.

Graham began pursuing political influence as his reputation grew, remarking at the 1952 crusade in Washington, D.C., that "I'm appealing to a higher-type social strata."[40] He found patrons and allies in the very rich, such as the Texas oilman Sid Richardson, who once called the Speaker of the House to personally advocate for Graham to be allowed to lead a religious service at the foot of the Capitol Building in Washington.[41] And while in his later years he attempted to present himself as a nonpartisan figure, Graham (a lifelong registered Democrat) would regularly court partisan political favor, seeking to provide counsel to presidents—with varying degrees of success. In a 1950 meeting, Graham did not impress President Truman, who felt he acted too familiar; Graham would later turn on Truman and belittle him to the press.[42] He had better luck with Eisenhower and other political figures who saw religiosity as a matter of national security during the Cold War. It was only after his own high-profile embarrassment during the collapse of the Nixon administration that Graham would learn to be more discreet with his political proclamations and would settle into a more subdued form of political influence (in stark contrast to the future partisanship of his son Franklin Graham, an ardent Trump supporter).

When Graham did focus on theology, it was informed by premillennial apocalypticism—how and when Jesus would return and the world would end.* While Graham was certainly a member of the New Evangelicals who sought to soften the image and content of their fundamentalist forebears, he still held to dispensational premillennialist beliefs about Christ's imminent return. Historian Matthew Avery Sutton puts it in the simplest terms: "Graham never doubted that the time was nigh."[43] Like so many premillennialists, Graham predicted a few dates: in 1950, he said it would be between two and five years (!), and in 1957, following the launch of Sputnik, he invoked the impending apocalypse once again.

There is something inherently nihilistic about this premillennialist worldview. It puts so little emphasis on addressing societal ills—why try to solve a difficult and unpleasant problem like segregation given that Christ is going to return at any moment and make it a moot point? Instead, an *individual* response to the gospel is necessary in order to assure *individual* salvation, and any large-scale issue, real or imagined, simply becomes another bit of proof to reinforce both your political opinions and your apocalypticism. Thus, in 1965, Graham published a book titled *World Aflame* that listed current events he considered signs

---

*   We use the word "apocalypse" to mean the end of the world, but if you weren't raised in the church, you might not know that it comes from the Greek word for "revelation"—as in the book of Revelation, from which people draw most of their (highly interpretive) ideas about the Second Coming.

of the apocalypse. They "included hydrogen bombs, the population explosion, increasing crime, sexual perversion, homosexuality, immorality, dependence on pills and alcohol, political turmoil, and a lack of true faith. The most controversial movements of the day, such as feminism, civil rights, and the battle against communism, served as additional signs."[44]

Lists like these, as imagined by Graham and other evangelicals, cast the movement's political opponents—who were often marginalized people advocating for equal rights—as harbingers of the apocalypse. This cosmology takes evangelicalism's in-group identity formation to a logical extreme; outsiders aren't just strange or bad people, they're the literal end of the world. We don't necessarily remember Billy Graham as an extremist figure, but this is rather extreme—and evangelicalism would only get more extreme in the years to come.

5

IT WASN'T *ROE*

THE RISE OF THE RELIGIOUS RIGHT

I spent so much time discussing Billy Graham in the previous chapter not just because he was midcentury evangelicalism's most prominent figurehead but also because he typified the movement. Graham's individual views and actions embodied the larger movement's views and actions, from his machismo to his Americanism to his telegenic charisma. He successfully harnessed the media of the era to promote a version of religion that combined American exceptionalism and capitalism into a consumerist package that didn't oppose the hegemonic power of capitalism and whiteness but rather celebrated them. But there is one view Graham held that may come as a shock even (or especially) to people who grew up saturated in evangelicalism: he was not against abortion.

How is it possible that Graham, with all his patriarchal blus-
ter and political ambition, was *not* a committed pro-life warrior?
While the idea of it is nearly inconceivable today, the truth is
that well into the 1970s, there was no evangelical consensus on
the topic of abortion; it was considered a "Catholic issue," as
strictures against abortion had been enshrined in the Catholic
catechism for centuries. Evangelicals, who defined themselves
partially in opposition to Catholicism, didn't see the issue the
same way. Graham himself "said in 1968, 'In general, I would
disagree with [the Catholic stance],' adding, 'I believe in planned
parenthood.'"[1] Nor did evangelicals balk when the Supreme
Court case *Roe v. Wade* legalized abortion nationwide in 1973.
In her book *The Power Worshippers*, journalist Katherine Stewart
writes:

> The 1971 convention of the Southern Baptists endorsed
> a resolution calling for the legalization of abortion to
> preserve the "emotional, mental, and physical health of
> the mother" as well as in cases of rape, incest, and
> "deformity." The convention approved the same
> resolution after *Roe*, in 1974, calling it a "middle ground
> between the extreme of abortion on demand and the
> opposite extreme of all abortion as murder," and again
> in 1976.[2]

How do we square unambiguous institutional approval of
abortion with the common perception that the current incarna-
tion of the evangelical movement first galvanized around *Roe* in
1973? To understand how myth came to replace truth, we must
turn our attention to Paul Weyrich. Though he was lesser known
in the public consciousness than his press-coverage-coveting

contemporaries and allies, his influence is profound. Weyrich was not an evangelical but a deeply conservative Catholic—so conservative, in fact, that he joined an Eastern rite Catholic church after deciding that Roman Catholicism had become too liberal. Like evangelicals, though, he had a flair for media, and he got his start as a political reporter and radio personality in Wisconsin before moving to Washington, D.C., in 1967. After spending time in the Beltway, journalist Sarah Posner writes, his two key insights were that "conservatives had failed to match what he believed to be liberalism's powerful institutions guiding policy making in Washington," and that "the old guard of the conservative movement was too focused on free market economics and not enough on moral, cultural, and religious issues."[3]

Weyrich wanted to fight back against the Democratic victories of prior decades, including the Civil Rights Movement, and he became convinced that conservatives should tap into the animating force of religion the way MLK and other civil rights leaders had. But Catholics, while obviously a large portion of the American population, didn't have the same kind of political power Protestants did. At the time, there had only been one Catholic president, John F. Kennedy, and some Protestants had considered his denomination a national security threat because they (irrationally) feared he'd take orders from the pope.[*] If Weyrich wanted to push his conservative agenda, he couldn't just rally Catholics—he'd have to find Protestant allies too. Evangelicals, who had proven so skillful at influencing culture and politics, and who had considerable media prowess, would make for powerful partners, but how could he persuade them they had common cause with him when they had such different

---

[*]   Even today, there has still only been one other Catholic president: Joe Biden.

stances on issues like abortion? He began conversing regularly with many of the media-savvy evangelical leaders who had sprung up in Billy Graham's wake, including Jerry Falwell and Pat Robertson, about what Stewart calls the "hot-button issues of religious conservatives" that "lay at the intersection of federal power, race, and religion."[4]

In the late '70s, Weyrich finally found the hot-button issue he needed. In his own words from 1990, "It wasn't the abortion issue; that wasn't sufficient"—rather, "what caused the movement to surface was the federal government's moves against Christian schools."[5] Christian schooling was under attack by the government! How so? Well, a series of Supreme Court cases ruled that Christian schools, from kindergartens to colleges, could not discriminate on the basis of race. The "segregation academies" evangelicals had established after *Brown v. Board of Education* could no longer stay segregated, and, notably, Bob Jones University lost its tax-exempt status. Again, Weyrich's own words from 1990 give a sense of how he spun the issue to avoid mentioning race: "This absolutely shattered the Christian community's notion that Christians could isolate themselves inside their own institutions and teach what they pleased."[6] Or, as religious historian Randall Balmer puts it, "evangelical leaders, prodded by Weyrich, chose to interpret the IRS ruling against segregationist schools as an assault on the integrity and sanctity of the evangelical subculture."[7]

As discussed earlier, Christian education had become an incredibly important part of evangelical culture and a crucial way of differentiating the subculture within society. Like nearly every potential threat, this one was treated as existential. One reason this tactic was effective was evangelicalism's rigorous cultivation of an in-group identity, which could easily be channeled into an us-against-the-world antagonism or a sense of aggrieved victimization. And sometimes evangelicals really were excluded or disrespected by mainstream society and mainline Protestants—I think, for example, of when mainline theologian Karl Barth laughed at the founding editor of the New Evangelical publication *Christianity Today* for believing in a literal virgin birth, quipping, "Did you say Christianity *Today* or Christianity *Yesterday?*"[8] But, needless to say, that kind of exclusion and disrespect rather pales in comparison to literal segregation. In the end, the principle that finally united conservative Catholics and evangelicals was just . . . racism.

This alliance would previously have been almost unthinkable. Bob Jones famously once said, "I would rather see a saloon on every corner than a Catholic in the White House"; now his university's tax status formed the linchpin in the union with Catholics. But conservative Christian leaders saw an opportunity to achieve their goals via "cobelligerent Christianity," and they took it.[9] Thus the movement known as the "religious right" (sometimes called the Christian right or the new Christian right) was born, and organizations like the Moral Majority, the Heritage Foundation, and Focus on the Family began to appear. A few conservative members of other faiths such as Judaism and Mormonism were involved in some of these organizations, but Catholics and evangelicals were the driving force.

This confluence of concerns about preserving whiteness and power led the religious right's two main denominational factions to join forces on certain matters they'd previously disagreed on, in what historian of religion, sex, and gender Megan Goodwin calls "the catholicization of public morality."[10] Prior to this, evangelicals and other American Protestants "as far back as the Puritans received ethical instruction that the primary purpose of sex between married partners should not be mere procreation, but increased intimacy and shared pleasure."[11] But now issues like contraception, abortion, abstinence, and sexual purity all became inextricable from the concept of "the family."

This was far from the first time evangelicals had used the metaphorical family as the justification for abhorrent ideology. Scholar Bradley Onishi has documented how, in the antebellum South, "evangelicals claimed that enslaved people were part of the family, the family was ordained by God, and thus to usurp its structure would be to go against God's plan for human-kind."[12] Now the concept was mobilized for a different purpose. This meant that changing cultural mores surrounding sexuality and gender were perceived as an affront to "the family," and any moves away from a white conservative sexual ethic were signs of "moral decline." Abortion was the perfect flash-point issue for this change in attitude because it let conservatives cast their misogynistic disgust with female sexuality as something holy and urgent. They could channel their sexual disapproval into accusations of literal murder, and if their opponents defended reproductive rights, it only proved they were depraved, bloodthirsty monsters.

Soon, it was much more popular to say that the religious right formed around "the family" and "the sanctity of unborn life" than around supporting school segregation into the early '80s. That version of the story conveniently obscured evangelicalism's real and very recent history of blatant racism, replacing it with a fake history of consistent, long-standing opposition to abortion. It made the racism seem trivial and the oppression of women seem divinely ordained since time immemorial. The pivot to abortion was strategic, as was the effort to bury the real motivations of the powerful individuals and institutions that steered everyday rank-and-file evangelicals.

When I was still one of those rank-and-file evangelicals, I was heavily indoctrinated into the belief that the religious right was founded on abortion. I didn't learn better until almost a decade after graduating from a Christian college, when I read an article written by Randall Balmer (whom I've quoted throughout this section) and discovered that the truth is readily accessible in the historical record and openly attested to by Weyrich and others. That the myth has survived for so long is a testament to the amount of work that has gone into spreading it. Evangelical leaders have the power to steer the attention of large swaths of people and alter the content of those people's lived, genuine faith. Learning that you've been manipulated not by the hand of God but by your fellow believers can be profoundly disorienting and discouraging. It forces you to either disavow a sincerely held belief or double down on your convictions, with major emotional, intellectual, spiritual, and social consequences.

But I'm getting ahead of myself. We'll get to the *ex*vangelicals soon. For now, let's stay with the evangelicals.

WITH CHRISTIAN SCHOOLS UNDER "ATTACK" by antisegregationists, some evangelical parents turned to a different form of education entirely: homeschooling. Even more than Christian schools, homeschooling let parents control exactly what their children encountered and learned about. It also further reified the concept of the idealized family: mothers didn't need to work, and children didn't need to go to school. Labor and education could be performed in their rightful place: the family home. But homeschool moms—they were and still are virtually always moms—didn't necessarily have a background in early education or pedagogy. They needed trustworthy sources to turn to for textbooks, curricula, and other educational materials, and several organizations founded in the early 1970s were ready to meet that need, including Accelerated Christian Education (ACE), Abeka Books, and Christian Liberty Academy School System (CLASS), plus, of course, Bob Jones University.

Two closely related schools of thought played an outsize role in the development of these homeschool curricula (which are also commonly used in private Christian schools): Christian reconstructionism and dominionism.* Without getting too into the weeds on the terminology, these are movements whose goal is to establish a Christian government that would enforce biblical law—that is, they want to *reconstruct* society so it's under the *dominion* of the Lord. If this sounds vaguely familiar, that's because these movements originated many of what we now refer to as "Christian nationalist" talking points.

The godfather of reconstructionism was R. J. Rushdoony, an archconservative Calvinist who, according to religious historian Julie Ingersoll, "developed and then helped popularize what he called a 'biblical worldview' " in which "the Bible speaks to every aspect of life and provides a blueprint for living according to the will of God."[13] While a statement like "the Bible speaks to every aspect of life" may seem abstract and innocuous, Rushdoony imagined a very particular kind of Christian nation, informed by Civil War–era "Southern Presbyterian theologian R.L. Dabney . . . an apologist for slavery; and a

---

* For a more thorough examination of these theopolitical projects, please refer to Julie Ingersoll's pivotal text, *Building God's Kingdom: Inside the World of Christian Reconstruction.*

defender of the agrarian patriarchal ways of life that characterized the Old South."[14] Reconstructionists present their highly prescriptive, patriarchal expectations of how government, society, and church should be ordered as *the* biblical worldview— and they have a strategy to submit all of human life to "the Lordship of Christ."[15]

This strategy is "two-pronged. There is the short-term effort to engage in electoral politics and then bring pressure on elected officials. The more long-term strategy is to 'raise up generations of leaders' with the skills and the worldview to 'usher in the Kingdom of God.'"[16] Children need to be steeped in these ideas at a young age so that they grow up to put them into action. Reconstructionists and evangelicals in general have been working to "raise up generations of leaders" for decades, first with Christian schools and then with homeschooling. The Christian curriculum companies established in the '70s gave parents a whole new alternative educational environment with which to resist modernism and propagate fundamentalist mores and beliefs.

These companies have persisted since the '70s. In the 2021 book *Hijacking History*, Kathleen Wellman writes: "With over a million students using its textbooks, Abeka Books is the largest US publisher of Christian textbooks and the largest provider for the homeschool market. . . . Its K–12 curriculum is now used in more than 10,000 Christian schools. . . . By 1998, over 225,000 families purchased their textbooks independently of schools."[17] And their reconstructionist influences have only become more entrenched. For example, an Abeka textbook on American history calls the United States "the greatest nation on the face of the earth" but says that "no nation can remain great without God's blessing."[18] An ACE textbook on the same subject reads: "The south suffered greatly both from the war and the period of reconstruction that followed but 'de land ob cotton' rose from the ashes to become the bible belt, a part of the country that has continued to stand firm on the fundamentals of Christian faith."[19]

The full academic, social, and psychological impact of Christian schooling and homeschooling—which often entail neglect or abuse—is beyond the purview of both this text and my own lived experience, but suffice it to say that homeschooling became an invaluable part of the evangelical media ecosystem and remains so to this day, turning generations of children into culture warriors ready to go to battle for the evangelical gospel of whiteness and power.*

FROM ITS EARLIEST DAYS, EVANGELICALISM has consistently prioritized sociopolitical ideology over faith, but as the religious right developed, the "religious" part became even more secondary to the "right." This is plainly illustrated in the way the movement vilified President Jimmy Carter. A devout Southern Baptist, his religious beliefs closely matched those of evangelicals, at least on paper. But they couldn't stomach his liberal policies, which included pardoning draft evaders, signing nuclear arms control agreements, and handing over control of the Panama Canal to Panama. The Bible doesn't exactly contain detailed commandments about nuclear arms, but that wasn't important to a movement that valorized "strength" and "masculinity" first and foremost.

Carter became such a boogeyman to them that decades

---

* One prominent example is the youth organization Generation Joshua, whose stated vision is "to assist parents to raise up the next generation of Christian leaders and citizens, equipped to positively influence the political processes of today and tomorrow." (Generation Joshua, "About.")

later, in 2009, conservative activist Grover Norquist anachro-
nistically blamed Carter for the very formation of the religious
right, saying, "it didn't get started in '73 with *Roe v. Wade.* It
started in '77 or '78 with the Carter administration's attack on
Christian schools."[20] In actuality, most of the relevant events
related to the desegregation of Christian schools happened before Carter took office in 1977; Bob Jones University lost its
tax-exempt status on January 19, 1976.[21]

In June 1980, Carter organized the White House Conference
on Families, in hopes that it would join liberals and conservatives together in common cause. That is not what happened.
Instead, in a *Washington Post* story on the conference, Paul Weyrich is quoted as saying that Carter "has the worst record for
family issues for any president in history"—possibly somewhat
of an exaggeration.[22] Conservatives balked at the mere inclusion
of their liberal counterparts and, as is their custom, refused to
participate. Du Mez writes:

> Fuming that conference organizers had excluded
> conservatives' issues—including banning abortion,
> defending school prayer, and opposing gay rights—from
> their final recommendations, conservative delegates
> walked out of the official conference in protest. The next
> month, they organized their own counter-conference in
> Long Beach, California, an event that united the forces
> of the pro-family Religious Right. [James] Dobson,
> [Phyllis] Schlafly, [Jerry] Falwell, and the LaHayes [Tim
> and Beverly] all spoke, rallying the troops.[23]

Ronald Reagan, in the middle of his presidential campaign,
saw an opportunity. He didn't come close to having the same

evangelical bona fides as Carter; he belonged to nonevangelical denominations (first Disciples of Christ, then Presbyterian) and wasn't a regular churchgoer. A contemporary source once said, "He goes to church several times a year—on the holidays. He just doesn't feel it's necessary to go every Sunday."[24] He had also been divorced and, as California governor, had supported the Equal Rights Amendment, signed a law legalizing abortion, and would not lend support to an anti–gay rights referendum. This might seem to be disqualifying among a group that was so "pro-family" it wouldn't countenance the mere presence of Democrats. But he was a staunch capitalist who, as a former Hollywood actor, embodied white masculinity, and it was becoming ever clearer that this was what evangelicals truly valued.

One month after the conservatives' alternative Long Beach Pro-Family Conference, Reagan addressed 15,000 pastors and other activists in August 1980 at a gathering of the newly formed Religious Roundtable in Dallas's Reunion Arena. He told them, in no uncertain terms, "I know this is a non-partisan gathering, and so I know that you can't endorse me, but I only brought that up because I want you to know that I endorse you and what you are doing."[25] If this framing seems like a rather small fig leaf trying to conceal the reality that the event *was* de facto partisan and was, in fact, hosting the presidential candidate of a political party, well, that didn't bother the religious right. This was an inflection point, and not in a mere symbolic manner—multiple contemporary and future architects of the conservative movements within evangelicalism and Republican politics were present, including Paul Weyrich, Jerry Falwell Sr., and even a young Mike Huckabee. For the first time—but not the last—white evangelicals rallied behind a divorced candidate whose prior positions seemingly ran counter to their stated values and helped elect him to the White House. Moving forward, the evangelical political culture by and large codified behind the GOP, a level of faithfulness and certitude still counted on by Republicans to this day.

One of the conference's organizers, who effectively fed Reagan the "you can't endorse me, but I endorse you" framing, was a man named James Robison. We've seen that, across the sweep of evangelical history, the movement has always been quick to adopt new media and use it to expand its sphere of influence, from dedicated publishing houses to radio broadcasts. Robison was a high-profile figure in the newest media wave: televangelism. He and other televangelists, like the Christian Broadcasting Network's Pat Robertson, took advantage of the new medium of cable broadcasting to build massive audiences over the course of the 1970s and '80s.

As their audiences grew, so did their political ambitions—if not for political office (as was the case for Robertson, who would run for president in 1988), then for political influence. In fact, the very idea for certain prominent conservative advocacy groups was born indirectly via televangelism. A television station had dropped Robison for making homophobic remarks on the air, fearing he had violated the Fairness Doctrine, a policy of the Federal Communications Commission (FCC) that required broadcasters to give airtime to both sides of controversial issues. In the year prior to the 1980 conference where Reagan spoke, Robison had met with Jerry Falwell, Paul Weyrich, and others after an anti–Fairness Doctrine rally, and thus the Moral Majority and the Religious Roundtable were born.[26]

Televangelists helped Reagan get elected (and the Fairness

Doctrine abolished), but their influence would eventually wane, largely due to scandals both sexual and financial. If you remember nothing else about the era, you probably remember Jim and Tammy Faye Bakker, who started out on Pat Robertson's Christian Broadcasting Network before spinning off to form their own network. They fell from grace when fellow televangelist Jimmy Swaggart accused Jim Bakker of having an affair with Jessica Hahn, a church secretary to whom Bakker had paid hush money. Bakker resigned and handed his ministry to Jerry Falwell. When Hahn later told her own story, it differed drastically from the initial framing of an affair: "In Hahn's telling, beneath the scandal and sensationalism was an act of violence, the manipulation and rape of a young woman, a preacher's abuse of power, and the betrayal of a faith community. Bakker's lawyer, meanwhile, claimed he was the victim."[27] (Swaggart would eventually be caught in his own sex scandal.)

Televangelism wasn't and isn't a purely evangelical phenomenon. In fact, the most famous televangelists, including Swaggart and the Bakkers, tended to be not evangelical but charismatic. The lines between charismatic denominations and evangelical ones can sometimes be blurry, and they share many theological similarities, including doctrines like biblical inerrancy, but the defining feature of charismatic churches is their emphasis on "spiritual gifts" like speaking in tongues and faith healing. (The use of the word "charismatic" in this context comes from the Greek word *charism*, meaning "spiritual gift.") Some televangelists straddled the line between the two camps, like Pat Robertson, a Southern Baptist who nonetheless incorporated charismatic worship practices into his ministry. In any case, TV shows and TV networks became one more arrow in evangelicals' media-savvy quiver.

The increasingly dominant conservatism of evangelical media did not occur in a vacuum. As historian Nicole Hemmer writes in *Messengers of the Right*: "Everywhere one looked in the 1980s, conservatism was on the rise."[28] In the early years of the first Reagan administration, certain conservative outlets wished for an even more conservative president and criticized Reagan using now-common ideological purity tests on issues such as abortion and gun control. This led to conservative infighting with more moderate pro-Reagan conservatives, though the two factions brokered an uneasy peace in unified opposition to a Cold War arms control treaty that favored negotiation over armed conflict. Neither branch of conservatism seemed to sway Reagan's administration, which didn't seem to see itself as beholden to media activism. But, as Hemmer writes, "Reagan may have governed in an era of limited media activism, but his administration helped ensure future presidents would face far different conditions."[29] Crucially, the Fairness Doctrine that had so irked Robison and Weyrich was repealed by Reagan-appointed FCC chairman Dennis R. Patrick in 1987. This would have far-reaching consequences for the conservative media empire, as we'll see in later chapters.

Clearly, the 1970s and '80s were a time when evangelicals formalized and consolidated power. They made strategic alliances with other conservatives, established official organizations, and intentionally wielded their influence in culture and politics. But not everyone fell in line during these decades. As we'll see in the next chapter, there were those who rebelled against evangelical conservatism and tried to reform the movement from the inside.

6

THE DREAM OF URBANA 70

PROGRESSIVE REFORM EFFORTS AND THEIR LIMITS

T hus far, I've given a brief survey of the history of American evangelicalism in the nineteenth and twentieth centuries, demonstrating how it grew into a movement based on power, capitalism, and whiteness. But as we saw in chapter 2, this path was not inevitable. Early American evangelicalism had wild roots that grew in all manner of directions. One of those directions eventually became the dominant strain we know today, but there were plenty of others that existed alongside it. In fact, though they usually haven't prevailed, more progressive versions of evangelicalism have always existed, and they're an important part of the movement's history. So, while prior chapters have looked at how today's dominant evangelical institutions and norms were built over time, in this chapter, we'll consider some of the reform efforts that emerged around the same time as the religious right and tried to steer evangelicalism in a different direction.

In many ways, you could say neo-evangelicalism itself started as a type of reform movement. Typified by preachers like Billy Graham, publications like *Christianity Today* (which counts Graham as its founder), organizations like the National Association of Evangelicals, and schools like the Fuller Theological Seminary, this movement sought to "differentiate itself from its fundamentalist forebearers by rallying conservative Protestants around both orthodoxy and a kinder, gentler cultural reengagement."[1] In historian Anthea Butler's words, it "promoted a forward-thinking Christianity that was not as staid as the fundamentalist versions of earlier times. In a striking shift, these new evangelical believers were willing to engage the world, media, and scholarship."[2]

However, as we saw in chapter 4, their reforms only went so far. As Butler writes, "their grip on the cultural and social visions they wanted to promote was pointedly circumscribed . . . by racial exclusivity," and "the political action they engaged in set them up to claim new power while also placing them . . . in opposition to the movement for civil and social rights for African Americans."[3] Take *Christianity Today*. According to its website, the magazine "set out to become, in Graham's words, a 'flag to follow' for believers who did not feel at home in progressive mainline congregations or in reactionary fundamentalist settings. It would 'restore intellectual respectability and spiritual impact to evangelical Christianity.' "[4] They may have been gentler and more willing to engage with the outside world than the previous generation's fundamentalists, but as the previous chapter illustrates, the New Evangelicals' seemingly moderate stance did not challenge the underlying beliefs or the politics of capitalism, patriarchy, and whiteness. Power was only successfully accumulated by people who played by those rules.

Where did this leave Black evangelicals? Black evangelicals have long been a part of the American religious landscape. You may remember from chapter 2 that some Black Protestant denominations were categorized as evangelical as far back as Robert Baird's 1844 book, *Religion in America*. But if Black and white evangelicals hold the same religious beliefs, isn't it odd, from a theological standpoint, that Black denominations would even need to exist? Butler explains it like this:

> The general expectation of white evangelicals in both the nineteenth and twentieth centuries was that nonwhite believers would take on the practices and viewpoints of white members and leadership, no matter the cultural context in which Black evangelicals had been born or raised. As a result, tensions surrounding race and ethnicity commonly lodged in harsh criticism of Black cultural practices of dress, singing, or worship expressions. In order for Black evangelicals to belong, they had to emulate whiteness.[5]

It was all well and good for Billy Graham to advocate for a "color-blind gospel" following the Watts riots, but in practice, the church's whiteness was still normative and exclusionary. Thus, while Black evangelicals have participated in evangelicalism broadly, many have developed their own traditions so they can practice their faith without being subject to the racism of white Christians. At the same time, Black evangelicals have, as we say in churchspeak, offered a consistent witness to white evangelicals for decades, asking them to reckon with the racism that plagues them.

One person offering this witness was Bill Pannell, a Black evangelical who'd had pastoral roles in a few different Christian organizations, including Youth for Christ, where Billy Graham got his start. Yet Pannell found that his passion for evangelical religious beliefs only got him so far in such organizations. In his 1968 book, *My Friend, The Enemy*, he describes in incisive language the racist limits of white evangelical acceptance he'd experienced: "I have no trouble believing you want me to be in your church to sing on Sunday. I have very little faith that you want me in your living room for serious discussion."[6]

In 1968, Pannell left Youth for Christ to become vice president of Tom Skinner Associates (TSA), an evangelical organization founded by Black author and evangelist Tom Skinner. The next year, he was joined by Carl Ellis as senior campus minister, and Ellis had big plans for an upcoming national event: Urbana 70.

Starting in the 1940s, the Urbana Student Missions Conference has been held every three years on the campus of the University of Illinois Urbana-Champaign—hence the name.* Sponsored by the InterVarsity Christian Fellowship, it gathers together Christian college students from around the country to educate them about and encourage them to engage in missionary work at home and abroad. After attending as a college student in 1967, Ellis, like many other Black attendees, was dis-

---

* Technically, the first Urbana was in Toronto, and in the 2000s, it changed location, first to St. Louis and then to Indianapolis, but it retains the name Urbana.

appointed by how thoroughly white the event was: "I didn't see anybody from my neighborhood there. I didn't see anyone talking about missions to the cities or about the concerns of the black population. And I said to myself, 'I hope these people aren't deliberately doing this.'"[7] To do something about this problem, he got his new boss, Tom Skinner, added to the list of speakers for the next conference in 1970.

Urbana 70 was already unusual in that frequent guest Billy Graham was not invited to speak that year, as younger evangelicals were put off by his close public association with Nixon.[8] But it went much further than that; the entire theme of the conference was "World Evangelism: Why? How? Who?" The event was, after all, ostensibly about global Christianity, and many young evangelicals wanted to take that seriously, to genuinely engage with Christians around the world instead of assuming they should or could export a white American Jesus.* The official list of topics included "U.S. racism," "social action," "student power," and "revolution."[9] Scholar Melani McAlister writes that a whole "series of speakers denounced racism, colonialism, and the generally self-satisfied attitude of the North American church," including Samuel Escobar, a theologian from Peru who called on attendees to expand their notion of "sin" to "one that took political issues seriously."[10]

But no one was more memorable than Tom Skinner, who pulled no punches in a barn burner of a speech excoriating white evangelical racism.

---

* Such soul-searching about the role of international missions had taken place earlier in other ecumenical circles, notably the 1932 text *Re-Thinking Missions: A Laymen's Inquiry After One Hundred Years*, but these young evangelicals in 1970 had been largely cut off from that tradition by prior schisms.

Understand that for those of us in the Black community, it was not the evangelical who came and taught us our worth and dignity as Black men. It was not the Bible-believing fundamentalist who stood up and told us that Black was beautiful. It was not the evangelical who preached to us that we should stand on our own two feet and be men, be proud that Black was beautiful, and that God could work his life out through our redeemed Blackness. Rather, it took [Black Power activists] Stokely Carmichael, Rap Brown, and the Brothers to declare to us our dignity. God will not be without a witness.[11]

Skinner fully embraced the theology of evangelicalism but rejected the notion that this should translate to support for certain political parties or economic systems.

The thing you must recognize is that Jesus Christ is no more a capitalist than he is a socialist or a communist. He is no more a Democrat than he is a Republican. He is no more the president of the New York Stock Exchange than he is the head of the Socialist Party. He is neither of that. He is the Lord of heaven and earth.[12]

Urbana 70 was a significant event, revealing a nascent evangelical left that would continue to grow through the 1970s, even as Paul Weyrich was casting about for conservative evangelical allies to form the religious right. One expression of that growth was the Chicago Declaration of Evangelical Social Concern. Published in 1973, it was developed under the leadership of a (white) Canadian theologian named Ron Sider and signed by fifty-three racially diverse evangelical leaders and thinkers, including Samuel Escobar, Bill Pannell, and Donald Dayton. It read, in part:

> We acknowledge that God requires justice. But we have not proclaimed or demonstrated his justice to an unjust American society. Although the Lord calls us to defend the social and economic rights of the poor and oppressed, we have mostly remained silent. We deplore the historic involvement of the church in America with racism. . . . Further, we have failed to condemn the exploitation of racism at home and abroad by our economic system. . . . So we call our fellow evangelical Christians to demonstrate repentance in a Christian discipleship that confronts the social and political injustice of our nation.[13]

The declaration soon led Sider to found Evangelicals for Social Action in an attempt to mobilize evangelicals to combat issues like racism and sexism based on biblical notions of justice. Over the next two decades, it would advocate progressive positions from a Christian perspective on matters such as nuclear armament, the Reagan administration's involvement in Nicaragua, and antiapartheid sanctions against South Africa. By 1999, it launched the Evangelical Environmental Network.

Nevertheless, despite the excitement of the early 1970s, the evangelical left never met with the level of success that the religious right would enjoy by the end of the decade. As theologian and author Isaac Sharp puts it, "the more influence [progressive evangelicals] gained, the more vicious and vocal their persistent critics became."[14] Progressives were maligned by conservative voices in broader evangelical circles as being Marxists and socialists. A century of free-market-capitalist, media-savvy, corporate evangelical culture was hard to overcome; when one side of a debate has wealthy backers, political influence, and a well-oiled media machine while the other doesn't, it's not a mystery who will ultimately come out on top. Liberal evangelicals simply could not compete in an environment that saw them as suspect from the outset. No matter how persuasive their arguments were, even if they appealed to the evangelical conscience and rooted their reasoning in the Bible, they couldn't instantly disperse it to faithful consumers through a dedicated network of print and broadcast media the way conservative evangelicals could.

What is notable about the progressive evangelicals is that their leaders were, almost to a man, well, men—and straight, mostly white men at that. Yet even for someone like Sider, who in addition to his progressive economic and racial beliefs maintained a "consistent life ethic" that opposed abortion as well as the death penalty, it wasn't enough. These men's evangelical pedigrees were consistently questioned, because no matter how deep their knowledge of the Bible, no matter how sincere their love of God, no matter how well reasoned their theology, they were not adhering to the true defining features of evangelicalism, namely, capitalism, nationalism, and whiteness. And if a progressive white man cannot be tolerated, what chance does anyone else have?

PARALLEL WITH THE FIGHT FOR racial justice within evangelicalism was a fight for gender justice as part of a movement that became known as Christian feminism or biblical feminism.

Within secular progressive enclaves,* it may be common to think of Christianity and feminism as diametrically opposed, but in many ways, the concept of Christian feminism is not a radical interpretation of Protestant doctrine. The Bible depicts plenty of strong women playing important roles, from Jael driving a tent stake through the head of an enemy general to Esther saving her people from genocide in Persia. In the New Testament, several female followers of Jesus are mentioned by name, including Mary Magdalene, who, unlike any male disciples, was present at Jesus's crucifixion and resurrection. The Apostle Paul mentions Junia as "prominent among the apostles" (Romans 16:7). At the same time, the Bible is rife with misogyny, not least of which is Paul's statement in 1 Corinthians 14:34–35 that "women should be silent in the churches. For they are not permitted to speak, but should be subordinate. . . . If there is anything they desire to know, let them ask their husbands at home. For it is shameful for a woman to speak in church."

Needless to say, that misogyny has an effect on evangelical women. In her book *Evangelical Christian Women*, about those who have dedicated themselves to improving women's quality of life within evangelical faith communities, religious historian Julie Ingersoll quotes a female faculty member at a conservative seminary who couldn't understand why God gave her the gifts of preaching and teaching, since she was born a woman and forbidden to use them. This led her to a terrifying conclusion: "So the only way, ultimately, that I could please God would be to kill

---

*   My use of language like "secular progressive enclaves" demonstrates how hard it can be to speak across the evangelical/non-evangelical divide. Someone who is not religious does not necessarily think of themselves as "secular," but someone who has spent time in evangelicalism understands intuitively what I mean.

myself. Because nothing I could ever do as a living human being, because of being a woman, could ever please God."[15] Christian feminism was a lifeline for many women within evangelical communities. Ingersoll writes: "They compared their discovery of the biblical feminist movement to finding home after being lost for years; the terms they use are quite like terms used to describe a conversion experience. Feeling alienated from the rest of Christendom, many of those involved found a surrogate church and family among their evangelical feminist sisters."[16]

Instead of turning to more liberal forms of Christianity, evangelical Christian feminists used astute biblical readings to try to reform evangelicalism from within. When cofounding the Evangelical Women's Caucus, originally as a subgroup of Evangelicals for Social Action, Nancy Hardesty wrote that "women should be allowed to exercise fully whatever gifts the Holy Spirit has endowed them with, including public leadership," that women should get equal pay and opportunities for advancement in the workforce and in education, and that "women should exercise equal rights and responsibilities with their husbands in the marital relationship and in regard to any children. A woman's homemaking should be considered of equal value with other work outside the home and compensated accordingly."[17] In a later book written with fellow EWC member Letha Dawson Scanzoni, she is "prochoice regarding abortion" and even "leaves open the possibility of lesbianism," because "though the scripture prohibited homosexual acts, 'neither Paul nor any other biblical writer speaks of a "homosexual orientation" or of an attraction for members of one's own sex.'"[18]

This last issue proved to be a sticking point. In 1986, after the Evangelical Women's Caucus voted to support civil rights for gay people, a more conservative faction split off and became the Christians for Biblical Equality (CBE). They were still quite liberal in comparison to most evangelicals, though, and are probably most famous for advocating for a concept known as egalitarianism. Egalitarianism argues that scripture supports full equality between men and women on the grounds that "the Bible, properly translated and interpreted, teaches the fundamental equality of women and men of all racial and ethnic groups, all economic classes, and all ages, based on the teachings of Scriptures such as Galatians 3:28: 'There is neither Jew nor Gentile, neither slave nor free, nor is there male and female, for you are all one in Christ Jesus.' "[19]

Unfortunately, Christian feminism encountered the same roadblocks as the broader progressive movement: regardless of their theological beliefs, their evangelical bona fides were constantly questioned. CBE was able to garner the support of a few big-name (read: male) evangelicals, but their acceptance was always conditional. In order to retain any influence, CBE members had to conform to the gendered and sexual norms of white evangelicalism, like being married and having children (and, of course, rejecting queerness). They could only proclaim women's equality if they didn't upset the patriarchal order too much. They could hold leadership positions only in certain contexts, and they still faced harassment, lack of opportunity, and oppression.

Furthermore, a backlash developed in response to these feminist efforts. In 1987, a group of conservative evangelicals including Wayne Grudem and John Piper met in Danvers, Massachusetts, for the purpose of combatting evangelical feminism and egalitarianism. There they formed the Council on Biblical Manhood and Womanhood (CBMW) and put out the Danvers Statement, which put forth a new philosophy they called "complementarianism," because it teaches that men and women, though equal in worth, have distinct, "complementary" roles ordained by God within scripture. As part of these roles, a husband was supposed to show "loving, humble headship" and a wife was supposed to show "intelligent, willing submission."[20] Additionally, "some governing and teaching roles within the church are restricted to men."[21] This meeting led to the eventual publication of the book *Recovering Biblical Manhood and Womanhood: A Response to Biblical Feminism*, edited by Piper and Grudem. An immediate beneficiary of the evangelical media promotional machine, it was named *Christianity Today*'s book of the year in 1992.

By the early 1990s, what is known as the "conservative resurgence"—or the "fundamentalist takeover," depending on one's viewpoint—was in full swing in the Southern Baptist Convention and beyond. (The SBC is the largest Protestant denomination in America, and its internal battles are illustrative of battles that take place across evangelicalism.) Women's ordination became a litmus test for orthodoxy at seminaries such as the SBC's flagship seminary, Southern Baptist Theological Seminary (also known as SBTS or Southern Seminary), where president Albert Mohler insisted that women were not eligible for ministry. This led to a purge of faculty, staff, and students who disagreed, and "the seminary lost approximately one-third of its faculty and one-half of its student body."[22]

But Mohler's side prevailed. Thirty years later, he continues to serve as president of SBTS, and his radio show and podcast, *The Briefing*, regularly maintains a position in the top twenty-five shows in the Religion and Spirituality category of Apple Podcasts. Both Piper and Grudem would go on to write multiple bestselling books each. A strident Calvinist, Piper would write titles such as *Desiring God* and *Don't Waste Your Life,* found DesiringGod.org, and become a founding member of The Gospel Coalition. Wayne Grudem's reference tome *Systematic Theology* is widely taught in conservative schools and purchased for personal use as a general theological text.

Meanwhile, Evangelicals for Social Action, the progressive group that grew out of Urbana 70, still exists today, but in 2020, it rebranded itself as Christians for Social Action, shedding the evangelical label due to its "political connotations."[23] The Evangelical Women's Caucus still exists, but for the same reason changed its name to the Evangelical and Ecumenical Women's Caucus and the name of its journal from *EEWC Update* to *Christian Feminism Today.* Unable to compete with the politically powerful and well-funded core of conservative evangelicalism, the dream of Urbana 70 and the Chicago Declaration had been thoroughly deferred. Decades later, the same questions and same concerns would be asked anew by the rising generation: Who holds the rights to the title of "evangelical"? Who can hold power and exert influence, and who can participate fully in the church and in society? By now, you may be able to guess the answer.

WHAT IS THE LEGACY OF these progressive reform movements today? Did they have any long-term effect on evangelicalism? If things had gone a little differently, could today's evangelicalism have turned out less radical and right-wing? In considering these questions, I think it's useful to look back at the progressive evangelical movements that came earlier—much earlier.

As discussed in chapter 2, there's no denying that American evangelicalism's roots in abolitionism run deep (even if its roots in slavery run equally deep, as also discussed in chapter 2). The evangelical pastor Jonathan Blanchard, for example, was a northern abolitionist who believed in "immediate abolition"—that is, he recognized that slavery was an urgent problem to solve, not something to be softened or phased out gradually in order to appease slaveholders.[24] In 1845, he took part in a public debate in Cincinnati regarding the sinfulness of slaveholding against the proslavery opponent N. L. Rice; the debate yielded a five-hundred-page book, which, despite its length, was popular enough to have several editions. Fifteen years later, when Blanchard became the founding president of Wheaton College, an evangelical institution, he ensured that the school proclaimed "the testimony of God's Word against Slave-holding," among other social ills, in its 1860 catalog.

When religious historian and Chicago Declaration signatory Donald Dayton wrote his influential 1976 text, *Rediscovering an Evangelical Heritage*, he was inspired by people like Blanchard. The book's original preface addresses Dayton's disappointment in the evangelical response to the Civil Rights Movement in the 1960s, which led him away from evangelical institutions—but when he later learned about the abolitionist strain of evangelicalism, he "discovered the sweet irony that this denomination was not unique, but shared a reformist heritage with other aspects of evangelicalism. I had been struggling with the wrong end of evangelical currents that had once reverberated with vitality and reform activity, but had over the course of a century fallen into a form of decadence."[25] In other words, evangelicalism already had a well-established anti-racist legacy for him to draw on—he just didn't know it had existed for many years.

Why didn't he know it existed? It's not as if a history of abolitionism was considered shameful or deliberately covered up.

EXVANGELICAL AND BEYOND   91

By the time of the Civil Rights Movement, virtually every white evangelical would agree that slavery was bad, even if they were otherwise extremely racist. But clearly this abolitionist history wasn't a significant source of pride either, or it would have been widely discussed and people like Dayton would have been aware of it without having to do scholarly research on it. The truth is that, for the evangelical movement as a whole, Blanchard and his ilk were simply not very interesting or relevant. The memory of this abolitionist legacy was kept alive among particular denominations, but abolition never became a font of inspiration in the evangelical public created by the network of Christian colleges, publishing houses, and radio preachers. That movement was concerned with advancing a gospel of individualism, patriotism, and capitalism, not with fighting for or celebrating a legacy of racial justice. Essentially, the progressive strain of evangelicalism that had existed in the nineteenth century lost the fight for dominance so badly that many people had never even heard of it.

Something similar is true of the movement around Urbana 70. It's by no means intentionally covered up—in fact, this chapter cites articles about it from *Christianity Today* and Wheaton College's archives. But it lost the fight for dominance even worse than Blanchard did; today's white evangelicals are largely still hostile to the ideas expressed in the Chicago Declaration nearly fifty years ago, so why would they be interested in exploring or promoting the legacy of those ideas within their movement? To the extent that they do, it's often at least partially a defense against accusations of racism: *How can you call us racist when we had Tom Skinner name-dropping Stokely Carmichael in 1970?*

But when today's conservative white evangelical apologists

are embarrassed by the actions of their more blatantly Christian nationalist contemporaries, they usually skip straight over Skinner and point all the way back to Blanchard. And while it's one thing for Dayton to write about the joy of discovering abolition as an example of evangelicalism's potential progressivism, it's quite another for conservative journalist (and former George W. Bush speechwriter) Michael Gerson to trot out the same example forty years later. In an April 2018 cover story for *The Atlantic*, Gerson expresses horror at evangelical support for Donald Trump but writes, "Some words, like strategic castles, are worth defending, and *evangelical* is among them."[26] He doesn't want to cede the term "evangelical" to Trumpists when its pedigree equally belongs to abolitionists like Blanchard.

Fair enough—but Blanchard lived 150 years ago. If evangelicals in 2018 are still pointing to abolitionists instead of any of the progressive reform movements that have happened in the intervening years, it would seem to indicate not a genuine desire for change but rather a form of deflection, of appealing to prior scions of virtue in order to distract from less exemplary contemporaries. If evangelicals like Gerson—or Tim Keller, in the *New Yorker* piece I quoted in chapter 1—truly wanted a more equitable, just version of their movement, they would support the people who have fought and continue fighting for those values within, say, the same century. But they usually don't, because they don't actually share those values; they object to outright slavery and segregation, but they still prefer the current racial hierarchy of white privilege to real racial justice.

In reality, the same was true of Blanchard himself. Following the outcome of the Civil War, he considered slavery "solved" and did not advocate for integration or other forms of African American equality (this was affirmed by the Historical Review

Task Force's report on race relations at Wheaton College, published in 2023).[27] That's not to detract from the commendable moral clarity of his abolitionism or the significant work he did for the cause. Rather, it's to acknowledge the very real limits of white abolitionists. In most cases, even though they were against slavery, they were still invested in whiteness. Following the Civil War and Reconstruction, the majority of Northern and Southern Christian abolitionists ceased their activist efforts and tolerated or even enforced racist practices such as sundown towns, mob violence, Jim Crow, and more. By giving in to the demands of white supremacy, abolitionists like Blanchard allowed their more racist evangelical contemporaries to accumulate the power and sway that would eventually make the movement what it is today. When commentators like Keller and Gerson try to rest on Blanchard's laurels instead of supporting today's evangelical reformers, they're doing the same thing.

7

BUILDING THE BUBBLE

THE REIGN OF EVANGELICAL CONSUMER CULTURE

The ability to deeply understand and adeptly use media has been key to the development of evangelicalism since the very beginning. From printing presses to radio shows to television networks, an ever-growing media web has helped develop and disseminate its preferred ideology, defeat internal dissent, and exert influence on wider American culture and politics. As the United States grew more consumerist, so too did evangelicalism, gradually integrating its media ecosystem into an identifiable *consumer* culture.

This highly developed consumerism, expressed in large part via books, music, and other media, blossomed from the 1970s onward, meeting the needs of white evangelical families who sought "godly" alternatives to popular culture. Organizations like James Dobson's Focus on the Family, founded in 1977, generated entire suites of products and services for this audience—books, radio and TV shows, cartoons, parenting advice, marital advice, and so on and so forth. This consumer culture didn't just promote evangelicalism's white capitalist agenda—it created a whole Christian bubble that evangelicals could live almost entirely inside, retreating from interaction with the outside world.

One major locus of this consumer culture was Christian bookstores. Historian Daniel Vaca writes that the commercial expansion of Christian bookstores was the realization of grander aspirations:

> For decades, figures like [Moody Bible Institute and
> Fuller Theological Seminary professor] Wilbur Smith
> had emphasized the notion that evangelicals composed a
> subculture or counterpublic that functioned in
> opposition to a dominant liberal culture and public.
> Smith and other midcentury 'neo-evangelicals' dreamed
> of a day when the evangelical book industry would be
> able to produce and circulate literature on such a broad
> scale that it would overwhelm liberal religious literature
> and its proponents.[1]

Beginning in the 1960s, evangelical publisher Zondervan began to do just that, building out its own chain of retail bookstores in suburban shopping malls. Zondervan opened its first Family Bookstore near its Grand Rapids, Michigan, headquarters in 1962; by 1980, it had sixty stores and by 1994, 153 stores across twenty-seven states—a retail footprint that put it in the company of Waldenbooks and other mass-market book chains of the era.[2] And this was just one of many Christian bookstore chains; others included Lemstone Books, where I worked in high school, and LifeWay Christian Stores, where I would work after college.

As you'd expect, these bookstores sold—and to the extent that they still exist in the age of Amazon, continue to sell— books as part of the preexisting evangelical media interchange of readers, schools, and publishers. During my tenure at Lemstone, the bestsellers included Bruce Wilkinson's *The Prayer of Jabez*, various Max Lucado books, Rick Warren's *The Purpose Driven Life*, and John Ortberg's *If You Want to Walk on Water, You've Got to Get Out of the Boat.** They helped police the boundaries of what was considered acceptable within evangelical circles, promoting certain (white, capitalist) visions of Christianity through the Christian Living category.

They also sold music, in particular a genre called Christian contemporary music, or CCM. Now, gospel music had been part of the fabric of the music industry since its inception, with dedicated Black gospel artists like Mahalia Jackson and Sister Rosetta Tharpe constituting the golden age of the genre in the 1940s and '50s, while major white artists like Elvis Presley and Johnny Cash sang gospel tracks or produced entire gospel albums. But CCM was different.

The genre was born out of Southern California's Jesus movement in the late '60s and '70s, an offshoot of the hippie movement whose followers were called the Jesus People or Jesus Freaks (a term that would later be appropriated by CCM

---

* Ortberg would later resign as pastor of a Bay Area megachurch after it was revealed that he allowed his son, John Ortberg III, to continue volunteering with minors at the church even after he'd "admitted to having obsessive sexual feelings about young children." (Swartz, "Menlo Church Leadership Acknowledges Abuse from Decades Ago.")

megastars DC Talk). When Jesus Freak Lonnie Frisbee met Chuck Smith, the pastor of Calvary Chapel Costa Mesa, they began signing bands and releasing music that would appeal to this particular demographic through their Maranatha! Music label. (The label would eventually branch into children's music; if you grew up with Psalty the Singing Songbook, you have Maranatha! Music to thank.) The introduction of rock instrumentation into church spaces would lead to the evolution of contemporary worship styles that persist to this day.[3] Meanwhile, rock bands *specifically marketed as* "Christian" acts began to tour. The best-known early breakout Christian rocker was another Californian, Larry Norman. Historians of the genre disagree about whether his album *Upon This Rock* could be considered the *first* Christian rock album, but it was certainly the first with identifiable broad commercial success. Norman would later distance himself from the industry, but his impact is still recognized.

The CCM industry's development would continue apace from the 1970s through to today, generating massive bodies of work and creating music cultures that could be deemed "safe" for evangelical adults and their children. What began as a regional movement would eventually gain widespread attention and investment, blossoming into a fully developed alternative music-media ecosystem that supplemented the preexisting mediums of books, radio, and television. Now evangelicals could isolate themselves further from mainstream society without feeling like they were losing out on the riches of pop culture—they could more fully be "in but not of the world," a Christian ideal based on Jesus's prayer in John 17. This supercharged the already existing division between the evangelical in-group, which was seen as godly and righteous, and the secular or otherwise nonevangelical out-group, which was seen as wayward, sinful, and, if not downright evil, certainly dangerous.

This strange parallel-universe music industry not only provided evangelicals with their own version of pop music, it also made it easier for Christian musical artists to succeed financially. Just as the evangelical media network had long disseminated certain ideas to a ready-made audience of millions, now it did the same with CCM, stocking Christian bookstores with CDs, selling concert tickets to youth groups, and so on. Additionally, many members of their audience were discouraged or even forbidden from listening to mainstream music, which assuredly helped sales. In his book on CCM, *Body Piercing Saved My Life*, Andrew Beaujon writes that major labels "had realized that this music was becoming an essential accessory to new Christians' lifestyles, creating a viable market, and those companies soon had sizable investments to protect."[4] Industry revenue grew by leaps and bounds during the 1980s and increased throughout the '90s; "between 1985 and 1995 Christian recordings grew by $298 million, or a 290 percent increase in sales," according to Don Cusic's book on the subject, *The Sound of Light*.[5] "By 1995 the revenues from the Christian music industry were estimated to be as high as $750 million per year."[6]

CCM became the soundtrack of millions of American youths, with Christian artists catering to every genre—folk acts like Caedmon's Call, vocal groups like Point of Grace, country acts like the Gaither Vocal Band and Steven Curtis Chapman, the sing-rap-talk stylings of Carman, singer-songwriters such as Nichole Nordeman and Jennifer Knapp, the ska punk of Five Iron Frenzy, rappers like Lecrae, and the harder punk and metal sounds of Tooth & Nail Records artists like Underoath, MxPx, and many more. Some acts even got so popular they had crossover hits on mainstream radio in the '90s and '00s, including Amy Grant's "Baby, Baby," Sixpence None the Richer's "Kiss Me," P.O.D.'s "Youth of the Nation," Lifehouse's "Hanging by a Moment," and Switchfoot's "Meant to Live."

Christian bookstores were key to CCM's success. "In 1985, about 90 percent of all contemporary Christian music was sold in Christian bookstores," and even as mainstream retailers like Target and Walmart started carrying CCM, Christian bookstores still accounted for the lion's share of sales (64 percent in 1995).[7] But the bookstores and the musical artists existed in tension with one another. Remember, Christian bookstores functioned as the vanguard of what was considered acceptable within evangelical culture, and they enforced the often vague and contradictory norms of evangelical orthodoxy in a concrete, dollars-and-cents manner—by pulling the work of artists who deviated from the norm off their shelves.

This happened from the onset of the CCM industry, when many stores refused to stock Larry Norman's album *So Long Ago the Garden* because its cover art hinted at Eden-style nudity. But the most common reason for censorship was any expression of queer sexual identity or support for LGBTQ+ people. For example, Marsha Stevens (now Marsha Stevens-Pino) arguably had as much of an impact on Christian pop music as Larry Norman did. Her band Children of the Day's album *Come to the Waters* sold half a million copies and helped establish the genre's viability. However, following the announcement of her divorce and the fact that she was a lesbian, Stevens's music was removed from Christian bookstores, and her contributions were largely sidelined (or wholly erased) in "official" Christian music histories.

It is hard to talk about these issues without invoking language such as "excommunicated," "expelled," "ostracized," and, yes, "canceled" to describe what was routinely done to Christian artists who refused to acquiesce to evangelical heteronormativity. Stevens was just the first CCM artist to receive this treatment for being openly queer. Ray Boltz, Jennifer Knapp, Trey Pearson, Vicky Beeching, and many others would follow suit, losing access to their audiences when they insisted on being their full selves. It was not always clear where the pressure to enforce "traditional" gender norms was coming from—the labels, the bookstores, or the evangelical customers themselves. It was likely a combination of all three. Decades later, former Caedmon's Call member Derek Webb would tell me on a podcast that, behind closed doors and off the record, there were plenty of people within the industry who were not as conservative as the products they created, but "the market" demanded their conformity. (A former Zondervan executive said the same thing to me about evangelical book publishing.)

Meanwhile, David Bazan (aka Pedro the Lion) broke the bounds of conformity in a different way, wrestling publicly with the strictures of what was allowed within the confines of CCM. His lyrics directly addressed the terrible internal strife some evangelicals felt about consumerism in songs like "Secret of the Easy Yoke," and the conflation of evangelicalism with the Republican party in songs like "Backwoods Nation." Eventually, he'd publicly declare he was no longer an evangelical Christian when he released his 2009 album, *Curse Your Branches*. Bazan's honesty provided much-needed catharsis for me and many others who struggled with our evangelical heritage; his impact on people within my cohort cannot be overstated. Yet, as a result of his outspoken positions, he was often excluded from the CCM ecosystem. He had to be highly creative with his promotion, pioneering the concept of "living room tours," in which he played intimate shows in fans' houses because, despite his popularity, it was hard for him to get booked in standard CCM venues.

Conversely, more conservative Christian products were endorsed and heavily promoted within the evangelical media ecosystem—not just music but books as well. In fact, books might have had even less leeway than music, because they weren't intended to replace the fun and romance of pop music but to formulate and advance ideology. While Sixpence None the Richer were singing "Kiss Me" on the radio, Joshua Harris's book *I Kissed Dating Goodbye* was selling more than 800,000 copies. Written when Harris was just twenty-one, it promoted the concept of "courtship" over dating, emphasizing the value of "sexual purity" and admonishing its adherents to be entirely chaste, engaging in little to no physical contact with the person they courted prior to marriage. Along with Elisabeth Elliot's *Passion and Purity* and Stephen Arterburn and Fred Stoeker's *Every Man's Battle*, *I Kissed Dating Goodbye* became a landmark text that foisted the unhealthy expectations of "purity culture" upon a generation, supplementing harmful youth-group comparisons of people who had premarital sex to pieces of gum that had already been chewed.

In purity culture, sexual guilt is the expectation, and the most basic parts of humanity are cast as dirty, sinful, even beyond the pale of what can be loved by God—until, of course, you get married. At that point, you're expected to switch from seeing sex as vile to seeing it as a holy part of marriage—literally overnight. Girls and women are the primary victims, but boys and men do not escape unscathed. As one woman told Linda Kay Klein in her book *Pure*, in purity culture, "women are taught their bodies are evil; men are taught their minds are."[8]

To authors like Harris and the Christian bookstores who sold their work, it didn't matter that this idea of human sexuality was deeply flawed, limited, and harmful.* Out in the real world, the sexual revolution may have happened, but inside the evangelical bubble, the real world didn't matter. In many cases, the real world was actually the enemy, and any progress made there caused evangelicals to strive for the opposite in their own world. For example, activist and author Emily Joy Allison argues that the post-*Roe* evangelical concern about abortion "is intimately connected to the birth of the modern purity movement. At its heart, abortion is a question of sexual control. Who will reproduce? Does it matter if they want to or not?"[9]

The more robust evangelical consumer culture grew throughout the '90s and into the 2000s, the more self-contained the bubble became. To an even greater extent than before, evangelicalism was defined more by membership in this in-group than by religious beliefs or practices. In her book *Evangelical Christian Women*, Julie Ingersoll builds upon a theory put forth by Barbara Wheeler, the former director of Auburn Theological Seminary, in 1995:

> Wheeler suggests that observers of evangelicalism
> consider that "it is not doctrine or ancestry or warm
> family feeling . . . but religious culture." Maybe, she
> continues, "the best definition of an evangelical is
> someone who understands its argot, knows where to buy
> posters with Bible verses on them, and recognizes names
> like James Dobson and Frank Peretti." Wheeler points

---

*   In 2019, Harris apologized for the harm his book had caused and announced that he had "divorced his wife and renounced his Christian faith." (Bote, "He Wrote the Christian Case against Dating. Now He's Splitting from His Wife and Faith.")

to the distinctively evangelical religious dialect, leaders and celebrities, self-help groups, and Christian service providers (e.g., chiropractors and dentists), as well as the extensive material culture of music, tee-shirts, bumper stickers, books, and jewelry, as evidence that evangelicals are culture makers.[10]

Kristin Kobes Du Mez comes to a similar conclusion in her book *Jesus and John Wayne.*

Many evangelicals who would be hard pressed to articulate even the most basic tenets of evangelical theology have nonetheless been immersed in this evangelical popular culture. They've raised children with the help of James Dobson's Focus on the Family radio programs or grown up watching *VeggieTales* cartoons. They rocked out to Amy Grant or the Newsboys or DC Talk. They learned about purity before they learned about sex, and they have a silver ring to prove it. They watched *The Passion of the Christ, Soul Surfer,* or the latest Kirk Cameron film with their youth group. They attended Promise Keepers with guys from church and read *Wild at Heart* in small groups. They've learned more from Pat Robertson, John Piper, Joyce Meyer, and The Gospel Coalition than they have from their pastor's Sunday sermons.[11]

However, the outside world inevitably sometimes still managed to intrude. And so, parallel to the media landscape of Christian bookstores and record labels, there arose a conservative news media empire in the '80s and '90s that could rewrite news events to better accommodate the requirements of the bubble.

Leading the charge was Rush Limbaugh, whose self-titled radio show debuted in 1984. Unlike the radio stars previously mentioned in this book, Limbaugh was not a preacher but a college dropout and former disc jockey who pivoted to political commentary. He broke from the elitist heritage of conservative commentators like William F. Buckley Jr., Henry Regnery, and William Rusher (all Ivy League graduates), rooting his content in entertainment rather than scholarship. This entertainment value, combined with the 1987 abolition of the Fairness Doctrine, led Limbaugh to commercial success that prior generations of conservative media activists could only dream of. Much as they would with Donald Trump in 2016, people (evangelical or otherwise) flocked to Limbaugh not because he had anything intelligent or insightful to say but because his bombastic, emotional delivery resonated with the listener's latent prejudices. If you agreed with him, his use of loaded phrases like "feminazis" made you laugh; if you disagreed, he made you furious. His polarizing, extreme takes sorted people into clear camps: the in-group (like those who called in to his show to offer "mega dittos") and a "liberal extremist," "wacko," immoral out-group.[12] Either way, just as with polemicists and shock jocks before and since, his ability to court controversy allowed him to gain and keep attention. To put it more bluntly, he gave voice to racism, sexism, homophobia, and other hateful viewpoints that his audience wanted to hear. He became so prominent that when Democrats tried to reinstate the Fairness Doctrine in 1993, the legislation was nicknamed the "Hush Rush" bill. It failed.

Meanwhile, the launch of Fox News in 1996 provided an entirely new outlet for conservatives. After trying to buy CNN and being spurned by Ted Turner, Rupert Murdoch decided to launch his own channel; he enlisted the help of Roger Ailes, who had worked at NBC's cable channel, America's Talking (MSNBC's predecessor). In her book *Messengers of the Right*, historian Nicole Hemmer writes that Fox News "borrowed heavily from the world of talk radio: personality driven, overtly partisan, and laced with a thin edge of vitriol."[13] The network also inspired "a surge of right-wing talk-radio shows" that "could be traced to a second wave of deregulation" in Limbaugh's wake.[14] In many ways, we still live in the world that Fox News created. Hemmer writes:

> As a result of deregulation, the three hours a day of Rush Limbaugh had become, by the 2000s, wall-to-wall right-wing talk. A slew of new hosts gained national syndication between 2000 and 2002: Sean Hannity, Michael Savage, Laura Ingraham, Bill O'Reilly, Glenn Beck. . . . A 2007 study of 257 news/talk stations by the progressive Center for American Progress found 91 percent of the programming was conservative, an imbalance they concluded was not market driven but a result of "multiple structural problems in the U.S. regulatory system."[15]

Not all of these commentators were evangelical, and nearly all emphasized partisan politics over religion qua religion. But by this time, evangelicalism writ large had made its dedication to preserving a white, capitalist, conservative in-group identity a clear priority. Prior chapters demonstrate just how consistently evangelicalism resisted calls for justice and significant change coming from the marginalized and disenfranchised in their own midst. After each would-be reform movement that grew was quashed or its members were deemed un-Christian, evangelical norms could be reinforced. By policing what was considered acceptable via evangelical consumer culture, they also policed what was acceptable evangelical thought and behavior. The way consumerism and media production developed at the end of the twentieth century supercharged this dynamic.

There are endless variations within this dynamic—some evangelicals would survey the world of evangelical media and still consider it "too worldly," for instance, while others might reject politics wholesale. But all these efforts went far in creating a unified vision and experience of the world, enabling an entirely alternative lifestyle that exists in parallel to the so-called secular world outside of it. The construction of these mental, social, commercial, academic, and church environments was so totalizing that many people have had no trouble at all living their lives entirely within the confines of white evangelical institutions and practices. And if you're raised within a bubble, you can't always see its distortions or feel its boundaries, until one day you press on the edge of the bubble and it bursts open.

8

HOLY GHOSTED

MY JOURNEY AWAY FROM EVANGELICALISM

When I prep people prior to interviewing them on my podcast, *Exvangelical*, I tend to tell them the interview will follow a typical three-act structure. Act I establishes their background, where they grew up, and what their exposure to and experience with evangelicalism was like. Act II discusses what led to their break with evangelicalism—was it a single cataclysmic event, or was it a slow death by a thousand cuts? Act III explores where they find themselves now in relation to religion and their current personal approach to spirituality.

As with many of my guests, my own break with evangelicalism came in fits and starts. We now call this "deconstruction"—the process of reexamining the religious beliefs you've been taught by your faith and ultimately arriving at a healthier place, whether that's following a less toxic form of Christianity or leaving Christianity altogether. But such a term wasn't in widespread use then, and it wasn't easy to find communities of people on similar journeys. In the first chapter of this book, I shared about my upbringing within evangelicalism until the age of about seventeen. Now I'll carry that story forward into Act II: my deconstruction.

AT SEVENTEEN, I FELT A call to the ministry. I was going to be a pastor, and nothing would deter me. My evangelical fervor was so strong that when it came time to look at colleges I *only* considered Christian schools. I toured Milligan College in Tennessee, where my mother had gone for a short stint before transferring to a state school in Indiana. I looked at Judson College in Elgin, Illinois, where my high school girlfriend would enroll. My confidence in my academics was too low to apply to Wheaton, the so-called Harvard of Christian colleges where my high school best friend would go—and besides, it was only half an hour away from my parents. (Distance wasn't a prerequisite, but like most college-bound teenagers, I wanted some individuation from my parents.) Other local Christian colleges like North Park (where another friend went) and Moody Bible Institute were out too, also due to proximity to home. Another of my friends from youth group had applied to Indiana Wesleyan University, so I did too. I visited and it felt right. And that's where I ended up going.

Both my parents were supportive of my choice of college and my sense of calling. My mother, however, gave me two pieces of practical advice. First, she told me to go to a Christian college, not a Bible college. Christian colleges require religious classes but generally offer a wider curriculum (filtered through a Christian lens), so students can use their degrees to get regular jobs in the secular world if they want to; Bible colleges tend to focus only on religious subjects, to the point that many aren't even accredited, and they tend to prepare students only for a profession within the church. Second, she told me not to major in ministry. I could pursue ministry as a career, but my degree should enable me to go down other paths if I changed my mind in the future. (This advice was rooted in family experience; her brother had been a minister before leaving for a different profession.) I followed the first bit of advice. As for the second, well, I entered college with a declared double major in history and biblical literature, so . . . you be the judge.

I was happy to go to college and was ready for the changes it would bring. High school had been dramatic; I was deeply involved in youth group, and the compounding effects of purity culture, raging hormones, and teen angst had taken their toll. I built up IWU in my mind as a utopian haven. Because we were all Christians—all of us, students and faculty alike!—with shared ethics, morals, and goals, surely we would live in harmony. Surely this would be heaven on earth.

Two things quickly shattered that vision of Indiana Wesleyan. First were the strict guidelines for the student body: a curfew for freshmen, no R-rated movies, mandatory chapel attendance, and so on. Dorms were segregated by gender, and you could only visit a dorm of the opposite sex during certain supervised hours. I had signed the statement of faith without really reading it, and I thought I had just promised not to drink or smoke. I was dismayed to learn about all these rules shortly after checking into my dorm for the first time. Like any student arriving at college, I was looking for independence and freedom. Now I realized I'd actually had more freedom at home, where, as long as I informed my parents where I would be, they trusted me to be responsible.

The second thing was that the September 11 terrorist attacks occurred during the first full week of school, utterly changing the tenor of my college experience and the direction of the world. Every freshman was required to take a class called World Changers (because we were supposed to change the world for Christ, you see). I remember how in that class that week, the professor showed us newspaper headlines about long lines at local gas stations, which people had flocked to because they didn't know if gas supplies would be cut off. He chided any of us who'd filled up our tanks the day before for our lack of faith. It was pretty harsh for an audience of teenagers reacting to an unprecedented global event—not to mention that, in retrospect, relying on God for the divine providence of gasoline, of all things, is an almost comically American-capitalist expression of Christianity.

But regardless of that memorable rebuke, even as first responders were still at the scene in New York and Washington, there was already an undercurrent running through the school: the expectation that we would be going to war.

I'D BEEN TOO YOUNG TO vote in the 2000 presidential election, but at the time, I was a de facto Republican. It was a rule of thumb among the adults in my life that politics was a contentious topic, so my family didn't necessarily discuss it explicitly very often, but I grew up with Rush Limbaugh playing in the background, and it seemed as if all the Christians I knew were Republican. It was part and parcel of our evangelical heritage. If others had another way of being, I didn't know it. But college should be a time for questioning, and my experiences on campus and in class were making me do exactly that.

Because I was a history and biblical literature double major, I took classes in both the history and religion departments. It was the juxtaposition of these courses, as well as the backdrop of the war on terror, that led to my first major faith crisis.

In my Bible classes, I was learning about how the Bible was constructed and developed over centuries. I learned to read the Bible in Greek and, as part of that, learned about how manuscripts were copied through the centuries. While our religion professors did have to sign the Wesleyan denomination's Articles of Religion, which included the doctrine of biblical inerrancy, inerrancy as such was not taught as a core belief. This gave my professors the ability to frankly discuss modern biblical criticism. Even an undergraduate exposure to this topic is enough to make the notion of biblical inerrancy crumble quickly. Additionally, in my other religion courses on church history, I was learning about the many ways that people lived out their Christian faith, which made clear that, contrary to what I'd been taught, the evangelicalism I was raised with was not the one true version of Christianity.

So, somewhat ironically, it was the religion department that gave me a more open-minded and historical understanding of Christianity; meanwhile, my history classes were focused on dogmatic indoctrination. The chair of our history department taught required classes on American history and Western intellectual and social history, in which he tried to instill in us what he called "the biblical Christian worldview." He was of small stature, but his voice boomed when he got passionate (which was often), and he had an authoritarian air that drew people to him. He taught about ontology, epistemology, axiology, and teleology, and argued that each of these had to be rooted in this biblical Christian worldview. He lionized the Puritans for founding a theocratic form of government; assigned readings by Andrew Jackson's racist, proslavery vice president, John C. Calhoun; and articulated an argument that Southern slave owners should have been monetarily compensated for the loss of their slaves after emancipation.*

He was also vehemently antiabortion. He taught a course based on the antiabortion book *Whatever Happened to the Human Race?*, published in 1979 and cowritten by the Christian apologist Francis Schaeffer and Reagan's eventual surgeon general, C. Everett Koop. In that course, we would read about "abortion, infanticide, and euthanasia," and the professor would rail against the evil of abortion and the Democrats who enabled it. When I asked in the course if, as Christians, we should extend grace to people who have abortions, he called them murderers and went on a rant.

The dissonance of these experiences was painful. As I learned more about the history of my religion and my scriptures, I became more conflicted about the militant, conservative faith exemplified in this "biblical Christian worldview" and its stark contrast to my understanding of Jesus, whom we called the Prince of Peace. My feet would lead me to the prayer chapel adjacent to the Christian Ministries building that housed most of my classes, where a sculpture of Jesus pleading with his father in Gethsemane was displayed. It was a great place to pray and have anxiety attacks.

This faith crisis reached its peak during my sophomore year

---

* I could not identify it as such at the time, but this terminology and outlook align with R. J. Rushdoony's Christian reconstructionist theology, as discussed in chapter 5. Clearly, it permeated Christian education beyond the homeschool movement.

as the American war machine ambled toward a justification for invading Iraq. As the "floor chaplain" in my dorm, I was supposed to do things like lead devotions, but I only managed to do so once or twice before deciding that I would just "do life with" the guys on my floor instead. My faith and my politics were skewing liberal, and at a place like IWU, that was not the majority opinion. At IWU, the student body was generally assumed to be as conservative as the administration, and there were several instances in my biblical literature classes where it was evident that the students were more fundamentalist than the professors teaching the class.

In 2004, I was, for the first time, old enough to vote in a presidential election, and I had a decision to make between George W. Bush and John Kerry. Unlike Trump, who would receive support from evangelicals despite being not at all a member of the faith, Bush was the real deal. He was a genuine born-again evangelical, converted by Billy Graham himself. Profiles of Bush would mention how if he said he would pray about an issue, he meant it. His faith appeared sincere and lived. Surely that meant I, as a Christian, had to vote for him. Everyone I knew was voting for him.

Nevertheless, I didn't want to vote for him. In his 2000 campaign, he'd espoused "compassionate conservatism," but this was largely abandoned following 9/11 as he increasingly used stark black-and-white language to describe the war on terror— including, very literally, "You're either with us or against us."[1] As my evangelical faith was shaken, I was becoming increasingly pacifist. I was also learning bits and pieces of the development of conservative evangelical politics that I've detailed in prior chapters and beginning to wonder why these politics were part and parcel of Christianity as I knew it.

I made the tortured decision to vote for John Kerry. As I walked away from the voting booth, I felt like a heretic, but I also knew I could not vote for Bush and the politics—and Christianity—he represented.

THOUGH I HAD ENTERED COLLEGE with the intent of becoming a minister, by the time senior year came around, I didn't bother applying to seminary or graduate school. At eighteen, I was on fire for God; by twenty-one, I was burned out. I felt I couldn't meaningfully lead a congregation if I didn't believe as I once had. After graduating college, I was unmoored. My sister, who is several years older than I am, invited me to live with her and her husband in Nashville. I got a job at a high-risk auto insurance company and tried my best to simply enjoy life without endless moral and theological crises. I was what they call "unchurched"—I hadn't gone so far as to renounce my faith, but I didn't belong to or regularly attend a church.

In 2006, my girlfriend Emily also moved to Nashville after finishing college. A scientist, she applied to several PhD programs. When she was accepted to Northwestern University, she found a liberal arts master's program there that she thought would appeal to me. It offered several possible emphases— including religious and ethical studies. By 2007, Emily and I were both in grad school at Northwestern, she full-time and I part-time. We got married that summer.

My grad school experience was markedly different from undergrad. In my first course, on the Progressive Era, I learned about the Social Gospel movement of the nineteenth century (mentioned in chapters 3 and 4 of this book). Later, I took a course called Moral Reform in America that contextualized the political debates surrounding abortion, gay marriage, and a host of other issues in ways that were new and revelatory to me. I took a course on the American West that dealt with both our mythologization of the concept as well as the realities of what white settlers had done to Indigenous communities. Then I took a class called Energy and the Environment, through which I discovered the writing of the incisive social critic, farmer, and writer Wendell Berry. These classes opened up for me an entirely new vision of the possibilities of both the Christian faith and the broader world. In particular, I discovered the creation-care theology movement, which located narratives of ecological stewardship within biblical texts and sought to protect the environment accordingly.

My flagging faith was reinvigorated, and I launched myself into it. Through a fellow IWU alum who had moved to the Chicago area, Emily and I heard of an Evangelical Free church and started attending there. We joined their "Green Team," which was focused on creation care and personal environmental practices. We read books by Michael Pollan as a group and went to farmers markets. We became heavily involved and even spoke in front of the church as part of our involvement in this group.

And then we had a series of weeks when we couldn't attend Sunday services or go to other events, and we just . . . faded away. No one called us or reached out as is standard in a church community, and given how involved we had become, this surprised us. We had thought we'd developed real relationships there, but it became clear they were shallower than we thought. We stopped going.

My interest in environmental issues stayed consistent, though. This was a period of intense public interest in climate change, characterized by the "We Can Solve It" ad campaign that featured Nancy Pelosi and Newt Gingrich on a couch calling for a bipartisan response to climate change. I decided I would finish up my master's studies, then apply to law school to become an environmental attorney. I took the LSAT on September 25, 2009. Five days later, I was laid off from my insurance job.

We were still in the throes of the Great Recession, and the same thing was happening to a lot of millennials. Concerned friends reached out, some of whom had begun attending a church in Rogers Park, the northernmost neighborhood of Chicago. They offered comfort and solace in a period when we needed it. We felt loved in a way we hadn't at our previous church, so we started attending. It met in a storefront on Sundays, but it also had active small groups, which it called root groups, that met during the week to share a meal and have a discussion. These root groups could be intergenerational, with other young people or older couples. When our lease ran out, we started looking at places in Rogers Park to move to. After an extended period of unemployment and short-term work for the 2010 census, a church member helped me get a part-time job at a LifeWay Christian Store, which served as the campus bookstore for Moody Bible Institute.

We were attracted to this church because of the community, but we didn't always agree with the theology that was taught. The lead pastor was a graduate of Moody Bible Institute, which, as you've likely gathered from previous chapters, is more conservative and fundamentalist than the Wesleyan and Methodist traditions that Emily and I were raised in.* There were expectations

---

* The Methodist branch of denominations, which includes today's Wesleyan and United Methodist denominations, is part of what is called the "holiness movement." These traditions have theological distinctions that separate them from, say, Baptists, but are quite often culturally evangelical, as typified by the previously

of "female submission" in marriage, and women were not allowed to serve as elders or deacons. Our pastor played antiabortion PSAs featuring evangelical celebrity quarterback Tim Tebow and his mother, and delivered sermons about how, before his conversion, he drove a friend to an abortion clinic, an act our pastor now regretted. Mark Driscoll (whom I will discuss in detail in the next chapter) was a popular author and podcaster among the church and small group leaders.

Even the preferred English translation of the Bible, the English Standard Version (ESV), was a marker of a more conservative evangelicalism; the advisory council overseeing the translation included Wayne Grudem and John Piper, whom I've previously discussed. The ESV was proffered as a market alternative to the New International Version (NIV), which was popular at the time but became yet another culture war battleground when it updated its language to be more gender inclusive. This translational choice was so significant within evangelicalism that *Christianity Today* published point/counterpoint debates for Sunday schools and small groups to discuss.[2]

The people we met at this church were good people and had become good friends, but we grew increasingly uneasy with the theological elements of our church life. Although we were heavily involved in the church community—coleading small groups, serving on the worship team, and volunteering in other ways—we never became official members of the church because Emily and I were egalitarian, which, as you'll remember from chapter 6, means we saw genders as equal. The church, however, was complementarian, viewing men as leaders and women

---

quoted Donald Dayton, who grew up in the Wesleyan tradition but was unaware of its abolitionist roots.

as "helpmeets" who must submit to their husbands' God-ordained authority. After the birth of our daughter, we knew this would become an even more contentious issue, as we would not allow her to be taught that she could or could not do something on account of how she was born—and most certainly not in the name of God.

In time, the Moody-trained pastor moved away after a health scare in his family, and another member of the church took over the lead pastor role. The church contracted, and given that we were close to the new leadership, we decided to finally tell them that our egalitarian beliefs were why we had never become official members of the church, despite serving in the worship team and leading a small group, among other activities. This disagreement drove a wedge between us. We met in private and were essentially told that we could leave. There would be no compromise regarding this belief.

Older couples in the church tried to broker peace and help us hold discussions on the topic. We planned to discuss the issue over the course of a year, but those dialogues broke down after the very first meeting. It became too much, and we decided to leave. We sent an email to the leadership, and that was that. Friends and acquaintances from church stopped reaching out. We lost our entire support network overnight.

In retrospect, we realized we'd seen a pattern of this type of "holy ghosting." The only people who left on good terms were those who moved away from the area. For anyone else, there was almost always a rupture with no healthy closure. And we realized that we had been complicit in similar behavior when others had left before us.

We never attended an evangelical church again.

9

A TALE OF TWO MARS HILLS

POLICING THE BOUNDS OF ORTHODOXY

I was not the only evangelical reexamining my faith in the early 2000s. A flurry of voices, mostly women, were starting to test the limits of evangelical acceptance via a new medium: blogs. In retrospect, the blogging era was relatively short-lived, but that doesn't mean it wasn't consequential. At a time when the internet had become widespread but social media was still in its infancy, blogs let anyone with an internet connection post their thoughts for anyone in the world to read—for free. Never before in human history had self-published writing been able to reach so many people so easily and cheaply. Of course, most bloggers would just post about the details of their everyday lives for an audience of a few friends, but many talented writers with something to say amassed large readerships and parlayed their blogs into professional careers in journalism or publishing. Many members of today's elite journalist class, now enshrined at bastions of American journalism like *The New York Times* and *The Wall Street Journal*, got their start as bloggers.

It's no surprise that evangelicals, with their extensive history of adopting and mastering new forms of media, began blogging. But what is surprising is that some of those evangelicals were not following the party line—they were using this new technology to make an end run around the now-behemoth Christian media industry in order to ask questions and express dissent. And people were listening. Sarah Bessey, who began her blog in 2005 and went on to write *Jesus Feminist* and other progressive Christian books, said in a 2017 interview, "The internet gave women like me—women who are outside of the usual power and leadership narratives and structures—a voice and a community. We began to write, and we began to find each other, we began to learn and be challenged, we began to realize we weren't as alone as we thought we were. Blogging gave us a way past the gatekeepers of evangelicalism."[1]

Bessey would later cofound the organization Evolving Faith with Rachel Held Evans, another progressive Christian who rose to prominence with her blog around 2007 and went on to author books like *Faith Unraveled* and *A Year of Biblical Womanhood*, even serving on President Obama's Advisory Council on Faith-based and Neighborhood Partnerships.* Other notable bloggers from this time period include Jamie Wright, who wrote about her family's experiences living as missionaries in Costa Rica on her blog, *The Very Worst Missionary*, and Jen Hatmaker, now known as a fierce advocate for LGBT+ Christians, who

---

* Evans died unexpectedly in 2019 due to an allergic reaction to antibiotics, a loss that is still felt deeply in the exvangelical community.

wrote books like *A Modern Girl's Guide to Bible Study*, had an HGTV show with her then-husband and five children, and received a profile in *Christianity Today* in 2014.[2] And though it may be somewhat surprising to fans of Glennon Doyle—author of the bestselling memoir *Untamed* and cohost of the megasuccessful podcast *We Can Do Hard Things*—she began her career with a progressive Christian blog called *Momastery* and even wrote a book about reconciling her marriage with her husband. (After its publication, she ended up divorcing him, coming out as queer, and marrying women's soccer star Abby Wambach.)

Throughout the 2000s and 2010s, these authors and creators would find wide audiences and develop their own conferences and organizations, such as Belong, the Wild Goose Festival, Why Christian?, and the aforementioned Evolving Faith Conference. Through their work, they explored what it might mean to be evangelical while also being feminist, pro-LGBT+, even pro-choice. In doing so, they utilized the media savvy that is part and parcel of evangelicalism to press evangelicalism itself to change.

They were also participating in a centuries-old Protestant tradition of women using novel media to challenge notions of authority. In *A People's History of Christianity*, Diana Butler Bass highlights how the printing press enabled women to publish their own pamphlets during the Reformation: "In the early days of the Reformation, Protestant women likened themselves to biblical heroines such as Judith and Deborah, taking up both pen and spoken word to correct the corruptions of the church."[3] Bass points to the example of Katharina Schütz, who wrote pamphlets in support of clergy marriage and other contemporary issues. Because women were not empowered to speak or be part of clergy, she also penned her defense of *why* she wrote:

She believed that speaking out is necessary for Christian devotion, that proclaiming truth demonstrates love of God and neighbor—especially if one's neighbor is spreading falsehoods. "To keep silence is not patience. To suffer is patience," she wrote. "By keeping silence I give him grounds to continue in his trumped up lies, and that, in my judgment, is against brotherly love." For Katharina, not to speak truth was to support error.[4]

Bass ultimately concludes that "the pamphleteers, like Katharina, were the bloggers of the sixteenth century, those whose words shaped religious rebellion by challenging traditional authorities and bypassing established channels of communication."[5]

In addition to the blogging movement, several books were published in the first decade of the 2000s that shed light on evangelical consumer and media culture, such as 2004's *Shaking the World for Jesus: Media and Conservative Evangelical Culture* by Heather Hendershot, 2006's *Righteous: Dispatches from the Evangelical Youth Movement* by Lauren Sandler, and 2006's *Body Piercing Saved My Life: Inside the Phenomenon of Christian Rock* by Andrew Beaujon. In a nod to just how all-consuming evangelical life is, Kevin Roose (now a technology journalist at *The New York Times*) went undercover and enrolled at Liberty University for a semester for his 2009 book, *The Unlikely Disciple: A Sinner's Semester at America's Holiest University*. This period was a time that seemed filled with possibility in American Christianity—and in evangelical Christianity in particular. It seemed that the staid political and social dynamics of evangelicalism might be truly up for debate in a way that they hadn't been for a generation. But the same sort of culture wars and policing of norms were still playing out, and these battles are exemplified by two celebrity pastors at two separate churches called Mars Hill.

WE START OUR TALE OF two Mars Hills in Seattle, Washington, where Mark Driscoll was raised Catholic, converted to evangelicalism in college, and founded Mars Hill Church in 1996 when he was just twenty-five. As lead pastor, Driscoll took the formula that had been used by "seeker-friendly" megachurches to appeal to boomers and Gen Xers and updated it with millennial flair. His church, writes Kristin Kobes Du Mez, "had the feel of a nightclub, filled with predominantly white twenty- and thirty-somethings with a penchant for tattoos, piercings, beer, and the local indie music scene."[6]

With his hypermasculine version of Christianity and shock-jock preaching style, he drew on the "muscular Christianity" of prior "macho" preachers like Billy Sunday and Billy Graham, but he took it much further: "Gone was any language of friendship, tenderness, and personal enrichment; Driscoll wanted nothing to do with the softer side of the men's movement. Instead he made a name for himself as 'Mark the cussing pastor.'"[7] He was known for using frank, graphic language about sex from the pulpit, and he notably claimed he had the spiritual gift of visions that let him see when someone had committed adultery or been sexually abused as a child. He once wrote about having a "revelation" of his wife "sinning sexually" in a dream:

> I awoke, threw up, and spent the rest of the night sitting
> on our couch, praying, hoping it was untrue, and
> waiting for her to wake up so I could ask her. I asked her
> if it was true, fearing the answer. Yes, she confessed, it

was. Grace started weeping and trying to apologize for lying to me, but I honestly don't remember the details of the conversation, as I was shell-shocked. Had I known about this sin, I would not have married her.[8]

Driscoll was a key leader in the New Calvinist movement, a resurgence of Calvinist thinking among younger evangelicals covered by *Christianity Today* journalist Collin Hansen in his 2008 book, *Young, Restless, Reformed*. At his height, Driscoll commanded major audiences, with Mars Hill reporting an average weekly attendance of more than 12,000 people.[9] Acts 29, the church-plant network* he cofounded in 1998, was successful as well. As of today, it includes more than seven hundred churches around the globe.[10] His books, including *Doctrine: What Christians Should Believe* (cowritten with Gerry Breshears) and *Real Marriage: The Truth About Sex, Friendship, and Life Together* (cowritten with his wife, Grace) were bestsellers. He was heavily promoted by the orthodox, nonprogressive side of the evangelical blogosphere, including the website of The Gospel Coalition, a church network founded by the pastors Tim Keller and D. A. Carson in 2005, where Driscoll served as a council member.

Meanwhile, in 1999, halfway across the country, a different Mars Hill Bible Church was founded in Grandville, Michigan, by a different sort of pastor.** Rob Bell was much more liberal

---

*   "Church planting" is a Christianese term for starting new churches—often but not always evangelical ones—in a given area. The biblical book of Acts, in which the Apostle Paul starts many new churches, only has twenty-eight chapters, so "Acts 29" is a relatively common name for organizations aspiring to be the "next chapter" in Paul's church-planting project.

** It's not as odd as it might initially seem that two separate megachurches include the name of a Roman god. In Acts 17:23, Paul reclaims a Roman altar inscribed

than Driscoll but no less popular for it. He had a strong evangelical pedigree—he attended Wheaton College for undergrad and Fuller Theological for seminary—and his debut book, *Velvet Elvis: Repainting the Christian Faith*, published in 2005 by evangelical publisher Zondervan, sold half a million copies.[11] Much like the Seattle Mars Hill, the Michigan Mars Hill was "one of the fastest-growing churches in the country" in the early 2000s, so clearly Bell's message was resonating.[12] Yes, his follow-up books, *Sex God* in 2007 and *Jesus Wants to Save Christians* in 2008, touched on issues that rankled conservative evangelicals, but he was a star in the more moderate-to-progressive areas of evangelicalism—known as the "emergent movement" at the time—alongside other leaders and authors like Brian McLaren and Tony Jones.[13]

That all changed in 2011 when Bell published *Love Wins: A Book About Heaven, Hell, and the Fate of Every Person Who Ever Lived*. In it, he embraces Christian universalism, a theological concept which holds that *all* people will be saved—not just evangelicals, not just Christians, but *everyone*. This was not some newfangled idea that Bell came up with on a whim; universalism is an aspect of Christian thought going back to the second century and is present in the writings of Church Fathers like Clement of Alexandria and Origen. But that didn't matter to the evangelical industrial complex. Bell's position at the edge of orthodox acceptance had finally become untenable.

Contemporary white evangelicals bemoan "cancel culture," but in reality, they have long practiced it. For the crime of asserting that God loves humanity enough to offer salvation to all,

"to an unknown god" for the Christian cause at a site called Areopagus—Greek for "Mars Hill."

Bell's books were removed from LifeWay bookstores and other Christian retailers. I experienced the swift corporate mandate firsthand: I worked at a LifeWay in Chicago at the time, and I was directed to pull all of Rob Bell's books from the shelves, along with the NOOMA films he made for church small groups. Evangelical bloggers from across The Gospel Coalition network and beyond posted takedowns of Bell, accusing him of heresy. (John Piper infamously tweeted a simple "Farewell, Rob Bell," which has lived on as a meme.) By the end of the year, Bell resigned from his own church and moved to California.

Luckily, Bell's story has a happy ending. He found success as a spiritual leader in LA, creating podcasts, writing books, and being interviewed by Oprah Winfrey. But my point is not about Rob Bell—it's about evangelicalism. It's about the cruelty of a movement that happily forgets its theology to accommodate capitalism and whiteness but absolutely loses its mind when someone proposes the idea of a God who loves people outside the evangelical in-group.

But the tale of two Mars Hills isn't over, because a few years later, Mark Driscoll got canceled as well, and the differences between the two events are instructive. Starting around 2013, Driscoll became embroiled in scandal after scandal—not for his misogynistic or homophobic messages but for a variety of other bad behavior. His Mars Hill employees, including senior leadership, accused him of being "domineering," "verbally violent," "arrogant," and "quick-tempered."[14] Blogs like *Joyful Exiles* and *Mars Hill Refuge* proliferated online, detailing the emotional and spiritual abuses experienced by church members, volunteers, and staff, and offering solace and community to people who had left. In November 2013, Janet Mefferd, a Christian radio host, accused Mark Driscoll of plagiarism in his book *A*

Call to Resurgence in an on-air interview; subsequent instances of plagiarism in other books surfaced.[15] It was reported that Mars Hill Church had bought *Real Marriage*'s way onto the bestseller list by using a firm called ResultSource to purchase thousands of copies and artificially inflate sales figures.[16]

Criticism of Driscoll and his Mars Hill began to snowball. On August 8, 2014, Mars Hill and Driscoll were removed from the Acts 29 church network; by August 24, nine church elders penned a letter asking Driscoll to step down; Driscoll resigned on October 14, and Mars Hill announced on November 3 it would dissolve entirely at the end of 2014.[17] While Driscoll was at the center of controversy, outlets such as LifeWay pulled his books from their shelves, and elite evangelicals who formerly championed him kept him at a distance while he was persona non grata.[18]

The difference in what it took to get Bell and Driscoll canceled is striking. Bell had transgressed theologically, while Driscoll, despite his many scandals, had only improperly *acted* upon his "correct" theology. Bell's embrace of an expansive theology that blesses all people with eventual salvation and reconciliation with God was deemed anathema and heretical, whereas Driscoll maintained proper theology but acted too severely. Apparently, in evangelical math, one book about everyone going to heaven is equal to multiple scandals encompassing everything from plagiarism to abuse.

And not long afterward, something strange happened: Driscoll's cancellation began to be revoked. By August 2016, Driscoll had set up a new church in Scottsdale, Arizona, called Trinity Church. By 2022, he was back on the evangelical speaking circuit, speaking at the Theos Conference alongside Acts 29 president Matt Chandler and high-profile author Eric Metaxas.

Driscoll remade himself as, essentially, a content creator and influencer, and evangelicalism slowly welcomed him back into the fold. In the end, his wrongdoings only earned him temporary scorn. They didn't outweigh what was truly important: a gospel of rigidity, exclusion, and cruelty. An October 2023 feature article on *Religion Unplugged* details how Driscoll's new church uses private security to intimidate and harass churchgoers who try to undermine his authority.[19] That seems unlikely to be a problem for evangelicals writ large; they don't take kindly to undermining authority anyway.

10

READING TWO CORINTHIANS

WHAT I GOT WRONG ABOUT TRUMP

As progressive evangelicals tested the bounds of orthodoxy online and offline in the 2000s and '10s, conservative evangelicals grew ever more reactionary. Given the political power they had amassed by this time, their radicalism played out not just in churches and on blogs but on the national stage as well.

For liberals, the election of the first Black president in 2008 was an animating political event. While Shepard Fairey's iconic HOPE posters now seem a little cringeworthy, at the time, hope really did feel palpable. Emily and I were living in Chicago and took the train to Grant Park, where Obama gave his victory speech to an adoring crowd. The energy was incredible. It felt like change was possible.

For conservatives, it was a different story. Republicans were

motivated to respond to a newly energized Democratic Party
and were not about to take the loss of the White House (and
Capitol Hill—Bush's GOP lost control of both houses of Congress in 2006) lightly. As conservatives, determined to learn
from their mistakes, shored up their weaknesses on the digital
front, Democrats rested on their laurels, assuming that broader
social trends and their recent victory would ensure future success. Obama's campaign was lauded for being savvy with media,
the new frontier of social media in particular. The feeling was
that by being young, hip, and on Twitter, Obama would naturally appeal to younger voters in a way the passé GOP couldn't.
This assumption severely underestimated the sophistication of
the conservative media machine and the nearly limitless money
undergirding it.

As journalist Anne Nelson writes in her book *Shadow Network*, conservative "digital strategy was fully integrated into
their own dedicated media sphere of broadcast and online
platforms—an option that wasn't available to the Democrats.
The radical right could stream its messaging through CBN [the
Christian Broadcasting Network], TBN [the Trinity Broadcasting Network], Salem Communications, Bott Radio, American
Family Radio, and hundreds of other outlets."[1] (All of the networks Nelson names here are Christian, with moderate to strong
evangelical leanings.) The 2010 Wisconsin gubernatorial race
was a successful test balloon for conservatives as their adaptive
strategies worked to undercut Democratic gains and elect Republican Scott Walker. In contrast, Nelson writes, "The liberal
response was feeble: liberal Air America, an internet radio service launched in 2004, lasted only a few years before it went
bankrupt and was dissolved in 2010. Although Air America and
left-leaning news outlets such as MSNBC often concurred with

Democratic positions, there was little to suggest that they carried unidirectional messaging, networked through other data platforms and apps."[2]

The amorphous idea of the "mainstream media" is often assumed to be liberal by people on both sides of the aisle, and it is true that more journalists vote Democrat than Republican, but that's not the whole story. One 2013 survey published in *Journalism & Mass Communication Quarterly* found that 28.1 percent of journalists identified as Democrats, as opposed to only 7.1 percent who identified as Republicans—but fully 50.2 percent identified as "independent," with another 14.6 percent identifying as "other" or "do not know/refused."[3] So while mainstream news sources may sometimes lean slightly left or give favorable coverage to Democratic political candidates, and while liberal and leftist news sources do exist, they aren't remotely comparable to the vast network of well-funded evangelical media sources that has been developing itself and honing its messaging for a literal century.

As weaponized media messaging spread, funding from wealthy conservatives poured in; for instance, the budget of Americans for Prosperity, a 501(c)(4) entity financed by the (non-evangelical) Koch brothers, "leapt from $2 million in 2004 to $15.2 million in 2008, and again to $40 million in 2012."[4] Members of the Council for National Policy (CNP) strategized on how to respond. Despite its neutral-sounding name, the CNP was, in Nelson's words, "founded in 1981 by a small group of archconservatives who realized that the tides of history had turned against them."[5] Throughout its history, the CNP has been highly secretive about its membership, but its member lists have been occasionally leaked to the press, and we know its founding members included leaders of the Christian Right such

as James Dobson (the head of Focus on the Family), Tim La-
Haye (who cowrote the bestselling Left Behind series), and
Paige Patterson (one of the key figures in the conservative resurgence that shifted the Southern Baptist Convention theologically and socially to the right in the 1980s).

Americans for Prosperity, the CNP, and other deep-pocketed
organizations, evangelical and otherwise, provided the funding
for a nascent right-wing movement that called itself the Tea
Party, after the Boston Tea Party, in an attempt to align itself
with what it saw as patriotic protests against tyranny in the tradition of the Founding Fathers. As Nelson puts it,

> the reinvigorated Tea Party lowered the standards of
> American political discourse. Protests erupted across the
> country over the spring of 2009, unleashing a cult of
> invective and incivility. When Democrats returned to
> their home districts for the summer recess to promote
> the Obama health care plan, Tea Partiers invaded their
> town halls and shouted down the legislators, bringing
> the proceedings to a halt. Their disruptions led to
> fistfights, arrests, and even hospitalizations. The protests
> were largely organized through Facebook and Twitter
> and amplified by Fox News and other right-wing
> outlets.[6]

This denigration of public political discourse was a contin-
uation of the same trends that had begun in the late '80s and
'90s when Rush Limbaugh's bombastic commentary went national. The problem would be exacerbated further by the extension of conservative media into digital spaces throughout the

era and the general acceleration of media through Web 2.0 social media platforms like Twitter and Facebook. With social media, everyone could be their own shock jock, conspiracy theorist, or ultra-right-wing pundit. Forget the Fairness Doctrine—conservatives were beholden to no one except a few inconsistently enforced hate-speech policies on social media sites. At the time, it seemed like a nadir; we didn't know what was yet to come.

Funding the Tea Party was not the sole strategy of the CNP and fellow conservative political activists—they also employed sophisticated usage of voter data, with evangelicals and other conservative Christians as key targets. Starting in 2004, the Family Research Council had begun publishing "iVoterGuides" that "routinely awarded high marks to conservative pro-gun, anti-tax Republicans for defending 'biblical values,' at the expense of Democratic candidates."[7] The FRC also ran a "ministry" called Watchmen on the Wall "to connect pastors with policy makers and legislators and to encourage the pastors to advocate for those Biblical values FRC believes should be advanced in America."[8] It expanded to include more than 75,000 pastors by 2006.[9]

The prize jewel of conservative activist data mining, however, was an organization called United in Purpose. Founded by Bill Dallas, who experienced an evangelical conversion while serving a prison sentence for grand theft embezzlement, the group amassed a huge voter database. Dallas himself said on CBN in 2016, "We have about 200 million files, so we have pretty much the whole voting population in our database."[10] How they gathered such a trove of data is unclear, but in her book *The Power Worshippers*, Katherine Stewart cites Chris Vickery, an independent researcher who came across leaked data on nearly 191 million voters that could be tied back to United in Purpose.[11] These data machines were initially spun up to support the presidential ambitions of evangelical and evangelical-adjacent politicians like Ted Cruz, but by mid-2016, the political winds were shifting to give support to a candidate who was decidedly *not* evangelical: Donald Trump.

WE CAN'T TALK ABOUT THE Obama years and how they led into the Trump years without talking about racism. Although white evangelicals evince offense at accusations of racism, the movement has a long history of unambiguous prejudice, racism, and even outright white supremacy. To be clear, this does not mean that every individual evangelical is an overt racist; as we've seen, there are many evangelicals who are people of color, and there have been strains of anti-racist activism within evangelicalism since the very beginning. Racism, however, is not solely an individual problem but a systemic one. And on a systemic level, evangelicalism consistently provides the theological justification for the racist thought and practice that forms the bedrock of American injustice. Slavery, Lost Cause ideology, Jim Crow, the fight to preserve segregation (and therefore to preserve whiteness as a category at the top of a racial hierarchy), the resistance to civil rights, and the battle against even acknowledging the role racism has played in forming our society—none of these are exclusively evangelical phenomena, but all have claimed to be divinely ordained using evangelical rationales.

Evangelicals would have opposed any Democratic president; by the '90s, it was essentially a tenet of the evangelical faith to vote Republican, and I had friends who quite earnestly prayed for me when they learned that I had voted for John Kerry in 2004. But the fact that Obama was Black triggered their racism and threw their right-wing extremism into overdrive. Despite Obama's well-documented attendance at Chicago's Trinity United Church of Christ, millions of evangelicals (and Republicans in general) wholeheartedly believed he was secretly Muslim (an idea that, to his credit, Obama's opponent John McCain refuted).[12] The so-called birther conspiracy theory claiming that Obama was born outside the United States gained so much traction that Obama felt the need to publicly release his birth certificate to prove it was false. And although it was overall a minority view, it became shockingly common to hear evangelicals refer to Obama as the Antichrist. It was as if, after marinating in the alternate reality of Fox News for the past two decades, they could no longer process objective facts. The Christian bubble dictated what was true, not the outside world. Obama did not fit their conception of white, capitalist, conservative Christianity, therefore he was clearly not a Christian and was maybe even the ultimate enemy of Christianity.

Outside the Christian bubble, the latent racism and white supremacy of American culture became more explicit and apparent. As social media became more prevalent and marginalized communities made use of it to draw attention to injustice through the use of hashtags like #BlackLivesMatter, the far right became more blatantly racist. In the lead-up to the 2016 election, openly racist provocateurs such as the "alt-right" neo-Nazi Richard Spencer garnered media attention. While many Republicans hope to distance themselves from this aspect of the conservative movement, journalist Sarah Posner has been able to trace its coevolution alongside Republican elites in her book *Unholy: How White Christian Nationalists Powered the Trump Presidency, and the Devastating Legacy They Left Behind*. She writes about a conference held two months before the 2016 election, attended by white nationalists like Spencer and Peter Brimelow—a former writer for *National Review* and policy aide/speechwriter for Orrin Hatch who had been personally introduced to Rupert Murdoch by William F. Buckley Jr. and stayed well-connected in Washington despite progressing to explicit white supremacy and founding the hate site VDARE.[13] At this conference,

> Brimelow quietly hinted at exactly that kind of
> influence—gradually changing minds by relentlessly
> injecting its ideas into the political discourse, eventually
> eroding their shock value, and pulling the political
> discourse to the right. . . . "Alt-right people do tend to
> live in D.C., do tend to do conservative think tank
> jobs."[14]

Such blatantly racist goals were not limited to mere rhetoric and abstraction at conferences; they were also aggressively and empirically pursued. Posner reports that white nationalist Steve Bannon, "while still at Breitbart but before formally joining the Trump campaign, worked with Cambridge Analytica to help it focus-group slogans and strategies. As early as 2014, the phrases 'drain the swamp,' 'build the wall,' 'deep state,' and, tellingly, 'race realism' were tested."[15]

But these ideas and actions were not originating in the evangelical movement per se. Some white nationalists were evangelicals, and vice versa, and there were certainly links between the two movements within the ecosystems of conservative politics and media, but they were not the same thing. In other words, the circles on the Venn diagram overlapped, but they were still two separate circles. And evangelicals would never vote en masse for someone as far outside their bubble as Donald Trump. Or at least that's what I thought.

AN INCREDIBLE AMOUNT OF INK has been spilled describing Trump's unexpected rise to the presidency (including in several of the excellent books I've cited throughout this one). For my purposes, I'm not interested in dissecting Hillary Clinton's campaign missteps or pontificating on the role of third-party candidates. What I want to elucidate is how white evangelicals came to support Trump, why this support was not the aberration it initially seemed, and why I—even as someone who thought I had examined evangelicalism from every angle—got it so wrong.

During this time period, Emily and I spent some time "unchurched" after our painful exit from our last evangelical church—and I began to notice that we weren't alone. A lot of Christian college friends I was still in touch with (or loosely connected to via social media) were no longer involved in evangelical churches. They had either left evangelicalism for a more progressive expression of faith or left religion entirely, and many, if not most, had adopted positions that are considered taboo in modern evangelical orthodoxy. The most common included an affirmation of queer people (many now identified as LGBTQ+ themselves), a reckoning with the effects of purity culture, and a distancing from the militant political conservatism that was part and parcel of the evangelical experience.

Even though my own experiences within religion had been

by no means positive, I was still drawn to religious questions. My interest, however, had shifted to why and how people changed their minds about it, especially with regard to leaving evangelical communities and faiths. Podcasting had gone mainstream—the 2014 debut of *Serial* being a watershed moment—and I had the idea to start a podcast exploring "the world inside and outside the evangelical culture," as my tagline would eventually say. I decided to call it *Exvangelical*, a contraction of ex-evangelical.

The first episode came out in July 2016, the week of the Republican National Convention, when Donald Trump officially accepted the nomination. It featured a conversation between me and my college friend Jonathan Dodrill, who had gone on to become an American religious historian. In that conversation, we both stated our belief that Trump would not garner the necessary support from white evangelicals to beat Hillary Clinton in a general election. We thought that white evangelicals as both individuals and a collective would follow the angels of their better nature. We were incredibly naïve, and incredibly wrong.

Clearly, we were giving evangelicals too much credit to live up to what we believed their moral standards to be, but that wasn't the only reason we thought Trump would fail among evangelicals. There was also the fact that he just so obviously wasn't from the evangelical world. He used vulgar language, he had been divorced, he had cheated on his wives, but above all, he had spent no time in any type of church, evangelical or otherwise. He flubbed his first attempts at courtship of the popular white evangelical vote and the support of evangelical power brokers. At the Iowa Family Leadership Summit in 2015, he claimed to be a churchgoer but said he had never asked God for forgiveness, denying the most basic tenet of Christianity.[16] When he spoke at Liberty University in January 2016, he swore and—more shockingly—referred to Second Corinthians as "Two Corinthians," evidence of his complete lack of biblical literacy.

These missteps were cause for concern. Trump was running against several evangelical favorites, including Mike Huckabee, Ted Cruz, and Ben Carson, all of whom had deep ties to various evangelical and adjacent faith communities. Huckabee was a Southern Baptist pastor, Ted Cruz's father was a Dominionist pastor, and Ben Carson was a Seventh-day Adventist whose 1992 book, *Gifted Hands*, was published by Zondervan (and developed into a 2009 movie starring Cuba Gooding Jr.). Regardless, Trump polled incredibly well throughout the primaries, and by May 2016, all the other candidates had dropped out in the face of his success. So, at the risk of millions of religious voters either opting out of the election or backing an independent candidate, the CNP and their coalition decided to join the winning team and back Trump.

By June 2016, Trump had learned—or at least someone had fed him the lines—to speak to evangelical concerns with more tact, voicing support for "the sanctity and dignity of life" (coded antiabortion language), "marriage and family" (coded anti-LGBTQ+ language) and "religious freedom" (coded pro-Christian-nationalism language). United in Purpose's Bill Dallas worked with evangelical pollster George Barna to organize a New York City meeting with undecided fundamentalists. They only targeted two hundred fundamentalist leaders, but around one thousand attended, from all around the country. Ben Carson, Franklin Graham, Mike Huckabee, Tony Perkins, and Ralph Reed of the Faith & Freedom Coalition all lent their support to Trump, and by the end of the evening, the crowd was increasingly convinced of Trump's viability, even though many people stopped short of endorsing him.[17]

By early July, Trump had added to the ticket as his running mate Mike Pence, who had grown up Catholic but had been born again in college. Pence's tenure as governor of Indiana was dogged by the effects of the Religious Freedom Restoration Act, which allowed for legal discrimination against same-sex couples and had been met with swift backlash from the business community, resulting in lost revenue for the state.[18] This seemed like a negative at the time, but in retrospect, it might have actually burnished his reputation among evangelicals. In any case, with his evangelical bona fides and strong ties to the religious right, he was a known quantity. Trump plucked Pence from Indiana and, in doing so, helped shore up support among a critical voting bloc. Things moved even more quickly from there.

On July 21, 2016, Donald Trump officially accepted the Republican nomination. For some evangelical leaders, this was a turning point. Despite his ungodly actions and his clear lack of religiosity, Trump was the Republican nominee, and a vote for the Republican nominee was a vote to uphold the white patriarchal capitalism so close to the heart of evangelicalism. By July 28, Wayne Grudem—you may remember him from chapter 6 as a pioneer of complementarianism and cofounder of the Council on Biblical Manhood and Womanhood—penned an article called "Why Voting for Donald Trump Is a Morally Good Choice."

Evangelical support continued to accelerate as the general election reached its final months but hit a speed bump with the *Access Hollywood* tape released on October 7 in which Trump discussed "grab[bing women] by the pussy." The crudeness of the language combined with the unrepentant description of infidelity (not to mention the implication of sexual assault) evoked a crisis of conscience for some evangelicals. Ralph Reed, Tony Perkins, Robert Jeffress, and other evangelical leaders were steadfast in their support, but Grudem published another article on October 9 called "Trump's Moral Character and the Election," in which he wrote forthrightly that "I cannot commend Trump's moral character, and I strongly urge him to withdraw from the election."[19] A mere ten days later, he had reconciled his concerns and published a final article called "If You Don't Like Either Candidate, Then Vote for Trump's Policies," in which he provided the justifications necessary to mollify any guilty evangelical's conscience. He couldn't endorse Trump's personality, but he wholeheartedly endorsed his politics.

> I overwhelmingly support Trump's policies and believe
> that Clinton's policies will seriously damage the nation,
> perhaps forever. On the Supreme Court, abortion,
> religious liberty, sexual orientation regulations, taxes,
> economic growth, the minimum wage, school choice,
> Obamacare, protection from terrorists, immigration, the
> military, energy, and safety in our cities, I think Trump
> is far better than Clinton. . . . Again and again, Trump
> supports the policies I advocated in my 2010 book
> *Politics According to the Bible.*[20]

At the end of the day, what Grudem truly valued wasn't faith or morality. It was the cruelty inherent in white capitalist evangelicalism. It was the conservative vision for America, for seeing a particular kind of Christianity favored and, in some ways, imposed on the American people through the rule of law. It was lowering taxes, glorifying and supporting military and police power, resisting environmental and worker protections, reducing access to health care, and discriminating against immigrants, women, and LGBTQ+ people—all of which were in line with this vision of faith. A century of cultivation around certain evangelical beliefs brought Grudem and other evangelicals to this conclusion.

And though there was certainly some hand-wringing, it seemed most evangelicals needed even less convincing than Grudem; Pew reported immediately after the election that 81 percent of white evangelicals supported Trump, forming a crucial voting bloc that helped elect him to the presidency.[21] Trump's words resonated with their view of a world under threat ("perhaps forever," in Grudem's words) from evil liberals, reinforcing all the conditioning that had been done over the past forty years by the religious right. Trump justified their vision of a country in decline, an apocalypse on the horizon, an America that could only be protected by enacting what they defined as "Christian" policy.

For a few clear-eyed commentators, especially religious historians familiar with the history I've outlined in this book, Trump's election was not surprising. But for many, including me, it was a shock that made us wonder how the very people who had formed our faith could rally behind a man whose personal impiety, contemptible treatment of others, and inhuman policies stood in such stark contrast to so many of the teachings of Jesus of Nazareth. I had spent my entire adult life grappling with the various contradictions and paradoxes found in the evangelical community. I had had enough "church hurt" to realize that evangelicalism didn't always live up to the ideals of love, forgiveness, and social concern it claimed to espouse—the conditional acceptance of our evangelical communities had made that quite clear—but it wasn't until Trump's victory that I began to comprehend what its true ideals were.

I knew evangelicals made excuses for certain people who furthered their conservative agenda, but I hadn't understood that Trump, who worshipped only himself, could be lauded as a legitimate leader and ushered into power while I and so many others—lifelong believers who had devoted so much time and effort to our faith—could be turned away for disagreements around gender roles and sexual ethics. The same forces that sparked the businessmen's revival over a century earlier had become more and more radical over the years until they reached their logical conclusion: a religion beholden to a cultural and political movement, a faith in which faith didn't matter if it led you outside the evangelical bubble.

That is not to say evangelicals aren't "true Christians." Put simply: if a person says they are Christian, they are Christian. As historian Chrissy Stroop never tires of pointing out on Twitter, Christianity is defined by Christians' actions and can take many forms, some good and some bad. Evangelicals attend church, they read the Bible, they pray—they're Christian. But, in the Trump era more than ever, it's clear evangelicalism's consistent history of sidelining moderate critics in favor of strident fundamentalism has made them increasingly authoritarian—and increasingly willing to support authoritarians.

For some people who were already deconstructing their faith, seeing such widespread and unabashed support for Trump within their congregations was the final straw needed for them to disassociate from their churches and their evangelical belief. Rachel Held Evans published a blog post on November 14, 2016, called "Life After Evangelicalism," in which she encouraged her readers. "You are not alone. You are not alone in your grief. You are not alone in your anger. You are not alone in your doubt, frustration, and fear. The community that introduced you to Jesus—that baptized you and named you a beloved child of God—has aligned itself with values you don't recognize, powers that oppress. It's an enormous blow, and it'll knock the wind right out of you."[22]

Trump's election was a catalyzing moment for conservative extremists, but it also catalyzed people who were already weary of white evangelicalism's conservatism to view it in a new light and decide it was no longer worth staying. Evangelical leaders did not listen to the would-be reformers Bill Pannell, Tom Skinner, and Evangelicals for Social Action in the '70s; to the evangelical feminist movement of the '80s and '90s; or to the voices of progressive bloggers or pastors like Rob Bell in the '00s and '10s. So why would they listen in 2016? What is the purpose of staying and trying to "reform the church from within" if the church has always been resistant to all efforts to do so, if the conservative strains have not only stamped out the progressive strains but grown ever more radically conservative? If the evangelical movement would readily support Donald Trump, of all people, what change would even be possible?

Across the country, people were determining whether to continue supporting these institutions with their tithes and their time, and they began expressing themselves and finding a sense of community online. People had been leaving white evangelicalism for decades, but those individual exoduses were invisible and often private. The stories that were public were largely limited to people who were able to acquire book deals to tell them. But now, with the advent of a mature social media ecosystem and a major social catalyst in Trump's election, millions of people were equipped to tell their stories on their own terms. As people's distrust in their churches grew, as they began to question and deconstruct their beliefs, they were able to turn to the stories of strangers online and find people with the same concerns and experiences. It was the beginning of a new counterpublic.

11

TALKING BACK TO EVANGELICALISM

THE FORMATION OF A COUNTERPUBLIC

P rior chapters have reviewed how several different groups fought for their right to be accepted within the evangelical movements and were denied. The widespread white evangelical support for Trump in 2016 was a moment of clarity for many would-be reformers; they no longer saw reform as possible. The relationship became antagonistic, and a legitimate counterpublic began to develop. "Counterpublic" is not a commonly known term, but I believe it offers considerable value in understanding the role that "exvangelical" and similar terms have had in steering the public conversation around religion and social issues over the past several years. (I know this is a bit academic, but bear with me—I promise I'm going somewhere with it.)

The notion of a counterpublic was first introduced by political theorist Nancy Fraser. Her 1992 article "Rethinking the Public Sphere" interrogates the work of Jürgen Habermas, who popularized the notion of the public sphere in his influential book on the creation of bourgeois liberalism in Western Europe, *The Structural Transformation of the Public Sphere*. Fraser characterizes the Habermasian public sphere as "a theater in modern societies in which political participation is enacted through the medium of talk," separate from "state apparatuses, economic markets, and democratic associations."[1] In layman's terms, you could think of it as something along the lines of "public opinion" or "public discourse." Fraser finds this framework useful but insufficient—the public sphere is not a singular, unified entity, she argues, but rather one public among many, and Habermas's conception of it made several discriminatory assumptions along the lines of gender, class status, and what constituted public versus private concern.

In sum, the notion of a public for white, landed, bourgeois men was classist, sexist, and racist, and therefore exclusionary, compelling those who had been excluded—such as "women, workers, peoples of color, and gays and lesbians"—to create their own alternative publics.[2] Fraser termed these alternative publics "subaltern [lower-status] counterpublics," which she defined as "parallel discursive arenas where members of subordinated social groups" could have their own discourse based on their own "identities, interests, and needs."[3]

In his book *Publics and Counterpublics*, Michael Warner builds on Fraser's work, writing that "a counterpublic maintains at some level, conscious or not, an awareness of its subordinate status. . . . And the conflict extends not just to ideas or policy questions but to the speech genres and modes of address that constitute the public. . . . The discourse that constitutes it is not merely a different or alternative idiom but one that in other contexts would be regarded with hostility or with a sense of indecorousness."[4] In other words, a given nondominant community forms a counterpublic where it can have its own conversations about its own interests in its own ways *because it has to*—the corresponding dominant community doesn't allow those conversations to happen in the main public sphere.

Further, Warner highlights why counterpublics are both so valuable to and so vulnerable for people who hold minority opinions in religious groups: "In some cases, such as fundamentalism . . . participants are not subalterns for any reason other than their participation in the counterpublic discourse."[5] By definition, an evangelical counterpublic discusses evangelicalism on the terms of nondominant groups like women, people of color, and LGBTQ+ people. Merely participating in that discussion, even if you're a straight white man, can be enough to threaten your status within the dominant evangelical public.

Warner's book was published in 2002, before the advent of the social web, but his assertion that "a counterpublic comes into being through an address to indefinite strangers" is certainly relevant, and researchers have since applied the concept of counterpublics to digital media.[6] The authors of *#Hashtag-Activism: Networks of Race and Gender Justice* directly invoke counterpublics when calling attention to the role hashtags have had in public discourse: "Throughout this text we use *hashtag activism* to refer to the strategic ways counterpublic groups and their allies on Twitter employ this shortcut to make political contentions about identity politics that advocate for social change, identity redefinition, and political inclusion."[7]

Basically, social media created an easy and convenient way

to form a counterpublic—members of a nondominant group could easily find one another on social media platforms and join relevant conversations via hashtags and other digital means. But the level of convenience does not mean that digital counterpublics are somehow "not real" or that they have no effect offline. Indeed, the authors of #*HashtagActivism* write, "We argue that this online activism leads to material effects in the digital and physical sphere. . . . These hashtag activists, occasionally maligned as 'slacktivists' or 'armchair activists' because digital activism is sometimes considered less valid than direct action and is mistakenly regarded as in competition with it, use hashtags to create social change."[8]

In the age of social media, especially in the wake of Trump's election, people questioning their evangelical faith were ripe to form a counterpublic online. In fact, in her book *Redeem All: How Digital Life Is Changing Evangelical Culture*, Corrina Laughlin specifically calls out the online aspects of the deconstruction movement as having "the potential to connect and galvanize counterpublics by highlighting and amplifying voices that speak out against the evangelical power structure represented by Bible colleges, churches, and parachurch organizations and other sites of cultural power."[9]

This is where the #Exvangelical hashtag comes in.

Two questions spring to mind: (1) How did a broadly dispersed group of people disillusioned with white evangelicalism evolve into something resembling a counterpublic (inclusive of, but not limited to, those who might use hashtags like #Exvangelical)? And (2) Why is this framework valuable for understanding how exvangelical/deconstruction narratives find purchase in public conversation? To answer the second question first, the counterpublic framework functions as a useful metaphor for something that is hard to grasp. As Ben Tarnoff writes, "The internet is too sprawling to squeeze into a single frame. There is no bird's-eye view of the internet. That's why metaphors matter. Some things are too small to see without a microscope; others are too big to see without a metaphor."[10] To answer the first question, let's look at how public discourse about evangelicalism evolved in the years surrounding Trump's election, eventually incorporating terms like "exvangelical" and "deconstruction" into a common parlance.

But before I get to any contributions I may have made to this discourse, I want to discuss some of the big conversations that have been occurring over the past decade or so, online and offline, as people create their own spaces to talk back to evangelicalism.

THE #METOO CAMPAIGN, STARTED BY activist Tarana Burke, was catapulted to the center of public debate following a viral tweet by actor Alyssa Milano in October 2017. #MeToo provided an outlet for women to share their stories of sexual abuse and assault, and—in an example of how online counterpublics intersect with offline action—it led to tangible consequences for serial abusers such as Miramax producer Harvey Weinstein. In November 2017, two former Moody Bible Institute students, Emily Joy Allison and River Paasch, were inspired by #MeToo to create the hashtag #ChurchToo, which they used to share Allison's story of being groomed by a youth leader in her church. It quickly went viral as more and more people, women in particular, came forward with their own stories of abuse occurring within the church.

It is important to note that clergy sexual abuse has a long

history and is by no means confined to white evangelicalism. However, the fundamentalist theology that demands male headship and female submission, combined with a culture that justifies and excuses male "mistakes," does mean that evangelical churches are prone to attracting abusers. This is not mere conjecture. In 2019, the *Houston Chronicle* published an in-depth six-part investigation into instances of sexual abuse within the Southern Baptist Convention, in which they found that since 1998, "roughly 380 Southern Baptist church leaders and volunteers have faced allegations of sexual misconduct. . . . That includes those who were convicted, credibly accused and successfully sued, and those who confessed or resigned. . . . They left behind more than 700 victims, many of them shunned by their churches, left to themselves to rebuild their lives. Some were urged to forgive their abusers or to get abortions."[11]

Prior to this bombshell report, sexual misconduct and abuse by other prominent male leaders across the evangelical spectrum had begun to come to light. In January 2018, Andy Savage, a megachurch pastor in Memphis, Tennessee, was accused of sexually assaulting Jules Woodson in 1998 when Woodson was a teenager and Savage was twenty-two.[12] (When Savage told his congregation about this, he did not frame what occurred as assault or abuse but instead called it a "regretful sexual incident from his past," apologized to *them*, and asked *their* forgiveness. He was met with a standing ovation.) In March 2018, Bill Hybels, the founding pastor of the famous "seeker-friendly" Willow Creek Community Church in suburban Chicago, was the subject of a *Chicago Tribune* investigation into his own alleged behavior, which "included suggestive comments, extended hugs, an unwanted kiss and invitations to hotel rooms."[13] Less than a month later, Hybels stepped down, and by May, Willow Creek's elders apologized publicly for having doubted women's allegations.[14] That same month, Paige Patterson—a major figure in the SBC—was ousted from his role as president of the Southwestern Baptist Theological Seminary after multiple incidents of mishandling sexual abuse throughout his career came to light.[15] Just one example: *The Washington Post* reported that while he was president of the seminary, he "encouraged a woman who said she had been raped not to report it to the police and told her to forgive her alleged assailant."[16]

#ChurchToo eventually garnered direct responses from some evangelical leaders. By the end of 2018, Wheaton College hosted a conference dedicated to the topic, but notably they did not invite Allison or Paasch, the creators of the hashtag, likely because one is a queer woman and the other is a queer nonbinary person. Beth Moore, a popular Bible study author and leader who maintained an uneasy relationship with the Southern Baptist Convention, disclosed that she too had been a victim of sexual abuse. Over the next few years, #ChurchToo became an ongoing movement and a method of critiquing systemic issues that affect a wide swath of denominations. It has helped bring survivors together and bring stories to light, not for the sake of scandal but for the sake of justice.

In 2021, Allison published the book *#ChurchToo: How Purity Culture Upholds Abuse and How to Find Healing*, which took aim at the underlying theology that perpetuates abuse. For her book, Allison interviewed Jules Woodson.

One of the last things Jules and I talked about in our interview was justice. The statute of limitations for the crime committed against Jules had long since passed. Like me, she had very little legal recourse when she came forward.

"What's justice for you?" I asked.

"Justice is ugly. Justice is not clean. Justice is not cookie-cutter," Jules said. "I knew that I would never see justice in the form of a legal case."

"Thankfully that's not the only kind of justice," I responded. "Because guess what happens when you type the name 'Andy Savage' into Google?"

"And that's my justice," Jules said victoriously. "I took my story back."[17]

FOLLOWING THE 2012 KILLING OF Trayvon Martin, cultural awareness of police violence and discrimination faced by Black Americans reached a tipping point due in large part to the activists on Twitter utilizing hashtags such as #BlackLivesMatter to boost stories that were not highlighted in more traditional media outlets. Just as #ChurchToo helped expand the work of #MeToo, new hashtags focused on racial justice soon expanded the work of #BlackLivesMatter into the evangelical counterpublic's discourse. Though there are what are known as "historically Black" Protestant denominations that exist outside of institutional evangelicalism, there are also plenty of Black evangelicals, and as previous chapters have shown, there have been several instances where Black evangelicals have sought to call their white siblings in Christ to account for their complicity in white supremacy. Those calls accelerated from 2016 onward, even as Black people lost faith that they would ever be heard. This led to more and more Black churchgoers disaffiliating from white-led churches. *The New York Times* called it a "quiet exodus."[18]

Black congregants may have left quietly, but it was white congregants' silence on issues of racism and injustice that was the root problem. Black leaders like Andre E. Johnson, a professor and pastor, tried to get them to speak up. In September 2016, after the police shooting of Keith Lamont Scott, Johnson started the hashtag #WhiteChurchQuiet, demanding to know where the white church was in the fight for social justice. He subsequently wrote of his intentions: "When I saw African American pastors and ministers marching with protesters and speaking out, yet again, on abusive police tactics, I found myself asking a different question: 'Where was the *white* church in all of this?' "[19]

This conversation continued in books like Austin Channing Brown's *I'm Still Here: Black Dignity in a World Made for Whiteness* and Jemar Tisby's *The Color of Compromise*. But the unwillingness of white denominations to enact meaningful change or even acknowledge the realities of racism throughout the 2010s eventually led to the 2021 #LeaveLoud hashtag campaign. Organized by the Black Christian collective the Witness, #LeaveLoud was kicked off in a March 8, 2021, episode of their podcast, *Pass the Mic*. In it, host Tyler Burns interviewed Witness founder Jemar Tisby, a high-profile Black activist in evangelical and Reformed circles, about his story of leaving white evangelical spaces. Tisby was forthright about the racism he experienced there and about why he felt it was important for other

Black Christians to be equally forthright.[20] He called on Black churchgoers to loudly share their stories of why they were leaving white-led Christian spaces, using the new hashtag.

The next day, the aforementioned Beth Moore, who is white, announced she was leaving the SBC due to the issues of misogyny and sexual abuse discussed earlier in this chapter. Hers was clearly a worthy cause, but unfortunately, the timing meant that the press that covers white evangelicalism (which takes up much of the attention of the small cadre of full-time religion journalists in the United States) put the spotlight on Moore, hamstringing the momentum that the Witness had hoped to build in the broader cultural conversation. The Witness remains undeterred and continues to cultivate both content and novel forms of community that center the Black Christian perspective, but racial justice in evangelicalism is always an uphill battle.

Others, like lenny duncan, a former pastor with the Evangelical Lutheran Church in America (ELCA), have begun approaching the problem from a different angle altogether. While duncan's first book, published in 2019, was called *Dear Church: A Love Letter from a Black Preacher to the Whitest Denomination in the U.S.*, their follow-up 2023 book was called *Dear Revolutionaries: A Field Guide for a World Beyond the Church*. In just a few years, duncan had concluded that the church couldn't be reformed from within, that racial justice had to be sought from beyond its walls. In an interview with *Publishers Weekly*, they said, "When I wrote *Dear Church*, I thought I could weaponize a kind of respectability as a pastor. Then came May 30, 2020, and I did my first shift as a trauma chaplain as police attacked protesters. . . . Everything I thought I knew and thought would work melted in the revealing of the truth."[21] Online or offline, in the church or beyond it, that truth is revealed over and over by the work of the counterpublic.

ANOTHER ISSUE WIDELY CRITIQUED BY the exvangelical counterpublic is purity culture, and it's no mystery why. The purity culture of the 1980s and '90s—communicated through books such as *I Kissed Dating Goodbye* and *When God Writes Your Love Story*, True Love Waits abstinence pledges, purity balls, purity rings, and countless explicit and implicit lessons at church and at home—is rooted in patriarchy, misogyny, queerphobia, and racism.* The consequences of these beliefs played out in the bodies and lives of the people who took those theologies seriously, which was millions of people—especially, though not exclusively, girls and women. As they grew into adolescence and adulthood, many of these people discovered just how cruel and inhuman these teachings were, and how out of step they were with how sexuality and relationships are embodied.

As social media matured, it became a discussion topic online. In 2013, Laura Polk began the No Shame Movement, an early hashtag and eventual website about purity culture. Prior to launching #ChurchToo, Emily Joy Allison and River Paasch ran a blog called *The Flawless Project*, where they documented their process of overcoming purity culture. The conversation

---

* For an example of how purity culture intersects with racism, consider the details of Bob Jones University's segregationist policies in the 1970s. Until 1971, they denied Black students admission outright. Then, under pressure from the IRS, they allowed Black students, but only if they were already married to a Black spouse. Finally, they allowed single Black students but strictly prohibited interracial dating. The school considered Blackness such a threat to white sexual purity that they lost their tax-exempt status over it. For more exploration of the role of racism in purity culture, see sources like Sara Moslener's book *Virgin Nation* and Angie Hong's article "The Flaw at the Center of Purity Culture."

around purity culture also broke into books, as multiple titles addressed purity culture directly, including Bromleigh McCleneghan's *Good Christian Sex*, Brenda Marie Davies's *On Her Knees*, and Linda Kay Klein's *Pure: Inside the Evangelical Movement That Shamed a Generation of Young Women and How I Broke Free*, the latter of which received widespread mainstream media coverage from outlets like NPR's *Fresh Air*.

Inextricable from the misogyny evangelicalism expresses through purity culture is its homophobia. They're two sides of the same coin: the obsessive desire to police other people's sexuality and gender expression in order to neutralize any threat to the idea that a specific type of straight male dominance is God's unquestionable will. There is endless discourse within evangelicalism about "sexual sin" because that discourse is necessary to uphold the heteronormative, patriarchal order; without an elaborate web of justifications constantly reinforcing the system, it would fall apart all too easily.

LGBTQ+ Christians have fought against this bigotry and for recognition within their faith communities for decades. Occasionally, the public has listened to what the counterpublic was saying. An early example of this, much maligned in conservative Christian circles, is the 1988 book *Living in Sin?: A Bishop Rethinks Human Sexuality* by the Episcopal bishop John Shelby Spong. Spong, and a few other clergy who observed how their lay members navigated sexual ethics and faithfulness, thought maybe it was time to start interpreting biblical injunctions against homosexuality the same way they interpreted biblical commands not to eat shellfish or wear clothing made from two different fabrics.

In the early 2000s and '10s, as queer people gained more legal rights and broader social acceptance in the United States, many nonevangelical churches began to reevaluate their stances on the issue. Multiple major mainline Protestant denominations underwent schisms over the validation of queer Christians, arriving at a variety of positions on whether congregants or clergy could be openly queer, whether same-sex marriages could take place in the church, and so forth. For example, the Episcopal church and the largest American Lutheran denomination decided to affirm queer people, causing scores of conservative churches to disaffiliate and realign with newly formed nonaffirming denominations. Meanwhile, within conservative evangelical denominations and parachurch organizations, the "homosexual question" was moot because of the evangelical interpretation of the so-called clobber passages, a set of six Bible verses that seemingly condemn homosexuality* which are used to "clobber" any attempts at dissent.

But the counterpublic has its own conversations about itself on its own terms, which is exactly what we see among queer exvangelicals. In 2008, the activist, scholar, and performer Peterson Toscano released the comedy special *Homo No Mo' Halfway House: How I Survived the Ex-Gay Movement,* which told of his experiences spending seventeen years in various forms of conversion therapy. Books rethinking the clobber passages from a theological perspective appeared, including *The Children Are Free: Reexamining the Biblical Evidence on Same-Sex Relationships* by Jeff Miner and John Tyler Connoley, *Torn: Rescuing the Gospel from the Gays-vs.-Christians Debate* by Justin Lee, and *God and*

---

* I say "seemingly condemn" for several reasons: our modern conception of sexual orientation didn't exist in the ancient world; the contemporary context of some of the verses is unclear; the English translations of some Greek and Hebrew words are controversial; and so on. Despite evangelical assertions to the contrary, there is rarely, if ever, a single, unambiguous reading of any part of the Bible.

the Gay Christian: The Biblical Case in Support of Same-Sex Relationships by Matthew Vines.

As time progressed, the queer Christian counterpublic spilled into the digital realm, where the LGBTQ+ faith activist Eliel Cruz began the hashtag #FaithfullyLGBT to call attention to the experiences of LGBT Christians. In the world of podcasting, Kevin Garcia launched *A Tiny Revolution* and Matthias Roberts launched *Queerology*, while Crystal Cheatham developed Our Bible App, offering a progressive and queer-affirming alternative to Bible apps like YouVersion's that default to conservative evangelicalism. Musicians such as Semler (a queer Christian) and Flamy Grant (a gay nonbinary Christian and drag queen whose stage name is a reference to CCM megastar Amy Grant) both successfully released albums that reached number one on the iTunes Christian music charts.[22] (Despite their commercial and critical success, they were spurned by the Dove Awards, the CCM version of the Grammys. They attended anyway, as an agitation as well as a proclamation that they belong in Christian spaces.)

These authors and artists continue to fight for their right to be part of the public conversation. Evangelical institutions, however, continued to hold the line even as both broader society and their own membership became increasingly accepting of queer relationships. At the same time, the counterpublic's work had an effect. Knowing open homophobia was now unacceptable to many people, evangelical churches often began to remain intentionally ambiguous about their convictions surrounding queer affirmation, defaulting to vague statements like "We love everyone as they are." A new cliché was born: when pressed by church members for clarity, leaders often ask to meet in private over coffee, where they inevitably reveal that their church believes in the same old "traditional view" of marriage and condemns homosexuality. This became such a common trope that the queer Christian musician Semler wrote a song called "Wanna Grab Coffee?" that reenacts these conversations, and an organization called Church Clarity started grading churches as either affirming or nonaffirming.

Other evangelicals were not so subtle. InterVarsity, the sponsor of the Urbana conference and one of the largest evangelical ministries active on college campuses, purged its organization of any employees who supported gay marriage in November 2016.[23] Similarly, when the Christian charity World Vision, one of the world's largest NGOs, briefly enacted "a policy change that would have allowed the non-profit to hire married gay and lesbian employees," it was met with a swift donor boycott organized by conservative evangelicals.[24] Unsurprisingly, the people who were willing to stop sponsoring needy children over an HR decision depicted themselves as the only ones protecting children from the true threat: the existence of gay people. Trevin Wax, a writer for The Gospel Coalition, wrote a piece called "World Vision and Why We Grieve for the Children," which cast all nonevangelical-approved relationships as the real tragedy of the situation.

> Children are the ones who suffer when society says
> there's no difference between a mom or a dad. . . .
> Children are the ones who suffer when Mom and Dad
> choose to live together unmarried. . . . Children are the
> ones who suffer when careers matter more than
> marriage. . . . Sex is our god. Children are our sacrifice.[25]

It's not hard to see why these attitudes about sex and sin drive people away from evangelicalism—and why such people are traumatized in the process. Indeed, many of the books that emerged during this time deal explicitly with trauma and trauma recovery, such as Teresa B. Pasquale's *Sacred Wounds: A Path to Healing from Spiritual Trauma*, Carol Howard Merritt's *Healing Spiritual Wounds*, and Jamie Lee Finch's *You Are Your Own: A Reckoning with the Religious Trauma of Evangelical Christianity*. Two of the cohosts on the podcast *The Liturgists* wrote books about learning to be fully present in one's body as part of the healing process: Mike McHargue with *You're a Miracle (and a Pain in the Ass)*, and Hillary McBride with *The Wisdom of Your Body*. Both look to non-Christian traditions and forms of knowledge such as psychology, neuroscience, "yoga, Tai Chi, martial arts, and breath work" for insight and wisdom.[26]

Whether by doing yoga or by sharing stories of abuse, in their own way, all the people I've highlighted in this chapter have followed their convictions beyond what the gatekeepers of evangelical orthodoxy would accept. They hint at the breadth and depth of responses to the effects of evangelicalism that were made all throughout the 2000s and 2010s. It was from this milieu that the #Exvangelical hashtag sprang, as you'll read in the next chapter.

12

#EXVANGELICAL

FINDING COMMUNITY ONLINE

I joined Twitter* back in 2009, primarily to follow comic-book creators. Over the ensuing years, I would become more and more enamored with the app. I could follow interesting people across all types of industries—comics, tech, public commentary—to learn more about their perspectives (or just because they posted funny memes). It was where the media set their agenda and sourced their stories, and where you had at least a chance to converse with influential people. It was also a place where a user could learn a lot about other cultures and perspectives by simply following along in real time.

I wasn't working in any public-facing fields like journalism, media, or government, but once my podcast launched and I

---

* I will not be calling it X.

began promoting it on social media, I started to build an audience. I started the podcast *Exvangelical* in July 2016, and by the time of the November election, I had begun to use #Exvangelical as a hashtag on Twitter.* I contend that what made this counterpublic different from the other internal reform movements that preceded it was social media's ability to render the invisible visible. People could go online and see that others were leaving too. It made the option to leave more tenable. And, indeed, as the hashtag gained traction, I began to make connections with other people who had left or been forced out of evangelicalism.

In the weeks leading up to the election, I somehow stumbled across the Twitter timeline of Chrissy Stroop, a fellow ex-evangelical and Hoosier. Stroop was an academic who studied (and had lived in) Russia, and combined with her insider knowledge of how white evangelicals operated politically and socially, this meant she was the right person to speak to at that moment in time. We became frequent collaborators, informally working together to push back on the standard narratives around white evangelical power that persisted in major media outlets, where religion reporters often regarded evangelicalism as inherently benevolent, if sometimes misguided. At the time, Twitter was a chaotic and lively place where any user might have a chance at snatching a moment of virality to build an audience or to start a conversation that would spill into mainstream coverage, much as #BlackLivesMatter and #MeToo had.

During the ensuing years, Stroop would develop related

---

* A since-abandoned blog called *Exvangelical* that seems to have independently coined the same term around the same time is not related to me.

hashtag campaigns, perhaps most notably #EmptyThePews, which she started in August 2017 following the Charlottesville Unite the Right rally and Trump's declaration that there were "very good people on both sides"—one side being literal Nazis. Despite a number of business leaders stepping down from Trump's advisory councils in protest, his evangelical advisory council remained steadfastly devoted. Stroop encouraged people on Twitter, "If you left Evangelicalism over bigotry and intolerance or this election specifically, please share your story w/ the hashtag #EmptyThePews."[1] The tweet went viral, and Stroop would later compile many responses in a follow-up article for *Religion Dispatches*, where she had become a regular commentator.[2]

She would also use Twitter to highlight various aspects of exvangelical experience with other hashtags, including #ChristianAltFacts, which built off Kellyanne Conway's use of the phrase "alternative facts" and highlighted the various implausible explanations common in evangelical culture; #RaptureAnxiety, which touched on the emotional effects of fearing an impending apocalypse; and #ExposeChristianSchools, which drew attention to harmful practices within Christian schools across the country. The latter hashtag gained enough traction that it prompted an article in *The New York Times*.[3]

Both Stroop and #ChurchToo creator Emily Joy Allison were repeat guests on my podcast. The three of us also appeared in the 2018 CBS Religion & Culture documentary *Deconstructing My Religion*, which brought attention to the burgeoning movement. And we were only one corner of that movement. As detailed in the previous chapter, an exvangelical counterpublic was steadily developing online. I found myself part of a new wave of creators who were all talking about the same issues with different frameworks and in different mediums—podcasts, Twitter, and soon, as we'll see in a moment, Instagram.

HERE, I WANT TO PAUSE to bring in another concept from media studies: networked publics. (Again, I know I'm being academic, but stick with me.) If a public is "a collection of people who understand themselves to be part of an imagined community," then networked publics are, in the words of media scholar danah boyd, "publics that are restructured by networked technologies. . . . They are built on and through social media and other emergent technologies."[4] Boyd conceives of networked publics as "simultaneously a space and a collection of people"—both the websites, apps, etc., where people communicate with one another *and* the people who are doing the communicating.[5]

According to boyd, there are certain characteristics that set networked publics apart from traditional publics (as defined in the previous chapter). In terms of the *space*, the architecture of networked publics provides

- persistence (meaning "online expressions are automatically recorded and archived"),
- replicability (meaning "content . . . can be duplicated" through retweets, screenshots, rip-offs, etc.),
- scalability (meaning content can go viral or otherwise be seen by a large number of people), and
- searchability (meaning people can find content using search engines or other search functions).[6]

In terms of the *people*, the dynamics of networked publics are defined by

- invisible audiences (meaning a person doesn't necessarily know everyone who'll be consuming their content),
- collapsed contexts (meaning a person doesn't necessarily know a speaker's background, what they're responding to, or other pieces of context), and
- blurred boundaries between public and private (meaning not just that things intended for private consumption can be made public but also that people care less about the distinction between public and private).[7]

If you've spent a lot of time online, you understand networked publics intuitively, and you probably participate in them intuitively as well. They're the water you swim in.* You're used to scrolling through posts made by friends and strangers alike, sharing others' posts (perhaps with your own commentary added), hunting down context to understand certain posts, and so on and so forth.

The exvangelical counterpublic is a networked public, and one of its most powerful tools is the hashtag. By 2019, the hashtag #Exvangelical was receiving more than 100,000 impressions on Twitter each day from organic use and engagement, which was more than I ever expected. But when it found its way over to Instagram, it exploded in popularity.

Like Twitter, Instagram uses hashtags to categorize posts, but unlike Twitter, there's a much larger character limit on posts, which means people frequently use multiple hashtags at a

---

* The value of media studies is that it gives us the language to describe our environments. It lets us become the fish in the old joke that says, "How's the water?" instead of the one that says, "What the hell is water?"

time. As a result, it became common to see #Exvangelical used as one star in a whole constellation of interrelated hashtags in Instagram captions. A single post might be tagged #Exvangelical #ExChristian #ExEvangelical #Deconstruction #ExvangelicalMemes #ProgressiveChristianity #ExJW #ExMormon #ExCatholic #ExFundie (and so on). The list might run for several lines. Someone searching for any one of those terms could quickly be connected to everyone searching for any other one of those terms—and that is an *enormous* audience. Not only is Instagram's active user base much larger than Twitter's (at least twice as big in 2019, by conservative estimates), but also exvangelical content began to blow up on the platform.[8]

Though I prefer text-based mediums and have never posted much on Instagram, accounts like Phil Drysdale, Science.Jesus .Memes, TalkPurityToMe, DirtyRottenChurchKids, YourFavoriteHeretics, DeconstructPod, GodIsGrey, and many more built followings in the tens of thousands. Counselors and therapists including the Religious Trauma Institute, Reclamation Collective, and Dr. Laura Anderson began using the service to discuss religious trauma, adverse religious experiences, and embodiment and other therapeutic practices. Still others, like my friend Kevin Garcia, use Instagram to discuss alternative spiritual communities for those who have left evangelicalism but now explore other practices.

A similar TikTok explosion wasn't far behind. TikTok also allows big blocks of hashtags that encourage bleed-over between related terms like, say, #Exvangelical and #Deconstruction. The platform's gigantic user base (more than one billion as of 2021), coupled with the algorithmic recommendations of its famous For You Page, meant that virality became achievable for a broader number of people than ever before. Seemingly any video had the potential to post big numbers. By August 2022, #Exvangelical had reached 985 million impressions. By December 2023, that had nearly doubled, to 1.7 billion impressions.

As on Instagram, TikTok creators like Melissa Stewart, April Ajoy, and Donnell McLachlan, along with musicians like Maddie Zahm and Semler, began to amass huge followings using hashtags like #Exvangelical and #Deconstruction. Of particular note is Abraham Piper, who gained more than one million followers in the space of a year or so with his engaging videos challenging evangelical theology and practice. (If his last name seems familiar to you, either you were raised evangelical or you've been paying close attention to this book; Piper's father is prominent evangelical author and pastor John Piper, who co-authored the complementarian Danvers Statement and founded the website Desiring God.)

Again, I prefer text-based mediums and haven't posted much on TikTok, so the success of the hashtag #Exvangelical there has very little to do with me personally. Most of the people using the hashtag, there or elsewhere, have no idea who coined it. I came up with a catchy word, but the idea behind it is much bigger than I am and resonates with many more people than my personal story ever could.

That's the power of a networked public. If you can capture an experience or idea in a short phrase and take advantage of the hashtag function built into social media platforms, your message can find purchase with people around the globe in a very short span of time. Evangelicals have always mastered every new wave of media technology, from the printing press onward, to spread their message of white capitalist theology, but that weaponized media savvy can cut both ways. Now people with evangelical media chops who are currently deconstructing can use new media technology to connect, discuss, question, learn. Instead of being isolated within the Christian bubble and saturated with toxic theology, we can use social media to discover just how many of us there are, to expose the abuses that have happened in our churches, and to realize better ways of life are possible. Whenever a person is ready to leave evangelicalism, there is now a vast counterpublic offering diverse perspectives for them to discover, from books to music to podcasts to documentaries, all illustrating the possibilities that exist beyond evangelicalism.

This community-finding aspect of online deconstruction is crucial, because community in and of itself is a significant part of the lived experience of evangelicalism—in ways both good and bad. Just as the borders of evangelical orthodoxy are guarded by its leaders and internally policed by its adherents, the in-group/out-group aspect of evangelicalism is a key part of maintaining group identity. Evangelicalism is often described as a "high-demand" or "high-control" religion. It can even come to resemble a "total institution," a term popularized by the sociologist Erving Goffman (and introduced to me by sociologist Bethany Gull) that indicates "a closed social system in which life is organized by strict norms, rules, and schedules, and what happens within it is determined by a single authority whose will is carried out by staff who enforce the rules."[9] The downsides of this kind of system are obvious, but when you're inside it, there are upsides too. The feeling of acceptance within an evangelical church can be incredible—whether it's through a shared meal at a pitch-in dinner in a church basement, the early morning camaraderie of a men's Bible study, the mountaintop experience of a church retreat, or the emotional bonding of a short-term mission trip, there's a sense of welcome and belonging that is hard to deny. This makes it all the more painful when you express doubt or deviate from the accepted norms and find yourself under suspicion from people you love. That sense of community—and one's place within it—is part of what is lost and grieved when one leaves one's church home.

Of course, we often leave those church homes because we realize they were never really homes at all, even if we have some positive feelings associated with them. Women, people of color, queer people, and trans and gender-nonconforming people are all marginalized and disempowered within white evangelicalism. If all or part of your self extends to one of these other identities and communities, your allegiance to and place in your evangelical community is questioned. This drives you to find acceptance elsewhere, including/especially online, which is the easiest place to find community when your offline community is racist, sexist, homophobic, or simply raises you to believe that you and everyone else alive deserve to go to hell.

For my part, I founded the Exvangelical Facebook group in 2017 as a Patreon perk for supporters of my podcast. However, as calls for a more private community continued to grow on Twitter, I opened it up to anyone. It ballooned from seventy members to seven hundred, then to three thousand, over the course of two years. By the end of 2023, it had grown to more than twelve thousand members.

Exvangelical was not the first group of its kind on the platform. For example, the group Raising Children UnFundamentalist was founded by Cindy Wang Brandt in 2015, while groups specific to particular denominations or communities cropped up to meet particular needs. Facebook groups have been a mainstay of deconstruction content because of their reach as well as their moderation tools. The Exvangelical group and its subgroups have clear moderation policies enforced by a team of volunteer moderators. The focus is to decenter the straight white male perspectives that are privileged in evangelicalism and be sensitive to content that might activate group members' trauma. This is not the focus of every group, and not every person agrees with our methodology or decisions, but we do our best to enforce them consistently. Thankfully, for us and for them, there is now an abundance of options for ex- and post-evangelical people; for example, the subreddit r/Exvangelical, which is not affiliated with me or my podcast, had grown to 18,000 members by December 2023.[10]

What changes for people joining these exvangelical online communities is the shift from total institution to "participatory culture," defined by scholar Henry Jenkins as a culture that "embraces the values of diversity and democracy through every aspect of our interactions with each other—one which assumes that we are capable of making decisions, collectively and individually, and that we should have the capacity to express ourselves through a broad range of different forms and practices."[11] That doesn't mean these online communities are always utopias of harmony and reason, but it does mean that, unlike in evangelicalism, exvangelicals can choose where, when, how, and if they participate. They can use their real name or stay anonymous. They can go wide on public platforms or stay in smaller private forums. And, crucially, if they feel the need to move on, either as their own personal growth continues or just because the conversations no longer interest them, they can *stop participating*. People will get into ideological arguments or petty squabbles in any environment, but in a participatory culture, the bounds of orthodoxy are not rigorously policed in every aspect of life. Exvangelicals don't have to live in a bubble anymore.

13

HASHTAG ACTIVISM

THE PROS AND CONS OF ONLINE MOVEMENTS

The critiques I and other exvangelicals have been exploring are not new in and of themselves. Even the very abridged history I've given in the first half of this book shows that there has always been resistance to the whiteness, capitalism, and patriarchy of American evangelicalism. But, like any movement, this one is unique to its time and place, and the most unique thing about it is that it has largely taken place online.

How much does it matter that the exvangelical movement is, to a large extent, digital? It's an old saw that technology is not inherently positive or negative; its value depends on how we use it. Indeed, much of this book explores just how true that is. Technology, particularly media technology, has been an indispensable part of creating and cultivating the evangelical worldview—and of fighting back against it. This extends to digital media and the cultures that it creates. After all, as danah boyd said when defining networked publics, "As social network sites and other genres of social media become increasingly widespread, the distinctions between networked publics and publics will become increasingly blurry. Thus, the dynamics mapped out here will not simply be constrained to the domain of the digital world, but will be part of everyday life."[1]

It can be tempting to subscribe to what internet theorist Nathan Jurgenson calls a "digital dualism" and believe that so-called real life is what happens offline.[2] From this flawed perspective, the things people say online don't matter because it's "just the internet." Activism isn't really activism, bullying isn't really bullying, and so forth—as soon as you log off, the words disappear, having no lasting effect "in real life." The truth is, as Jurgenson puts it in his book *The Social Photo*, "digitality is not inherently unreal."[3] A friendship or an argument may be conducted differently online than offline, but its fundamental elements of connection or conflict remain the same; it is still a real friendship or a real argument.

In essence, the internet has become a new "third place," an idea first explored by the sociologist Ray Oldenburg to describe gathering places other than home (the "first place") and work (the "second place")—for example, pubs, churches, and libraries are third places.[4] If you have ever joined a subreddit, been part of a Tumblr fandom, played fantasy sports, played an MMORPG, or found a hashtag you related to—like #Exvangelical—you have found an online third place. It's a place where you can work out a part of your identity in a way you can't do in person or just goof off with people who understand the same jokes about niche experiences.

This is especially important for people leaving the church,

who lose that important offline third place—and often most of their offline social network along with it. In *Because Internet*, Gretchen McCulloch writes that "the lure of cyberspace [is] . . . the promise that somewhere out in the world, you could find other people who matched your unique weirdnesses, or at least understood your niche passions. But to send someone a message, you need to find them first, and for that, you need some sort of shared space that several people can drop in on."[5] In the case of exvangelicals, the "unique weirdnesses" are deconstruction, and the spaces they can drop in on are hashtag discussions, private Facebook groups, subreddits, and so on.*

According to researcher Mario Luis Small, the loose, distributed, mediated nature of online third places is particularly important for people in search of confidants. He writes that "rather than consistently turning to their spouses, friends, or family, people will often studiously avoid their inner circle for many of the issues they most care about, precisely because the expectations involving many of these relationships make them too close for comfort."[6] Instead, people regularly "confide deeply personal matters to individuals they are not close to, even to those they barely know."[7] Again, this is relevant to everyone, but especially to people questioning or abandoning their faith. Confiding secret doubts or disagreement with orthodoxy to other church members risks significant social consequences, whether that's as simple as being accused of sin or as severe as being disowned, divorced, or disfellowshipped.** The internet gives

---

* In fact, the first episode of *Exvangelical* I recorded with Chrissy Stroop was titled "Weird Everywhere," based on a comment she made in our conversation about how exvangelicals are cultural misfits because they don't know how to belong in either evangelicalism or the broader "secular" culture.

** "Disfellowshipped" is a term more commonly affiliated with Jehovah's Witnesses (whom most evangelicals do not consider Christian) but may be used by other

people a place to explore deconstruction with other people going through the same process.

Social media can take the place of church in ways beyond social connection as well. In his book *IRL*, Chris Stedman, a writer and religion researcher (and former humanist chaplain), writes:

> Has social media become our new church—the place we
> turn to in search of answers about where we fit in and
> what makes us who we are? It can certainly feel like it. As
> author Briallen Hopper says in a conversation with the
> Revealer, there are countless ways for "forms of media to
> become religion: ecstatic consumption, collective textual
> study, cultural edicts about what is or is not permissible
> to consume, the instinctive clutch of your phone in your
> pocket as if it were a handful of beads."[8]

All of this is to say that online phenomena are no less real for being online. The exploration of identity and spirituality as well as the formation of community in online spaces is inherently valid. Social media and hashtags like #Exvangelical have enabled thousands of people to discover they're not alone and deprogram from toxic religion.

Nevertheless, I don't want to paint exvangelicals as uncomplicated do-gooder heroes fighting against the fundamentalist bad guys. Online third places are no more inherently utopian than offline ones. If the anonymity and loose connection of the internet make it easier to find kindred spirits, they also make it

---

denominations or churches to describe people who are forced out of church life due to "sin." The effect is severe and intentionally isolating.

easier to dehumanize and be cruel to others.* It's much harder to insult someone to their face when you can visually see their reaction—not to mention that in a face-to-face interaction you can't call up an army of your followers to join in on the bullying at a moment's notice.

There are other significant shortcomings to networking that occurs primarily online. All those attributes of networked publics that make hashtags so powerful—persistence, replicability, scalability, and shareability—can also exacerbate conflict and drama. People may respond hastily in ways they later regret, but their words can be archived forever, go viral, or be duplicated and shared privately or publicly. The asynchronous nature of today's internet also means that the speed of online discourse can be simultaneously too fast and too slow, as people respond to things they're reading out of chronological order and out of context. Due to that same context collapse, even when we're engaging in the same digital spaces, we're not always engaging in the *exact same* digital spaces; we can bring different experiences, reasoning, and assumptions to the same events and not even realize it. Ultimately, the very architecture of social media means that when we disagree with one another, there's very little to do other than create more online content to disagree about—and the companies that host these interactions are not terribly interested in the much less lucrative process of fostering healthy personal growth or encouraging complex social needs like reconciliation.

Exvangelicals talk a lot about trauma, because we're discovering—through our own experience, through therapy,

---

* Just as books about the internet's effects on our attention spans have become their own genre, so have books about online shaming—including books like Jon Ronson's *So You've Been Publicly Shamed* and Cathy O'Neil's *The Shame Machine*.

through the content of other exvangelicals—that we've experienced a lot of it. We also traumatize one another, kicking up drama online for a variety of reasons, not least of which is that we learned most of our coping mechanisms and conflict-resolution skills in the deeply unhealthy environment of the church. It turns out that people are human wherever they go. The language of "therapy speak" has coursed its way through popular culture throughout the 2010s, yet despite the accompanying understanding of trauma, we still often downplay the effect of trauma that happens online. At one point, I too felt these types of conflicts were less important because they were disembodied—but that's incorrect. The fact that they play out through mediated apps does not make them less stressful; in some ways, it actually increases the stress, because we can't see or respond to the person we're in conflict with *as a person*, which dehumanizes both parties.

And even if you're not physically in the same space as the other person, trauma has a profound physical effect within your body. Have you ever been in a fight on the internet? You read something that activates you. The stress and anxiety start in your chest, around your heart. You inhale a sharp breath, and the anxiety spreads up and back, through your chest to your shoulders. You lean forward and start typing—maybe something vicious. Maybe you backspace and write something more neutral, maybe you don't. Hitting reply. Waiting for the other person's response. And when it's worse than you predicted, the cycle begins again until your entire nervous system is burned out. Traumas and conflicts experienced in online spaces are real, emotionally and physically.

I wish I could say that exvangelical spaces are safe havens where everyone gets along perfectly, but the reality is that they can be as problematic as any other space inhabited by humans. It's not something that makes me happy, but it's something that I want to face with honesty. I don't like that the word "exvangelical" has become nearly as pejorative as the word "evangelical" for some people. I don't like that people seeking to heal from the racism, sexism, and queerphobia of evangelicalism can end up encountering those same problems in exvangelical spaces. Online interactions are just as real as offline ones, even if screens and servers and thousands of miles stand between us, because they're all conducted between humans, with all the positives and negatives that entails.

Exvangelicals are trying to do something good and necessary, and not always succeeding. But if deconstruction teaches exvangelicals anything at all, it should teach us humility—that there is so much we do not know, so much yet to learn, and so much more to the world and to one another than the simple teachings of fundamentalism would have us believe. This learning process is not always smooth, and sometimes people hurt and get hurt along the way. To deny that reality is to have learned nothing. It all matters, the good and the bad.

ONE FUNCTION OF DIGITAL THIRD places is social relationships, as we've seen. Another is social action. Gretchen McCulloch writes:

> Oldenburg also points out how third places have been essential to forming the kinds of large, loose-knit social groups that are the core of new social movements, such as the agora in ancient Greek democracy, taverns around the American Revolution, and coffeeshops during the

Age of Enlightenment, which parallels how Twitter was used for the Arab Spring or the Black Lives Matter protests. You can't fit enough dissenters in your living room to make a revolution out of close ties alone: you need the larger, looser network of a third place.[9]

The exvangelical movement has a social cause: to oppose and counteract the bigotry and harmful theology of the white evangelical church. And much in the same way digitality affects exvangelical discourse for better and for worse, it affects the exvangelical cause for better and for worse as well. On the level of the individual, being online gives the exvangelical movement incredible power and reach, for all the reasons I've explored so far. With the simple act of clicking on a hashtag, anyone anywhere can open up a whole new world for themselves. It has never been easier for people to learn all the ways in which conservative Christianity serves whiteness and capitalism or to understand why the way they were raised may have constituted spiritual abuse.

But in terms of accomplishing sociopolitical goals, there are also drawbacks to conducting a movement that primarily exists online. First of all, the elements of networked publics that make righteous movements powerful and effective do the same thing for competing movements by bad actors. Over the past ten years, we've seen the rise of #BlackLivesMatter and #MeToo, but we've also seen the orchestrated misinformation campaigns of the Russian state that contributed to Donald Trump's election. We've learned about the Cambridge Analytica scandal, in which social media users' data was used without their knowledge to create psychographic profiles in order to serve hyperspecific political ads that contributed to Trump's election. We've witnessed an online antivax movement that has led to untold numbers of unnecessary deaths from COVID-19. We've seen the rise of QAnon, and a coup attempt orchestrated on social media platforms such as Facebook and Parler.

For the average internet user, it's not always easy to distinguish between truth and fiction when encountering the content created by these movements. I think of the innocuous videos uploaded to Cameo by celebrities like actor Elijah Wood and boxer Mike Tyson that were deceptively edited and used in a Russian disinformation campaign to smear Ukrainian leader Volodymyr Zelensky as a drug addict—when content can be that decontextualized and purposely twisted away from its original intent, how is anyone supposed to keep track of what's what?[10] We are all pulled from one moment to the next, our personal crises unfolding in tandem with an information overload about various global crises. There are valid concerns about the rapid-fire pace at which we learn information and the collapsed context in which we learn it online. Whether it's a global news item or just a beef between two people you vaguely know on Twitter, you have to become a digital forensics expert. What was the inciting incident? Who did and said what? Is this indicative of other issues? It spirals from there, and soon enough, there's a conversation *about* the conversation and whether the conversation should be happening at all. The window of time in which all this takes place can be perilously small, and at every step of the way, there are a million other things vying for your attention. It's all so much all the time. It can be overwhelmingly daunting.

Lamentations about the demise of our attention spans in the digital age are their own literary genre. In his book *The Shallows,* journalist Nicholas Carr writes, "Whether I'm online or not, my mind now expects to take in information the way the Net distributes it: in a swiftly moving stream of particles. Once I was a scuba diver in the sea of words. Now I zip along the surface like a guy on a Jet Ski."[11] And that book came out in 2010—the problem has only deepened since then. This is partially an inherent function of digital social networks, but our distractible minds are increasingly directed by a force that's more subtle and insidious: social media platforms' need to drive engagement in order to keep advertising dollars rolling in.

The algorithms that platforms use to deliver content are opaque to us, the users. Yet what the consumer perceives as a simple and perhaps random process—thumbing away at a smartphone screen, scrolling the infinite feeds—is tailored specifically to elicit continued engagement. Facebook has even demonstrated that it has the capacity to intentionally affect the mood of its users. In 2014, it was revealed that two years prior they had "manipulated the news feeds of over half a million randomly selected users to change the number of positive and negative posts they saw. It was part of a psychological study to examine how emotions can be spread on social media."[12]

What is it that these algorithms serve us? Are they promoting thoughtfully considered, balanced, true arguments about current events? The answer, broadly speaking, is no. The evidence shows that they're much more likely to promote radicalizing right-wing content. Studies indicate that YouTube's autoplay features routinely suggest more radical content in order to maintain engagement; the *efficacy* of this content is up for debate, but the algorithm's preference for suggesting it is not.[13] On Facebook, the research group Cybersecurity for Democracy reported in March 2021, just two months after the January 6 insurrection, that "far-right accounts known for spreading misinformation are not only thriving on Facebook, they're actually more successful than other kinds of accounts at getting likes, shares and other forms of user engagement."[14] That same month, it was also shown that there were more than two hundred militia groups using the product to organize, and that Facebook was amplifying their reach by automatically creating pages for them—something it had previously done for ISIS in 2019.[15]

That doesn't mean that the people in charge of social media platforms are all trying to inculcate the world with right-wing propaganda (although in the case of Elon Musk, I think that's probably not far from the truth). But it does mean that those people are not incentivized to stop spreading right-wing propaganda to users, because the platforms profit off it. Sure, they employ some moderators, but even a robust moderation team can only do so much to stem the tide, and throughout 2023, all the major tech platforms actually cut back on moderation efforts through both layoffs and curtailed services.[16] On top of that, the tools the companies use to reap this profit—content-serving algorithms, data profiles, and so on—have been intentionally weaponized by malevolent state actors outside the United States, private companies within the United States, and Christian nationalist activists working in conjunction with GOP presidential campaigns. It is very, very difficult to fight against money and power on that scale regardless of the medium.

Back in 1967, foundational media theorist Marshall McLuhan wrote, "In an electric information environment, minority groups can no longer be contained—ignored. Too many people know too much about each other. Our new environment compels commitment and participation. We have become irrevocably involved with, and responsible for, each other."[17] He was talking about television, and he was right, but clearly racism and other forms of bigotry persisted past 1967. Simply *knowing more* about each other was no guarantee that we would demonstrate *more care* for each other. The increased awareness brought about by encountering minority groups on TV wasn't enough to solve all the pernicious problems that remain with us. McLuhan's quote is equally true about social media today, but the same limits apply, and for the same reasons. Movements like #Black-LivesMatter and #MeToo have had tangible effects on our culture, but systemic racism and misogyny remain in place, because they are just that: systemic, and backed by vast amounts of money and power.

If we think back to the successes and failures of past progressive reform movements within evangelicalism, we see much the same pattern. Urbana 70 activists, Evangelicals for Social Action, Christians for Biblical Equality, and others all eventually ran up against the hard fact that evangelicalism was an increasingly rich and politically powerful institution with expanding media mastery and cultural influence. We have seen that, although their efforts were valiant, their impact was limited. The exvangelical movement is not a reform movement per se (the "ex" is right there in the name), but it exists within that lineage. So it makes sense to ask: What effect has it had on the evangelical church? That's what we'll delve into in the next chapter.

14

STAND BY TRUMP

THE CHURCH'S RESPONSE TO EXVANGELICALS

The exvangelical movement, the deconstruction movement—whatever you want to call it—caught on at a time when evangelical moral authority was at its nadir but evangelical political power was at its zenith. What impact has it had on evangelicalism? How has the church reacted? Has it prompted anger, introspection, defensiveness? Where does the church currently stand on the criticisms the exvangelical movement has leveled at it and on the exvangelical movement itself? And has the exvangelical movement—or anything, really—moved evangelicals to reevaluate their loyalty to Trump?

For a while, the evangelical church could ignore the supposed "threat" of deconstruction, but by 2021, elite evangelicals started responding directly—the counterpublic had begun to elicit a response from the public. In April of that year, The Gospel Coalition published a book of antideconstruction essays called *Before You Lose Your Faith: Deconstructing Doubt in the Church,** featuring essays from Trevin Wax, Rachel Gilson, and Karen Swallow Prior, among others. In June, megachurch pastor David Jeremiah preached a sermon on the subject with the word "exvangelical" displayed in massive letters behind him. In it, he called exvangelical TikTokkers "a sign of the end times" and advanced a criticism that predates any hashtag: that those who leave the church were clearly never true believers to begin with.[1] This idea is not only dismissive, it's just plain wrong. As I wrote for *Religion Dispatches* at the time:

> Throughout his sermon, David Jeremiah utilizes scripture passages from 1 John and elsewhere to paint exvangelicals like me as apostates and false teachers. In doing so, he says the recent visible rise of exvangelical content online is a sign of the end times. He claims we were never believers. This is categorically false. He doesn't know who I am, but I know him: I sold his books when I worked at Lemstone Books, the Christian bookstore in my town. He quotes John Walvoord's definition of apostasy; I read Walvoord's book *Every Prophecy of the Bible* with great zeal. I attended college with the goal of becoming a pastor, and read 1 John in Greek. His facile use of scripture to delegitimize my

---

*   Note the subtlety in the wording of both the title and the subtitle. *Before You Lose Your Faith* implies that all those who question evangelicalism also lose their faith entirely instead of moving toward a new form of faith. *Deconstructing Doubt in the Church* orients doubt toward the church itself instead of a person's individual faith—and the church is often presented by apologists as a "fallible, human institution" in juxtaposition with God.

experience and that of untold others is insulting and dehumanizing.

Megachurch pastor Matt Chandler took a similar tack, saying in a sermon, "I contend that if you ever experience the grace and mercy of Jesus Christ, actually—that that's really impossible to deconstruct from."[2] He also added another common and equally insulting theory: that people leave the church merely because it's trendy. "You and I are in a day and age where deconstruction and the turning away from and leaving the faith has become some sort of sexy thing to do," he said.[3]

Meanwhile, Joshua Ryan Butler, who contributed to *Before You Lose Your Faith*, wrote a blog post for The Gospel Coalition titled "4 Causes of Deconstruction," which presented four more ridiculous but sadly common explanations for why people deconstruct: "church hurt," "poor teaching," "desire to sin," and "street cred."[4] Of these, only "church hurt" has any merit. People do often begin a journey away from the church after being abused or otherwise mistreated. But the problem is not that a few unlucky parishioners sometimes encounter the rare "bad apple" of a church*—it's that abuse and mistreatment are built into evangelical theology and endemic to the institution. They cannot be solved by, as Butler suggests, grieving and moving on. The rest of Butler's points get increasingly ludicrous. "Poor teaching" is a euphemism for teaching he disagrees with, and

---

* Versions of the phrase "One bad apple spoils the barrel" were commonly used in sermons throughout the 19th century to indicate that bad behavior quickly spreads beyond one individual. In the 20th century, when we started purchasing individual apples, it shifted to mean the exact opposite, and has since been used to deflect critiques of systemic issues (like police violence) onto individuals. There's a sermon there about how capitalism and institutional bias have shifted our perspectives, that's for sure. (Cunningham, "A Few Bad Apples.")

needless to say, no one is questioning their belief system and uprooting their entire life just because they think sinning is fun or "doubt is hip."[5] Arguments like these refuse to engage with deconstruction in an honest or serious way. The fact of their existence seems to indicate that deconstruction is too big a phenomenon for evangelicals to ignore, but they insist on ignoring everything people in the movement say.

Yet, as much as Butler has tried to dismiss the deconstruction movement, it has had an impact on him. Not too long after that blog post, Butler would publish an excerpt from his forthcoming book about "God's vision for sex" that "offered repeated descriptions of sexual intercourse in spiritual terms, most of them characterizing sex as a man bestowing a holy gift to a woman and comparing that to the relationship of Jesus and the church."[6] "The excerpt led to public outcry," with critics like Beth Felker Jones charging that the passage "does not dig into Ephesians" as it claims to but rather "turns it into a rhapsody over a very male-centered experience of sexual intercourse."[7] The passage itself was so controversial, and the theological backlash emanating from both the exvangelical counterpublic and the evangelical public so thorough, that TGC was forced to make an apology, and Butler was removed from his leadership role at its Keller Center for Cultural Apologetics.[8] He soon resigned his role as a pastor as well.[9]

Perhaps the deconstruction movement can't take 100 percent of the credit for that—evangelicals can be squeamish about any discussion of sex, whether they agree with it theologically or not—but I think we can see the fingerprints of hashtags like #ChurchToo and #Exvangelical here, along with those of earlier Christian feminist movements. Even those still within the evangelical fold who continue to engage with evangelical audiences are more emboldened to speak their convictions out loud. As a result, leaders can now sometimes experience negative repercussions for being too obvious about their misogyny in certain ways. That may not be a huge victory, but it's something.

AS SOMETHING AKIN TO THE evangelical paper of record, *Christianity Today* has published multiple pieces that engage deconstruction—or at least they claim to. On the surface, these *CT* pieces appear more cerebral and serious. They acknowledge some of the church's flaws. They use big words, employing theological language more commonly heard in seminaries than in Sunday schools. But when you take a closer look, they do the same thing as the blog posts and sermons mentioned earlier: they pretend to defeat exvangelical arguments with well-reasoned theology while in actuality refusing to listen to what exvangelicals are really saying.

In an October 2021 piece titled "The Church Needs Reformation, Not Deconstruction: A Short Guide to the Exvangelical Movement," Tish Harrison Warren offers advice to people considering deconstructing their faith. Her first suggestion is to "distinguish between deconstruction and reform"—essentially, to be the change you want to see in the church rather than leaving it.[10] Unfortunately, as documented in prior chapters of this book (and as so many exvangelicals know from personal experience), the evangelical movement writ large does not desire meaningful reform. It has routinely rejected reform efforts. Warren also advises potential deconstructors, specifically "white Christians," to "avoid inadvertently centering white, Western voices" and "listen more to evangelical people of color" who have stayed in the church.[11] The idea of reversing this and asking Christians to listen to evangelical people of color who have left the church does not seem to be relevant to her, and she's a million miles away from confronting the idea that, on an institutional level, the American evangelical church prizes whiteness above nearly all else.

Like so many critics of deconstruction, Warren is happy to admit that the church is flawed—or, in her words, "a sinful institution"—but she doesn't care to hear what the flaws actually are.[12] This makes it all the more infuriating when she says that "many of those who most vocally deconstruct Christianity jettison a thin version of American fundamentalism and mistake it for the whole tradition" and that they need to "assess the actual faith, not a truncated version of it."[13] If you don't listen to what exvangelicals are saying, it's easy to declare they just don't know what they're talking about and that joining a different Christian tradition would solve their problems. If Warren herself "assessed the actual deconstruction movement and not a truncated version of it," she might have to acknowledge that those who leave evangelical faith do so with both knowledge and experience. Some exvangelicals do join other versions of Christianity after deconstructing. Others feel those versions have their own disqualifying flaws, often extremely similar to the flaws of evangelicalism. Still others identify as Christians without joining a particular tradition—and are often told they're not "true Christians" because of it. (Remember how Rob Bell was branded a heretic for embracing universalism?) None of these people seem to exist in Warren's conception of deconstruction.

In a 2022 *Christianity Today* cover story called (eye-rollingly) "Wait, You're Not Deconstructing?," Kirsten Sanders approaches the topic from a slightly different angle, taking it upon herself to dictate to exvangelicals what deconstruction *should* be: "Deconstruction should be the task of articulating this difference between what we can know and where we must simply trust. . . . The process should dismantle certainty where it is not proper. But that does not mean faith will be dismantled."[14] Like Warren's, her argument centers on ignoring the reality of deconstruction. She does not quote any of the exvangelical podcasters, authors, or other content creators she says are ubiquitous on her Instagram feed, though I am sure many would have happily participated. Instead, she imagines a fantasy version of deconstruction in which people are allowed to ask questions about Christianity just as long as they arrive at the answers the church has predetermined are best for them.

It may be a little unfair of me to single out *Christianity Today*. The thing I'm taking issue with, which is far from unique to *CT*, is this paternalistic notion that exvangelicals just don't understand Christianity well enough or we'd obviously come to the "correct" conclusions. This purports to be the sophisticated, informed response to exvangelicals, appearing in high-minded publications, but in truth, it's just as flippant as saying deconstruction is the "sexy thing to do." I'm sure this line of argument is partially motivated by genuine (though condescending) concern for the souls of exvangelicals, but I'd also guess that the people making this argument struggle to honestly grapple with the idea that the belief system they've dedicated their lives to might be found wanting, morally bankrupt, or just not true. I don't exactly blame them—as exvangelicals know all too well, that realization can be extremely difficult. But we didn't come to it casually, and we can't be dismissed casually either.

THERE IS ONE *CHRISTIANITY TODAY* piece I want to highlight that doesn't follow the aforementioned pattern: a 2021 essay by Russell Moore called "My Dad Taught Me How to Love the Exvangelical." Moore's grandfather was a pastor, which means his father grew up a PK (the Christianese abbreviation for "pastor's kid") who saw the darker sides of church life, as most PKs do. Moore's father was not "against the church or religion" but had "spotty church attendance" and discouraged Moore from going into ministry because, he said, "I just don't want to see you get hurt the way they hurt my dad."[15] Moore writes that, in retrospect, he realized that "I judged my father too much for what I saw as a deficient spirituality—because I didn't know what it was like to experience what he had."[16]

This realization taught him to listen to what exvangelicals were actually saying rather than dismissing them out of hand, and although he doesn't go so far as to say that leaving the church might be the right choice, he acknowledges exvangelicals' criticisms as legitimate. When he spoke to them, he found that "they had been hurt. They saw the church turn against them because they wouldn't adopt as Scripture some political ideology or personality cult. Some had seen people they trusted revealed to be frauds or even predators. Not one of them walked away because they wanted to curry favor with 'elites' or because they wanted to rebel."[17]

I credit Moore for being compassionate rather than dismissive. Unfortunately, by 2021 he had already lost most of his credibility among conservative evangelicals. For people familiar with the evangelical world, this was an unexpected development. As a Southern Baptist pastor and a dean at the Southern

Baptist Theological Seminary, Moore wasn't exactly known for being progressive. He served as a chairman on the complementarian Council on Biblical Manhood and Womanhood, and he opposes abortion and homosexuality. He subscribes to the usual evangelical doctrines like biblical inerrancy. He had even broken out as a darling of the conservative mainstream media, earning profiles in *The Wall Street Journal*, where, during the Obama administration, he called on evangelicals to move from "moral majority to prophetic minority."[18]

In 2016, though, Moore emerged as a Never Trumper. He was no liberal, but he wrote (in the archconservative *National Review*, no less) that "Trump's vitriolic—and often racist and sexist—language about immigrants, women, the disabled, and others ought to concern anyone who believes that all persons, not just the 'winners' of the moment, are created in God's image."[19] Regardless of whether white evangelicals supported Trump vocally or through clenched teeth, to resist Trumpism within evangelicalism remains an uphill battle. As a letter later leaked to the Religion News Service revealed, that wasn't Moore's only uphill battle. He was also fighting the way the SBC was handling accusations of sexual abuse and calls for racial reconciliation within the church.[20] For Moore, these fights culminated in his 2021 resignation not just from his positions within the SBC but also from the denomination entirely.[21] Even a man with his qualifications could not survive in a space that sheltered abusers but would not brook any discussion of social justice.

After his resignation, Moore decamped for a "pastor in residence" position at a nondenominational evangelical church in Nashville and became editor in chief of *Christianity Today*. As when I wrote about Rob Bell in an earlier chapter, my point here is not to drum up sympathy for Moore personally. He still holds well-compensated positions of power and authority, if somewhat less powerful and authoritative than his previous ones. My point is that, since 2016, the white evangelical church has had the chance to reconsider its theopolitical alliance with Trump and change its course. It had a whole counterpublic calling for reform and repentance, if not reconciliation and redemption. It had leaders like Russell Moore and Beth Moore (no relation) willing to stand up for what was right. Various problems and their solutions were being clearly articulated. And instead, in that time, it doubled down on supporting Trump and sticking to its theological guns. Even as evangelicals criticized exvangelicals for faulty theology, they increasingly boiled their own theology down to Trumpism and dominance.

And, really, why wouldn't that be the case? Trump gave evangelicals nearly unlimited power to enact their Christian nationalist agenda. At the 2019 Values Voter Summit, Family Research Council president Tony Perkins said to the crowd: "What makes the difference in this administration is that we're not on the outside looking in, we are on the inside working out."[22] Trump was savvy enough to reward evangelicals for their political support (or perhaps simply narcissistic enough to reward the people who fawned over him), and he installed people with conservative evangelical bona fides throughout the administration, including Jeff Sessions as attorney general, Sarah Huckabee Sanders as press secretary, Mike Pompeo as secretary of state, and Ben Carson as secretary of housing and urban development. Secretary of education was Amway heiress Betsy DeVos, whose family has been funding conservative evangelical initiatives for decades, championing voucher programs and "education reform" in what is essentially a modern twist on the Christian segregation academies of the past.[23]

Trump also made good on promises to appoint conservative justices to the Supreme Court, which ensured conservative victories at the highest level of the judiciary for the foreseeable future. This culminated most clearly in the overturning of *Roe v. Wade* in 2022, which has already had horrific effects nationwide, but it's felt in other decisions that preference evangelicals as well. The plaintiff in *303 Creative LLC v. Elenis*, for instance, sued for the right to deny wedding-related services to a same-sex couple. It turned out the couple who requested design work for a wedding website was completely fictional—the man who supposedly sent the inquiry not only *didn't* send the email but also was married to a woman—but the court's decision still made it legally permissible to discriminate against minority groups based on religious belief.[24]

Trump's effect on evangelicalism extends far beyond his campaign and administration. His incessant lying inoculated both the Republican Party and white evangelicals against the effects of political and social shame. His capacity for duplicity extends so far beyond any concept of hypocrisy that the word "hypocrite" doesn't even really apply; he has no morals to be hypocritical about, just ego and a desire to be worshipped that his followers (which include many evangelicals) are happy to fulfill. He made it acceptable to be unapologetically authoritarian, a trait evangelicalism needed no help cultivating.

In Trump, evangelicals found a resonant apocalypticism—a belief that members of their in-group embody all that is good, their enemies embody all that is evil, and they have to defeat their enemies by any means necessary to prevent society from falling into ruin. The real-world consequences of this type of thinking became apparent in the QAnon conspiracy theory that ravaged evangelical churches and other communities. Though not explicitly Christian, it echoed dispensational premillennial-ism eerily closely, with its fixation on secret signs and symbols that, if correctly interpreted, would reveal a higher plan to re-ward the faithful and punish the wicked. Similarly, as Trump mismanaged the COVID-19 response, some evangelical churches were emboldened to refuse compliance with orders to not wor-ship in person. In 2020, during the height of lockdown, worship pastor and failed congressional candidate Sean Feucht hosted super-spreader events.

This attitude soon curdled into full-on antivax conspiracy theories—again, not exclusive to evangelicals but certainly com-mon among them. Even a few years earlier, that might have been shocking. What part of vaccinations and other public health measures during a pandemic go against Christian doctrine? A century earlier, in response to the Spanish flu outbreak, churches of many denominations readily complied with governmental re-quests to suspend regular services in the interest of public health.[25] But with Trump in power, the Christian bubble was more emboldened than ever to act in its self-interest without re-gard for anyone else's well-being. Especially during the peak of the pandemic, it was almost as if the rejection of reality became a tenet of the religion. Truth had become defined by what Trump and other in-group leaders said, not by the observable world.

Taking advantage of this dynamic, in the run-up to the 2020 presidential election, Trump began seeding the idea that if he lost, it meant the election results were fraudulent. And, indeed, when he was soundly defeated, he refused to concede, made baseless claims that the election had been stolen, and embarked on an elaborate campaign to overturn it. The story of how Trump publicly and privately pressured government officials to commit crimes and negate official vote counts is an important one. But for the purposes of this book, the more interesting event is the failed insurrection of January 6, 2021. On that date, egged on by Trump's tweets and spearheaded by white nationalist groups like the Proud Boys, thousands of pro-Trump rioters violently stormed the Capitol in an attempt to prevent Congress from counting the votes from the Electoral College and formally declaring Joe Biden president. The mob failed at achieving that goal but succeeded in interrupting the proceedings and vandalizing and looting the Capitol building while members of Congress fled to safety. Four people died, and countless more were injured.

Christian nationalist iconography and rhetoric were on full display during the attack. Rioters waved the Christian flag and homemade crosses alongside Trump flags and Confederate flags. Flags, banners, signs, and clothing bore messages like JESUS IS MY SAVIOR, TRUMP IS MY PRESIDENT; MAKE AMERICA GODLY AGAIN; GOD, GUNS, TRUMP; and GOD CHOSE TRUMP TO SAVE USA.[26] Images of the Virgin Mary and Jesus—sometimes wearing a red MAGA hat—were common, as were Bibles and signs with various Bible verses.[27] Even the faux-pagan imagery used by Jacob Chansley, the so-called QAnon Shaman, did not preclude Christian nationalism; once the mob had taken control of the Senate chamber, Chansley led a Christian prayer from the dais that concluded thusly: "Thank you for allowing the United States of America to be reborn. Thank you for allowing us to get rid of the communists, the globalists, and the traitors within our government. We love you and we thank you. In Christ's holy name we pray! Amen."[28] And this list is only scratching the surface.*

---

* For a more detailed account, see *Christian Nationalism and the January 6, 2021 Insurrection*, a report by the Baptist Joint Committee for Religious Liberty and the Freedom from Religion Foundation.

While Christian leaders of all stripes were quick to condemn the violence of that day (at least the ones who didn't directly participate in it), the groundwork had already begun to be laid to turn the event into a myth. Religious studies professor Bradley Onishi wrote in *The New York Times* that the events of January 6 function as a starting point for a new civil religion akin to the Lost Cause framework that arose in the South following the Confederacy's defeat in the Civil War.[29] The Lost Cause rewrote history to say the Civil War was not about slavery but about so-called Northern aggression against a noble Southern way of life. It supplied its followers with "rituals and symbols . . . of Confederate civil religion" such as "the funerals of Confederate soldiers, the celebration of Confederate Memorial Day, the pilgrimages made to the hundreds of Confederate monuments."[30] Likewise, MAGAism has its own rituals and symbols—Trump rallies, Trump flags, Jon McNaughton's stylized Trump portraits—and the insurrection acts as "the myth and symbol of . . . Trump's lost cause."[31] It "creates the foundation for a collective memory based on a separate national identity held together by the tragic stealing of his presidency and the evil of his opponents."[32] And, like the Lost Cause, it is grafted onto Christianity by Christians who have fused religion and nationalism: "Its gospel is spread through houses of worship every Sunday. For some evangelicals . . . Trump is a divinely ordained savior uniquely able to save the nation from ruin."[33]

The problem is that Christianity is already based around a divinely ordained savior, and it's not supposed to be Donald Trump (though many memes circulating online portray Jesus and Trump in loving embraces that equate the two, with Jesus lending some of his heavenly authority to Trump here on earth).

Nor is Christianity supposed to be centered on whiteness, capitalism, or the Republican Party. Yet, collectively, evangelicals act in the public sphere and through their political choices as if those were the concerns closest to the heart of the evangelical church in America. While this phenomenon is by no means new, it has reached new extremes.

When I first pitched this book in the wake of Trump's loss, I was hopeful about the trajectory of the country. I no longer thought it was possible to change the evangelical church for the better, but I believed it could be defeated. In March 2021, I published a post called "The End of White Evangelical Hegemony" proclaiming that white evangelicalism had lost control of the narrative, especially with regard to religion and public life in the United States. I still think that's true—the conversations around religious belief are more diffuse and diverse than ever—but hegemony is not solely about narrative control. It is about other, more consequential forms of power. And in those arenas, radical evangelicals and Christian nationalists continue to secure victories and enact sophisticated plans to maintain their influence over American life. Recent Supreme Court decisions, the ascension of Mike Johnson to the position of Speaker of the House, and the growth of movements such as the New Apostolic Reformation all speak to the power they maintain. For now, white evangelical hegemony persists. But the fight is not over.

THE NEED FOR NEW METAPHORS

THE FUTURE OF THE EXVANGELICAL MOVEMENT

Think of white evangelicalism as a house built in the 1800s and rarely kept up beyond the most basic maintenance. When my wife and I were looking for apartments in Chicago, we saw many such buildings. The walls, doorjambs, and crown molding were absolutely caked in paint. Old telephone cable, not used for twenty years, lined the baseboards along the wall. Lighting and outlets were scarce. Evangelicalism is like that—painted over but not updated, then sold to residents as if it were not only suitable for contemporary life but, in fact, the only acceptable place to live.

Now imagine growing up in a home like this, one that has been in the family for generations, and only learning as an adult that, in addition to being outdated, it has always had multiple structural problems: the exterior walls are infested with termites, the paint in your nursery has lead in it, the electrical wiring is overtaxed, and the asbestos-lined walls must be abated. In order to keep living on your own property, you have to tear down so much of what you knew. The familiar things of childhood and adolescence that you have deep sentiment for must now be thrown away, replaced, or refurbished.

This isn't just a major logistical challenge; it's also deeply emotional. It involves going room to room, picking up and reminiscing about small objects, packing them up, saving what you can. There is deep and abiding grief there that must be processed. Yes, there are periods of glee and anger too, when you, say, smash a rotted wall with a sledgehammer—but by and large, this is melancholy work. In addition to your feelings about your own life, you also wonder how your ancestors, your parents and grandparents, lived in these conditions, not knowing that it was harming them too. It's only when you start to rebuild that you start to enjoy your dwelling place again—and you get to decide what remains.

Imagining faith as a building is nothing new; Jesus himself does it in the conclusion to the Sermon on the Mount in the book of Matthew. So perhaps deconstructing a house is not the most original metaphor for deconstructing one's religion. Nevertheless, it does the work that metaphors do in helping the human mind comprehend abstract concepts. To me, metaphors are not mere decorations; they are intrinsic to our existence. As George Lakoff and Mark Johnson write in *Metaphors We Live By,*

> Metaphor is pervasive in everyday life, not just in
> language but in thought and action. Our ordinary

conceptual system, in terms of which we both think and act, is fundamentally metaphorical in nature. The concepts that govern our thought . . . also govern our everyday functioning, down to the most mundane details. Our concepts structure what we perceive, how we get around in the world, and how we relate to other people. Our conceptual system thus plays a central role in defining our everyday realities.[1]

Just because something is abstract doesn't mean it can't have real meanings and consequences. Feelings, thoughts, sensations—all these things are physical reactions to chemical processes in our bodies, but they create an infinite interior space we call consciousness, manifesting as images (visual or otherwise) in our mind. They codify to become words, and words change the course of humanity by letting thought leap from mind to mind. In the creation myth of the Gospel of John, we are told it was *the Word* there in the beginning, that, in fact, "the Word was God" (John 1:1). In the Genesis narrative, God creates the world through *speaking*. Over the course of human history, spoken words became *script* and were first etched in stone and clay and vellum and papyrus before they became *print* and formed the basis of literate societies. Now words are shared on screens—spoken on television, read on social media, typed as text messages, heard on podcasts. When you consider the story of humanity, told through language and passed through time, the supposedly abstract comes home to rest in your throat, in your heart, in your lungs, in your hands. You are made up of metaphor in the same way you are made up of carbon.

I believe that for those of us who were shaped by evangelicalism—which is so many of us, including those who were not raised within it but have been subject to its influence on politics and culture—it is time to look for new metaphors. In our current environment, the primary constant is change, and the pace of change is accelerating. To hold fast to unchanging belief makes us brittle and hollows us out. As Sophie Strand writes in *The Flowering Wand*, "Myths that stay the same don't survive. Or worse, they make sure we won't survive by reinforcing extractive behavior no longer tailored to our ecosystems. They don't adapt to changing climate and shifting social conditions."[2]

One potential source for a new metaphor can be found in the philosopher Timothy Morton's notion of hyperobjects. (If you've made it this far in the book, you already know this is where I'm going to get academic for a bit.) In *Hyperobjects: Philosophy and Ecology After the End of the World*, Morton (who uses they/them pronouns) defines hyperobjects as "things that are massively distributed in time and space relative to humans"—that is, objects so big and so long-lasting that they exceed the boundaries of human perception and thus can be described as "hyper" relative to objects that exist on a more human scale.[3] A single plastic cup is just an object, but *plastic* is a hyperobject; there is an unfathomably large amount of it, and it will last an incomprehensibly long time. Technically, the quantity and lifespan of all existing plastic are both finite, but they are so massive that a human can't directly perceive or even really imagine them. To think about plastic, we have to approach it from many angles, some scientific, some philosophical, some artistic, some economic, and so on.

Morton's definition of hyperobjects is exceedingly flexible: "A hyperobject could be a black hole . . . or the Florida Everglades. A hyperobject could be the biosphere, or the Solar

System. A hyperobject could be the sum total of all the nuclear materials on Earth."[4] But overall, they're primarily concerned with using the framework of hyperobjects to describe the simultaneous immensity and elusiveness of climate change, a process so intricate and massive that it is rendered invisible and incomprehensible, even as it directly intrudes upon our lives.

I contend that evangelicalism is a hyperobject as well. As the previous chapters have shown, its past stretches back well beyond the lives of our parents and grandparents, and it will outlast our lifetimes. Its influence extends into capitalism, politics, governance, media, and our mental and social lives. It informs our biggest ideas about the cosmos and our smallest ideas about ethics. It is huge and multifaceted, and living inside of it is a holistic experience.

Viewing evangelicalism this way has been immensely useful during the process of writing this book. It has helped me articulate why we require so many lenses, perspectives, and vantage points just to begin to grasp the totality of it. Its true impact, experience, and consequences can only be "seen" through historical, biblical, feminist, Black, queer, racial, gender, class, technological, and media-aware lenses. We have to employ all these approaches and more, in tandem, keeping intersectionality and a variety of interdisciplinary methodologies in mind, with a certain degree of remove and a certain amount of context. The cover of *Hyperobjects* shows an iceberg in profile, revealing how its small above-water peak hides its immense underwater depths. This image of a massive, slow *thing* helped me to visualize why it is so hard to reform or oppose evangelicalism. You can't just toss an iceberg aside, especially if you mistakenly believe it's only as large as what you see above water.

And although most evangelicals would probably dismiss the

framework of hyperobjects out of hand, I find that it has reso-
nances within Christianity itself. It is present in Paul Tillich's
concept of God as the ground of being, and in Paul's invocation
at Areopagus (aka Mars Hill) that "in him we live and move and
have our being" (Acts 17:28). Morton's invocation of apocalyptic language is also immediately evocative for most people who
lived in evangelicalism. "Hyperobjects," they write, "are directly responsible for what I call the end of the world."[5] Yet
Morton conceives of "the end of the world" not in the way people usually mean it but rather in a way that challenges the very
notion of "the world."

For Morton, the world is an "aesthetic effect based on a
blurriness and aesthetic distance."[6] In essence, it is a certain
view of life that places some things in the foreground and others
in the background so we can understand them—if not logically,
then at least consistently. From this point of view, the world
ended in 1784 with the advent of the steam engine and the introduction of the hyperobject we call carbon-based fuel. The
world also ended in 1945 with the birth of atomic weaponry,
another hyperobject. You might think of it a bit like the R.E.M.
song: it's the end of the world *as we know it*. And the world as we
know it ends over and over again.

But Morton does not let that reality lead them to nihilism.
Yes, hyperobjects impose on us and encapsulate us, but viewing
enormous natural and social phenomena like this comes with
opportunity. Instead of feeling tossed around by the winds of
fate, we can face the complexities of those winds with honesty
and clarity. Instead of feeling a vague sense of doom and guilt
about plastic, we can acknowledge how it works as a hyperobject
and change our actions accordingly. I think Morgan Meis sum-
marizes it well in a *New Yorker* profile of Morton.

Morton writes that we must cultivate a "spirituality of care" toward the objects of the world—not just the likable parts but the frightening ones. . . . Instead of burying nuclear waste, we might store it aboveground, in a visible place, where we can learn to take more responsibility for it—perhaps even building an aesthetically interesting enclosure. . . . At a minimum, Morton thinks that this kind of caring could cure us of the idea that we are in control; it might show us that we are part of a vast network of interpenetrating entities. . . . At a maximum, Morton seems to feel that this omnidirectional, uncanny form of care could help save the world.[7]

I think this "spirituality of care" speaks directly to the lived experience of exvangelicals in that it builds on the apocalyptic notions that still haunt our psyches, but it also returns to us our agency. The apocalyptic outlook is often part of our first world-view, and it stays with us even as we change. My undergraduate philosophy professor once asked us to look out the window and describe what we saw. After we did so, he commented that no one said, "I see glass." He said—another metaphor—that this is how our inherited worldviews work. We don't realize our vision is mediated by anything, even when that something is an impass-able barrier. Frameworks like hyperobjects let us acknowledge we are seeing the end of the world through a window, which means that—often with the help of others—we are now free to try looking at the same scene through a different window, or through a telescope, or maybe even by standing up and going outside.

Much of this book has been about the major systemic issues

that plague us. Those problems are larger than any one person or group of people could hope to solve, and they'll require immense investments of time, money, attention, and effort to overcome. The solutions will need to be as diffuse and multifaceted as the powers and principalities that maintain our current state of affairs. At the same time, as the examples in this book have taught us over and over, we as individuals will be ground down before we can hope to grind away at these problems. We are human and need human comforts, including spiritual practices and other forms of self-care.

I am increasingly convinced that a person's individual "religiosity" is a unique part of their neurodiversity that depends on their predispositions, their exposure to religion and philosophy, their experiences of trauma (or lack thereof), and so forth. If evangelicalism were spiritually satisfactory, exvangelicals wouldn't have left in the first place, but at the same time, many of us experience something like a God-shaped hole in our lives. To use a metaphor from the book of Romans, we're like a wild olive shoot that needs to be grafted to a living root. Essayist Meghan O'Gieblyn writes about her own loss of faith thus: "To leave a religious tradition in the twenty-first century is to experience the trauma of secularization—a process that spanned several centuries and that most of humanity endured with all the attentiveness of slow-boiling toads—in an instant."[8] Therefore, it is valuable to consider the experience of losing the "enchanted" view of the world provided by evangelicalism, especially when it is coupled with the ever-shifting realities wrought by increasing technological complexity and dependence. I recognize that even if some find it useful, the metaphor of the hyperobject will not fully meet the spiritual needs of most exvangelicals. I don't expect it to. The growing number of people leaving evangelicalism are not bound for the same destination—they are dispersing to various practices and traditions or to no tradition at all.

For those interested in continuing to cultivate a sense of Christian faith, there are ample possibilities, including liberation theologies, queer theologies, trauma-informed theologies, and embodied theologies. There are Black and anticolonial theologies created by and for people of color (which white exvangelicals can and should also learn from). While each of these theologies offers a new sense of vitality for former evangelicals, they do require that certain beliefs die off. That can be a difficult process, but on the other side of it, one finds many new ways to believe.

For those who no longer find any type of Christianity tenable, they may shift toward focusing on other forms of community and engaging in other aspects of social and political life, in a way that is more relationally healthy than the all-consuming aspects of evangelical culture. Still, many exvangelicals no longer have ties to their faith of origin but want to cultivate meaningful spiritual practices. For those who desire them, there are thankfully many other religious and secular practices that can imbue our lives with meaning. This has been the work of writers and creators like lenny duncan, who, as I mentioned in chapter 11, served for years as an ELCA pastor before resigning their call. In their book *Dear Revolutionaries: A Field Guide for a World Beyond the Church*, they offer new ideas for spiritual actions, such as building altars in our homes with symbols that connect us to the divine and humanity, doing ancestral work to discover people of valor in our own personal lineages, and devoting our attention to our local communities and immediate neighbors. Likewise, as a speaker, spiritual coach, and the author of the book *What Makes You Bloom: Cultivating a Practice for Connecting with Your Divine Self*, Kevin Garcia explores various non-Christian practices intended to help exvangelicals heal and reconnect to the spiritual.

Other visions of new personal spiritual practice have been explored in works of fiction. In her novel *Parable of the Sower*, Octavia Butler envisions a religion called Earthseed, in which the idea of God is identified as change and the construction of God is in the hands of the worshipper. When one shapes change, one shapes God. I find this perspective incredibly honest and insightful; it sees the concept of God as both immanent and inscrutable, and it decides to return agency to the believer all the same. The big-T truth of God is less important than the mental construct it allows by extending our ethics to an infinite, all-encompassing expanse, in the same way that many existing pantheistic traditions do. That Earthseed is self-aware to this extent is a strength. If fiction is a lie that tells the truth, perhaps fictional religion can be lies that provide useful truths as well.

IN HIS BOOK *White Too Long: The Legacy of White Supremacy in American Christianity*, Robert P. Jones highlights the work of researchers Michael O. Emerson and Christian Smith, which has found that white evangelicals have a "restricted . . . moral vision" based on viewing every problem and every solution through the lens of personal sinfulness.[9] Emerson and Smith write, "Absent from [evangelical] accounts is the idea that poor relationships might be shaped by social structures, such as laws, the ways institutions operate, or forms of segregation."[10] Walking away from evangelicalism means losing not just a certain form of spirituality but also a certain set of ethics. And so again, we must look outside of evangelical tradition to make up for our inherited deficiencies, seeking ethics that honestly appraise the world and its systems rather than trying to cram it into the simplistic framework of sin. To do that, these ethics must account for rapid social and technological change.

The steadfast evangelical commitment to never changing is not a virtue but a vice, and one that is costing them and us dearly. It is not a good thing that Harry Emerson Fosdick's description of the fundamentalists of his time in the 1920s applies just as well to the fundamentalists of the 2020s. By routinely refusing to revisit what they have deemed "orthodoxy," they have reduced themselves to circling the same issues again and again, methodically rejecting new information and reinforcing their worldview. Their commitment to remaining in the 1920s alienates and isolates them. It leads to a faith that stifles growth instead of encouraging it. But as Thich Nhat Hanh writes, "Our faith must be alive. It cannot be just a set of rigid beliefs and notions. Our faith must evolve every day and bring us joy, peace, freedom, and love."[11] Stubbornness is not a fruit of the Spirit. Because of evangelical stubbornness, everyone in the country is stuck having the same cultural conversations again and again throughout the twentieth and twenty-first centuries. We cannot keep allowing such intransigence to wind back the clock in our churches, our government, or our daily lives.

It is here that I think the work of philosophers like Shannon Vallor can help us. Vallor's book *Technology and the Virtues: A Philosophical Guide to a Future Worth Wanting* provides an in-depth comparative study of Aristotelian, Buddhist, and Confucian ethics in an effort to adapt those traditions to today's complex moral environment. As the name suggests, Vallor's book is mindful of the role technology has had in shaping, changing, and compli-cating society in the late twentieth and early twenty-first centu-ries. She acknowledges that the techno-utopia envisioned by mid-twentieth-century futurists and sold to us by technology firms has not come to pass. Instead, we have a fractured-yet-connected, information-saturated environment and enormous global problems (one might call them hyperobjects) like climate change and income inequality.

Yet technological progress does not slow. In retrospect, so-ciety may not have been "ready" for the seismic and sudden changes wrought by the mobile computing era—and it may not be "ready" for the digital paradigms based on AI or virtual/aug-mented reality that seem to be on the horizon. But there's no use in ignoring reality: "While we face a future that remains cloaked in a technosocial fog," Vallor writes, "this need not mean that we go into it unprepared or ill-equipped, especially when it comes to matters of ethical life."[12] She takes it as a given that "human social practices, including our moral practices, have always been intertwined with our technologies," and that, in this sense, the twenty-first century CE is not so different from the fifth century BCE.[13] We already have what we need to face this moment in history, because we have always had it.

Vallor proposes twelve "technomoral virtues"—honesty, self-control, humility, justice, courage, empathy, care, civility, flexibility, perspective, magnanimity, and technomoral wisdom— that can be adapted to various traditions.[14] This adaptability is key, because "it leaves room for a virtue ethic that is pluralistic (open to more than one mode of expression of human flourish-ing) and malleable (adapted to the needs and affordances of the present human condition and environment)" and thus represents "humanity's best chance to cope and even thrive in the midst of the great uncertainties and vicissitudes of technosocial life that lie ahead."[15]

This moral vision is diametrically opposed to evangelical presuppositionalism, which, true to its name, *presupposes* certain axioms (like the existence of God or the inerrancy of the Bible) and rejects out of hand any arguments that don't comport with them. Whereas presuppositionalism is rigid and inflexible, virtue ethics such as those proposed by Vallor are pliant and flexible. A presuppositionalist would argue that this is tantamount to unmoored moral relativism that can justify anything—theft, murder, whatever. What they'd fail to see is that by orienting itself around flourishing rather than a set of arbitrary presuppositions, virtue ethics allows practitioners to be moral while also being mindful of the complexity of the world. Presuppositionalism is simply not up to the task.

QUESTIONS ABOUT THE USE OF technology in politics, media, religion, and culture remain open-ended and consequential. What safeguards exist to prevent another weaponization of data like that of Cambridge Analytica? How will local pastors who struggled to address the influence of QAnon in their congregations be able to manage a more literal difference in worldview if their congregants can apply a Christian nationalist augmented-reality filter to the entire world via smart glasses? Will these technologies and the media they transmit deepen existing divisions, or will they enable new connections across these divides? Today's platforms have not been immune to weaponization by authoritarian or fascist groups and governments, which breeds little confidence that they will develop the buffers necessary to resist such efforts in tomorrow's media.

In order to face the personal and social challenges ahead of us, we will have to grow beyond our fundamentalisms. We will also have to grow beyond our transitional identities and practices. What is next for us, as individuals and as a people? How do we move forward with our own personal practices, and how do we work to structure our society in a way that is resistant to the most virulent and violent strains of Christian nationalism?

In my estimation, we must look far and wide for the answers to these questions, and we must not be afraid if our answers fail in part or in total. The only true failure is a failure to try.

CONCLUSION

When I first started the *Exvangelical* podcast, I didn't know what it would grow into. It was an extension of my own drive to understand the world and in particular the part of the world and its traditions that formed me. That work was always, in a way, laden with melancholy. To break with your faith of origin, even for another expression of faith, is no small thing. Still, I had no concept of how much soul-searching it would send me on or how it would deepen my own search for answers. I didn't know that my own fascination with evangelical religion and politics would connect me to people across the world with the same concerns and struggles. It is my hope that this book has helped people with and without the lived experience of evangelicalism to understand those concerns and struggles a little bit better.

The past decade has made clear that so much of our social and political life is at best highly precarious and at worst actively harmful to the most vulnerable among us. The number of simultaneous crises we face—police violence and militarization,

racism, homophobia and transphobia, economic inequality combined with a rapidly rising cost of living, housing insecurity,
unequal access to health care and education, epidemics of lone-
liness and isolation, the climate crisis—is overwhelming and
enough to make anyone feel hopeless.

Yet I choose hope.

I choose hope even as I recognize the limitations of our current communities and tools. Evangelical church leaders know
that their ranks are shrinking, and scholars have begun study-
ing ex-believers of all kinds. Our reasons for leaving are varied,
as has been covered in detail in the preceding pages—
overpoliticization, authoritarianism, abuse, and a stifling dogma
that favors those born straight, white, and male. These churches
know they are dying, but it is a slow death.

At the same time, even though the transitional communities
we find and create online are not the same as those we leave,
they can be stifling in a different way. This can lead to misun-
derstanding and real trauma that, for exvangelicals, has echoes
of what they felt when they lost their church community. Navi-
gating that process is specific to each individual, and each person should do what is healthy for them, especially as their
deconstruction process continues into new stages and other
spiritual, mental, or physical needs make themselves known. To
be clear, the centuries-old churches and publics of evangelicalism aren't directly comparable to nascent exvangelical communities and counterpublics in terms of impact, but that doesn't
excuse or minimize any harm that might occur in exvangelical
spaces, which need to be judged on their own merits.

Yet I still choose hope because I believe that the hard-fought
lessons exvangelicals have learned can benefit society. As individuals and as a loose cohort, we demonstrate that it is possible

to change your mind, and in doing so, change your life. In our current polarized state, this is no small feat. We are living proof that there is a desire for change from our religious and political leaders that can no longer go unnoticed or be denied, and that when a situation is no longer tenable, people can abandon it. The emergence of hashtags like #Exvangelical, #Deconstruction, #ChurchToo, #LeaveLoud, #ExMo (short for ex-Mormon), #ExJW (short for ex–Jehovah's Witness), and many others has helped to raise awareness of the systemic issues rampant within evangelical institutions and belief, and the impacts they have had on individual lives.

This heightened public awareness has led to the documentaries *Let Us Prey*, *Shiny Happy People*, and many others, directing the attention of broader audiences to the threat of Christian nationalism and the damage of purity culture. The rotten spoils of decades of culture warring are on full display, and anyone can contrast them with the fruits of the Spirit and draw their own conclusions. I hold out hope that this heightened public awareness will one day lead to true public investment in resilient institutions that can withstand the threats of Christian nationalism, unchecked capitalism, and systemic racism. I hope this because the world as we know it has already ended, and we can try anything, big or small, to make the new world we wake up to each day a little better in whatever capacity we can.

Throughout the course of my time producing the *Exvangelical* podcast, I have gone from pursuing more progressive strains of Christianity to having little personal interest in any kind of theology. The best metaphor I can come up with to describe this change is that, well, those nerve endings are shot. Through this work, I have directly experienced so much grief and indirectly witnessed so much more that questions about

God no longer animate my soul. At times I grieve that too, but I have made a sort of peace with it. I am now far more concerned with how people change their minds and how their beliefs motivate them to act in the world. I remain open to the possibility that a new faith of sorts will return, but it is not my primary concern. I have gone from believing in the Protestant doctrine of the "priesthood of all believers" to believing in a universal consortium of nonbelievers—and of those who go through periods of belief and nonbelief, around and around, in widening circles.

I hope that the words and ideas I've compiled here have provided some aid in understanding the world we've inherited and that we now work to shape. This work is being done—by exvangelicals online, by local congregations, by me, by you—as a part of a lineage that stretches back to the nineteenth century. I hope that by telling some stories from that lineage I have helped tie together some of the many disparate elements that affect us and provided a sense of continuity and history. I hope I've shed some light on what might need to come in order to resist creeping Christian nationalism and imagine new futures.

I also hope that we will continue to pursue the construction of new institutions even as we seek to remediate and reform the civic and ecclesial ones that fail us today. That may involve the development of what the activist and writer Noel Ignatiev calls "a period of dual power," an in-between phase when both current societal institutions (such as established churches and governments) coexist alongside the institutions that challenge them and will eventually revolutionize them.[1] Further, we must be cognizant of what philosophy professor Olúfẹ́mi O. Táíwò calls "elite capture," which is when established institutions try to co-opt counterpublics and subsume dissent, reducing the crucial work of so-called identity politics to a matter of performative deference. Táíwò calls for us instead to practice "a constructive approach to politics" that

> does not ask us to ignore our own interpersonal, symbolic, or material needs, even though it does ask us to be disciplined in how we relate those to the needs of the struggle and the scores of people and generations that are not immediately present. . . . It asks us to be planners and designers, to be accountable and responsive to people who aren't yet in the room. In addition to being architects, it asks us to become builders and construction workers: to actually build the kinds of rooms we could sit in together, rather than idly speculate about which rooms would be nice.[2]

Such organizational work will take attention, and capital, and a commitment to repudiating the simplistic, fundamentalist Christian nationalist vision for the world. This effort will take all of us. It will take people having the same or similar conversations, in different circumstances and with different people. It will require customization for different audiences. But in the end, the very act of repudiating white evangelicalism is valuable on its own—especially when it leads to the affirmation of more expansive views of life.

In 2020, I commissioned new artwork for my podcast. As I wrote on Instagram when debuting that artwork, I gave the artist, Jenna Luecke, a simple prompt: a design that would explore the idea of something dying away so something new can grow. The image she created, of flowers and plants growing from a decaying Bible, expresses the various ways that those of us who've left white evangelicalism have found our own distinct ways to flourish. We may all have been rooted in similar experiences, but we find our own expressions of new growth. And that diversity is beautiful—as is the growth that is possible. Yes, you may be exvangelical, but you are many things beyond that as well, and you have much to offer beyond stories of your trauma. There is still so much work to do. But there are so many ways to approach it, and so many people to do it with, and so many ways to rest and find joy along the way too.

For all these reasons, I choose to place my hope in those who forge new paths from the old, making new metaphors, imagining worlds beyond evangelical, beyond exvangelical, beyond binaries of belief and disbelief, beyond belonging and rejection. I will carry it all with me—the shame, guilt, hurt, and grief, and the joy, peace, and healing too. And thanks to the people I have met, the stories I have heard, and the histories I have learned, I will know I am not alone. Neither are you.

ACKNOWLEDGMENTS

M y first and deepest thanks go to my family. To Emily, my wife and partner and best friend, I could not have written this book or lived this life without you. I am so thankful for the ways we have grown together, and I love you more than I can ever express in a single paragraph, so I will spend the rest of my days telling you: I love you. To my daughter, Sophia, you are my inspiration and my hope and my joy, and you are your own too. I cherish being your father, laughing with you, and seeing you grow into yourself each and every day. I love both of you with my whole heart.

To my parents, Mark and Diane, my sister, Heather, her husband, Brian, and their children, I am so grateful for your steadfast support. You demonstrated what faith looked like, and I am thankful for your love. To my grandparents and all my extended family, thank you for being in our lives.

To all my teachers, professors, and pastors who had a hand in molding me, who broadened my worldview and encouraged me to keep writing, I thank you. Thank you to Rural Mission and First United Methodist Church in Crawfordsville. Thank you in particular to Dr. Kenneth Schenck, Dr. Mary Brown, Dr. Nicola Beisel, Dr. Timothy Eberhart, Rev. Lynn Denison, Rev. Scott Field, and Rev. Debra Bullock for your kindness, wisdom, and intelligence.

Thank you to all the people who went before me and spoke truth to power in their own place and time. Thank you to all the thinkers and writers and musicians who influenced me. Thank you for sharing your visions with the world. Thank you to David Bazan and Pedro the Lion for providing the soundtrack for my own journey out of evangelicalism.

Thank you to all the current, former, and future moderators and admins of the Exvangelical Facebook group. Your commitment to making a place where people can share and explore their experiences of leaving evangelicalism means more than I can say. That space remains what it is because of you all.

Thank you to all those who have been members of the Irreverent Media Group: Kevin, Sarah, Josie, Tori, Justin, Mason, Roberto, Anna, Bradley, Janice, Adrian, Josh. Thank you Dan and Mike for being constant friends, and to the BNO crew, Jon, Elliott, Alex, and Dylan. Thank you to Chrissy Stroop, Liz Kineke, and Julie Ingersoll. Thank you to my agent, David Morris, for providing solace when it felt like this project might not see the light of day. Thank you to my editor, Lauren O'Neal, for wrangling my words and ideas into something cogent and presentable. I truly cannot imagine having finished this book without you. Thank you to everyone at TarcherPerigee for allowing me to share this book with the public.

Thank you to all the people across the social web who have used hashtags like #Exvangelical to share your stories and challenge the dominant narratives about religion and society. Thank you to all the internet friends and strangers and acquaintances I have learned from along the way.

Finally, thank you to everyone who ever appeared on *Exvangelical* or *Powers & Principalities* and shared even a small portion of your stories with me and my audience. No matter where your journey has taken you, I am so thankful that you entrusted me with your story along the way, and I trust that your vulnerability helped someone be courageous in their own lives. It certainly helped me be more courageous in my own.

NOTES

INTRODUCTION

1. Berry, *The Art of the Commonplace*, 306–7.
2. Hannah-Jones et al., *The 1619 Project*, xvii.
3. Piper, *Book Was There*, 23.

CHAPTER 1

1. Pew Research Center, "In U.S., Decline of Christianity Continues at Rapid Pace."
2. Worthen, *Apostles of Reason*, 16.
3. Noll, *Scandal of the Evangelical Mind*, 8.
4. Boorstein, Bailey, and Zauzmer, "Would Billy Graham Be Disgusted by Evangelicals Today?"
5. Smith, "More White Americans Adopted Than Shed Evangelical Label During Trump Presidency, Especially His Supporters."
6. Keller, "Can Evangelicalism Survive Donald Trump and Roy Moore?"
7. McCrummen, Reinhard, and Crites, "Woman Says Roy Moore Initiated Sexual Encounter When She Was 14, He Was 32."

8. Keller, "Can Evangelicalism Survive Donald Trump and Roy Moore?"
9. Keller.
10. Keller.
11. Noll, *Scandal of the Evangelical Mind*, 8.
12. Butler, *White Evangelical Racism*, 4.

CHAPTER 2

1. Dayton, introduction to *Rediscovering an Evangelical Heritage*, 12.
2. Dayton, 12.
3. Dayton, 12.
4. Dayton, 12.
5. Morone, *Hellfire Nation*, 100–1.
6. Morone, 102.
7. Morone, 103.
8. Morone, 101.
9. Martin, "Slave Bible from the 1800s Omitted Key Passages That Could Incite Rebellion."
10. Kendi, *Stamped from the Beginning*, 31–32.
11. Jones, *White Too Long*, 1.
12. Jones, 1–2.
13. Dayton, *Rediscovering an Evangelical Heritage*, 59.
14. Dayton, 61.
15. Dayton, 64.
16. Dayton, 64.
17. Jones, *White Too Long*, 92.
18. Butler, *White Evangelical Racism*, 2.

CHAPTER 3

1. Gloege, *Guaranteed Pure*, 3.
2. Gloege, 19–20.
3. Gloege, 20.
4. Gloege, 20.
5. Gloege, 22.
6. Gloege, 22.
7. Gloege, 23–24.

8. Gloege, 24.
9. Kruse, *One Nation Under God*, 5.
10. Vaca, *Evangelicals Incorporated*, 34.
11. Gloege, *Guaranteed Pure*, 56.
12. Gloege, 55.
13. Gloege, 123.
14. Gloege, 174.
15. Gloege, 174.
16. Frykholm, *Rapture Culture*, 105.
17. Sutton, *American Apocalypse*, 43.
18. Gloege, *Guaranteed Pure*, 105.
19. Gloege, 105.
20. Eisenstein, *The Printing Press as an Agent of Change*, 701–2.
21. Eisenstein, 702.
22. Bass, *A People's History of Christianity*, 167.
23. Vaca, *Evangelicals Incorporated*, 27.
24. Gloege, *Guaranteed Pure*, 148.
25. McKinney, "The Fundamentalist Bible School as an Outgrowth of the Changing Patterns of Protestant Revivalism, 1882–1920."
26. Vaca, *Evangelicals Incorporated*, 11.

CHAPTER 4

1. Gloege, *Guaranteed Pure*, 177.
2. Gloege, 177.
3. Rood, "The Untold Story of the Fundamentals."
4. Gloege, *Guaranteed Pure*, 177.
5. Tillich, *Systematic Theology*, 3.
6. Gloege, *Guaranteed Pure*, 10.
7. Gloege, 180–81.
8. Laats, *Fundamentalist U*, 66.
9. Laats, 54.
10. Laats, 54.
11. Du Mez, *Jesus and John Wayne*, 17.
12. Stephens, "The Klan, White Christianity, and the Past and Present."
13. Sutton, *American Apocalypse*, 40.
14. Kruse, *One Nation Under God*, 5.
15. Kruse, 5.

16. Butler, *White Evangelical Racism*, 37.

17. Kruse, *One Nation Under God*, 10–11.

18. Kruse, 10.

19. Kruse, 12.

20. Jewish Telegraphic Agency, "Los Angeles Minister Urged to Apologize for Broadcasting Anti-Semitic Falsehood."

21. Seligman, "The Franklin Prophecy."

22. Butler, *White Evangelical Racism*, 35.

23. FitzGerald, *The Evangelicals*, 171.

24. FitzGerald, 172.

25. Du Mez, *Jesus and John Wayne*, 26.

26. FitzGerald, *The Evangelicals*, 175.

27. FitzGerald, 176.

28. Du Mez, *Jesus and John Wayne*, 23.

29. Du Mez, 23.

30. Du Mez, 26.

31. Du Mez, 26–27.

32. Butler, *White Evangelical Racism*, 43.

33. Kruse, *One Nation Under God*, 37.

34. Kruse, 37.

35. Butler, *White Evangelical Racism*, 42.

36. Butler, 45.

37. Curtis, *The Myth of Colorblind Christians*, 35.

38. Butler, 47.

39. Curtis, 39–40.

40. FitzGerald, *The Evangelicals*, 177.

41. Kruse, *One Nation Under God*, 54.

42. Kruse, 52–53.

43. Sutton, *American Apocalypse*, 328.

44. Sutton, 330.

CHAPTER 5

1. Stewart, *The Power Worshippers*, 67.

2. Stewart, 67.

3. Posner, *Unholy*, 101–2.

4. Stewart, *The Power Worshippers*, 60.

5. Balmer, *Bad Faith*, 49.
6. Balmer, 49.
7. Balmer, 50.
8. Worthen, *Apostles of Reason*, 15.
9. Goodwin, *Abusing Religion*, 22.
10. Goodwin, 16.
11. Goodwin, 22.
12. Onishi, *Preparing for War*, 67.
13. Ingersoll, *Building God's Kingdom*, 14.
14. Ingersoll, 16.
15. Ingersoll, 21.
16. Ingersoll, 21–22.
17. Wellman, *Hijacking History*, 22.
18. Smietana and Miller, "How the Battle over Christian Nationalism Often Starts with Homeschooling."
19. Klein, "The Rightwing US Textbooks That Teach Slavery as 'Black Immigration.'"
20. Gilgoff, "Exclusive: Grover Norquist Gives Religious Conservatives Tough Love."
21. Cloud, "Bob Jones University vs. United States."
22. Rich, "Carter Opens Conference on Families."
23. Du Mez, *Jesus and John Wayne*, 101.
24. Anderson, "Reagan: Religious in His Way."
25. Reagan, "James Robison: National Affairs Briefing."
26. Matzko, *The Radio Right*, 227.
27. Du Mez, *Jesus and John Wayne*, 128.
28. Hemmer, *Messengers of the Right*, 252.
29. Hemmer, 257.

CHAPTER 6

1. Sharp, *The Other Evangelicals*, 32.
2. Butler, *White Evangelical Racism*, 35.
3. Butler, 36.
4. *Christianity Today*, "Our History."
5. Butler, *White Evangelical Racism*, 60.
6. Butler, 62.

7. Gilbreath, "A Prophet Out of Harlem."

8. McAlister, *The Kingdom of God Has No Borders*, 64.

9. Wheaton Archives and Special Collections, "'World Evangelism: Why? How? Who?' A Backward Look at Urbana '70."

10. McAlister, *The Kingdom of God Has No Borders*, 64–65.

11. Butler, *White Evangelical Racism*, 61–62.

12. Wheaton Archives and Special Collections, "'World Evangelism.'"

13. "Evangelicals on Justice: Socially Speaking . . ."

14. Sharp, *The Other Evangelicals*, 214.

15. Ingersoll, *Evangelical Christian Women*, 1.

16. Ingersoll, 36.

17. Cochran, *Evangelical Feminism*, 13.

18. Cochran, 29.

19. CBE International, "About CBE: Our Mission and Values."

20. The Council on Biblical Manhood and Womanhood (CBMW), "The Danvers Statement."

21. CBMW, "The Danvers Statement."

22. Ingersoll, *Evangelical Christian Women*, 54.

23. Sider, "New Name, Same Mission."

24. Wheaton College, "Historical Review Task Force Final Report," 35.

25. Dayton, *Rediscovering an Evangelical Heritage*, 51.

26. Gerson, "The Last Temptation."

27. Fea, "Wheaton College Study on Race."

CHAPTER 7

1. Vaca, *Evangelicals Incorporated*, 156.

2. Vaca, 155.

3. Stowe, *No Sympathy for the Devil*, 8.

4. Beaujon, *Body Piercing Saved My Life*, 27.

5. Cusic, *The Sound of Light*, 384.

6. Cusic, 384.

7. Cusic, 384.

8. Klein, *Pure*, 346.

9. Allison, *#ChurchToo*, 26.

10. Ingersoll, *Evangelical Christian Women*, 13.

11. Du Mez, *Jesus and John Wayne*, 7.

12. Sedensky, "Rush Limbaugh, 'Voice of American Conservatism,' Has Died."
13. Hemmer, *Messengers of the Right*, 266.
14. Hemmer, 266.
15. Hemmer, 267.

CHAPTER 8

1. CNN, "You Are Either with Us or Against Us."
2. *Christianity Today*, "The TNIV Debate."

CHAPTER 9

1. Miller, "Women Bloggers Spark an Evangelical 'Crisis of Authority.'"
2. Shellnutt, "Jen Hatmaker Brings Her 'Super-Christian' Family onto Reality TV."
3. Bass, *A People's History of Christianity*, 167.
4. Bass, 168.
5. Bass, 169.
6. Du Mez, *Jesus and John Wayne*, 193.
7. Du Mez, 194.
8. Driscoll and Driscoll, *Real Marriage*, 12.
9. Mars Hill Church, *It's All About Jesus*, 8.
10. Acts 29, "Find a Church."
11. Gardner, "An Evangelical Icon Finds Salvation in West Hollywood."
12. Smietana, "At the Other Mars Hill Church, New Co-pastors Hope to Build a Faithful Future."
13. Crouch, "The Emergent Mystique."
14. Kraft, "Dave Kraft, Mars Hill Church and Mark Driscoll."
15. Merritt, "Mark Driscoll Accused of Plagiarism by Radio Host"; Throckmorton, "On the Allegations of Plagiarism Against Mark Driscoll."
16. Kellogg, "Can Bestseller Lists Be Bought?"
17. Acts 29 Network, "A Message from the Board of Acts 29 Concerning Mark Driscoll and Mars Hill Church"; Bailey, "'Step Down'"; Bailey, "Exclusive: Mark Driscoll Resigns from Mars Hill Church"; Smith, "Mars Hill Church to Dissolve."

18. Kellogg, "Pastor Mark Driscoll's Books Withdrawn from 180 Christian Stores."
19. Moody, "Mark Driscoll's Safe Space: How the Embattled Pastor Built a New Church."

CHAPTER 10

1. Nelson, *Shadow Network*, 168.
2. Nelson, 168.
3. Weaver, Willnat, and Wilhoit, "The American Journalist in the Digital Age."
4. Nelson, *Shadow Network*, 153.
5. Nelson, xvi.
6. Nelson, 154.
7. Nelson, 134.
8. Dias, "Watchmen on the Wall."
9. Nelson, *Shadow Network*, 135.
10. Christian Broadcasting Network, "Brody File Exclusive: Evangelical Leader Says It's 'Still to Be Determined' Whether Evangelicals Will Show Up Strongly in November."
11. Stewart, *The Power Worshippers*, 174–75.
12. Pew Research Center, "Growing Number of Americans Say Obama Is a Muslim."
13. Posner, *Unholy*, 77.
14. Posner, 78.
15. Posner, 75.
16. Boorstein, "Trump on God: 'Hopefully I Won't Have to Be Asking for Much Forgiveness.'"
17. Nelson, *Shadow Network*, 197.
18. WTHR-TV Channel 13, "Indiana's Corporate Leaders Call for Action on RFRA."
19. Bailey, "'Still the Best Candidate'"; Grudem, "Trump's Moral Character and the Election."
20. Grudem, "If You Don't Like Either Candidate, Then Vote for Trump's Policies."
21. Martinez and Smith, "How the Faithful Voted."
22. Evans, "Life After Evangelicalism."

CHAPTER 11

1. Fraser, "Rethinking the Public Sphere," 57.
2. Fraser, 67.
3. Fraser, 67.
4. Warner, *Publics and Counterpublics*, 119.
5. Warner, 121.
6. Warner, 120.
7. Jackson, Bailey, and Welles, *#HashtagActivism*, xxviii.
8. Jackson, Bailey, and Welles, xxxii.
9. Laughlin, *Redeem All*, 141.
10. Tarnoff, *Internet for the People*, preface, Kindle.
11. Downen, Olsen, and Tedesco, "20 Years, 700 Victims."
12. Haag, "Memphis Pastor Admits 'Sexual Incident' with High School Student 20 Years Ago."
13. Pashman and Coen, "After Years of Inquiries, Willow Creek Pastor Denies Misconduct Allegations."
14. Pashman, "Willow Creek Elders Apologize for Casting Doubt on Women's Allegations Against Founder Hybels."
15. Shellnutt, "Paige Patterson Fired by Southwestern, Stripped of Retirement Benefits."
16. Bailey, "Southern Baptist Leader Encouraged a Woman Not to Report Alleged Rape to Police and Told Her to Forgive Assailant, She Says."
17. Allison, *#ChurchToo*, 161.
18. Robertson, "A Quiet Exodus."
19. Johnson, "#WhiteChurchQuiet."
20. Tisby, "Leave LOUD."
21. Grossman, "Salvation Is Showing Up: PW Talks to Lenny Duncan."
22. "Grace Semler Baldridge | 'Preacher's Kid' Going #1 on iTunes Chart"; Daw, "Meet Flamy Grant, the Drag Queen Carving Out Her Own Lane in Christian Music."
23. Dias, "Top Evangelical College Group to Dismiss Employees Who Support Gay Marriage."
24. Rhodan, "Christian Group That Flip-Flopped on Gay Marriage Loses Donors."
25. Wax, "World Vision and Why We Grieve for the Children."
26. McBride, *The Wisdom of Your Body*, 16.

CHAPTER 12

1. Stroop, "If you left Evangelicalism over bigotry and intolerance or this election specifically, please share your story w/ the hashtag #EmptythePews."
2. Stroop, "I Created the Hashtag #EmptythePews Because It's Time for Evangelicals to Walk Out of Toxic Churches."
3. Levin, " 'Everyone Was Taught to Be Accepting.' Readers Share Stories of Their Christian Educations"; Stroop, "Setting the Record Straight on #ExposeChristianSchools."
4. boyd, *It's Complicated*, 8–9.
5. boyd, "Social Network Sites as Networked Publics," in *A Networked Self*, 41.
6. boyd, 46.
7. boyd, 49.
8. Molina, "Twitter Overcounted Active Users Since 2014, Shares Surge on Profit Hopes"; Enberg, "Global Instagram Users 2019."
9. Cole, "What Is a Total Institution?"
10. r/Exvangelical (subreddit).
11. Jenkins, Ito, and boyd, *Participatory Culture in a Networked Era*, 2.

CHAPTER 13

1. boyd, "Social Network Sites as Networked Publics," in *A Networked Self*, 55.
2. Jurgenson, *The Social Photo*, 68.
3. Jurgenson, 77.
4. McCulloch, *Because Internet*, 220–21.
5. McCulloch, 220.
6. Small, *Someone to Talk To*, 6.
7. Small, 6–7.
8. Stedman, *IRL*, 33.
9. McCulloch, *Because Internet*, 223.
10. Burgess, "Elijah Wood and Mike Tyson Cameo Videos Were Used in a Russian Disinformation Campaign."
11. Carr, *The Shallows*, 6–7.
12. Goel, "Facebook Tinkers with Users' Emotions in News Feed Experiment, Stirring Outcry."

13. Tufekci, "YouTube, the Great Radicalizer."

14. Martin and Jarvis, "Far-Right Misinformation Is Thriving on Facebook. A New Study Shows Just How Much."

15. Miller, "Hundreds of Far-Right Militias Are Still Organizing, Recruiting, and Promoting Violence on Facebook."

16. Alba, "Social Media Companies' Moderation Efforts Lost Steam in 2023."

17. McLuhan and Fiore, *The Medium Is the Massage*, 24.

CHAPTER 14

1. Chastain, "Exvangelical TikTokkers Aren't a Sign of the End Times, but Here's What Evangelicals Need to Understand About 'The Falling Away.' "

2. Jackson, "Matt Chandler Responds to Deconstruction Controversy."

3. Jackson, "Matt Chandler Responds."

4. Butler, "4 Causes of Deconstruction."

5. Butler, "4 Causes."

6. Smietana, "Josh Butler Resigns as Pastor Following TGC Article Backlash."

7. Smietana, "Josh Butler Resigns."

8. Gospel Coalition staff, "Beautiful Union Book."

9. Smietana, "Josh Butler Resigns as Pastor Following TGC Article Backlash."

10. Warren, "The Church Needs Reformation, Not Deconstruction."

11. Warren, "The Church Needs."

12. Warren, "The Church Needs."

13. Warren, "The Church Needs."

14. Sanders, "Wait, You're Not Deconstructing?"

15. Moore, "My Dad Taught Me How to Love the Exvangelical."

16. Moore, "My Dad."

17. Moore, "My Dad."

18. Riley, "Russell Moore: From Moral Majority to 'Prophetic Minority.' "

19. Moore, "Donald Trump Is Not the Moral Leader We Need."

20. O'Donnell, "Russell Moore to ERLC Trustees: 'They Want Me to Live in Psychological Terror.' "

21. Wingfield, "Russell Moore Leaves ERLC for *Christianity Today*, Highlighting the New Schism Within SBC."

22. Posner, *Unholy*, 261.
23. Stewart, *The Power Worshippers*, 193.
24. Grant, "The Mysterious Case of the Fake Gay Marriage Website, the Real Straight Man, and the Supreme Court."
25. Hicks, "How Churches of Christ Responded When the 1918 'Spanish Flu' Killed Millions."
26. Seidel, "Attack on the Capitol: Evidence of the Role of White Christian Nationalism," in *Christian Nationalism and the January 6, 2021, Insurrection*, 27–40.
27. Seidel, "Attack."
28. Seidel, "Attack."
29. Onishi, "Trump's New Civil Religion."
30. Onishi, "Civil Religion."
31. Onishi, "Civil Religion."
32. Onishi, "Civil Religion."
33. Onishi, "Civil Religion."

CHAPTER 15

1. Lakoff and Johnson, *Metaphors We Live By*, 3.
2. Strand, *The Flowering Wand*, 43.
3. Morton, *Hyperobjects*, 1.
4. Morton, 1.
5. Morton, 2.
6. Morton, 11.
7. Meis, "Timothy Morton's Hyper-Pandemic."
8. O'Gieblyn, *God, Human, Animal, Machine*, 43–44.
9. Jones, *White Too Long*, 97.
10. Jones, 98.
11. Nhat Hanh, *Living Buddha, Living Christ*, 136.
12. Vallor, *Technology and the Virtues*, 10.
13. Vallor, 78.
14. Vallor, 78.
15. Vallor, 10.

CONCLUSION

1. Ignatiev, *Treason to Whiteness Is Loyalty to Humanity*, chap. 39, Kindle.
2. Táíwò, *Elite Capture*, 118.

BIBLIOGRAPHY

Acts 29. "Find a Church." Acts29.com, accessed January 1, 2024. https://
www.acts29.com/find-a-church/?_church_map=-86.082579%2C-180
%2C76.66931%2C180.

Acts 29 Network. "A Message from the Board of Acts 29 Concerning Mark
Driscoll and Mars Hill Church." Acts 29 blog, August 10, 2014. https://
web.archive.org/web/20140810083820/http://www.acts29network.org
/acts-29-blog/a-message-from-the-board-of-acts-29-concerning-mark
-driscoll-and-mars-hill-church/.

Alba, Davey. "Social Media Companies' Moderation Efforts Lost Steam
in 2023." *Bloomberg*, December 26, 2023. https://www.bloomberg.com
/news/newsletters/2023-12-26/social-media-companies-moderation
-efforts-lost-steam-in-2023.

Allison, Emily Joy. *#ChurchToo: How Purity Culture Upholds Abuse and How
to Find Healing*. Minneapolis: Broadleaf Books, 2021.

Anderson, Jack. "Reagan: Religious in His Way." *Washington Post*, July 19,
1980. https://www.washingtonpost.com/archive/opinions/1980/07/20
/reagan-religious-in-his-way/4dc2e898-e35a-47cc-b9a2-9238d77f6048/.

Bailey, Sarah Pulliam. "Exclusive: Mark Driscoll Resigns from Mars Hill
Church." Religion News Service, October 15, 2014. https://religionnews
.com/2014/10/15/exclusive-mark-driscoll-resigns-from-mars-hill-church/.

————. "Southern Baptist Leader Encouraged a Woman Not to Report Alleged Rape to Police and Told Her to Forgive Assailant, She Says." *Washington Post*, May 22, 2018. https://www.washingtonpost.com/news /acts-of-faith/wp/2018/05/22/southern-baptist-leader-encouraged-a -woman-not-to-report-alleged-rape-to-police-and-told-her-to-forgive -assailant-she-says/.

————. "'Step down': Full Text of Mars Hill Pastors' Letter to Mark Driscoll." Religion News Service, August 28, 2014. https://religionnews .com/2014/08/28/step-full-text-mars-hill-pastors-letter-mark-driscoll/.

————. "'Still the Best Candidate': Some Evangelicals Still Back Trump Despite Lewd Video." *Washington Post*, October 8, 2016. https://www .washingtonpost.com/news/acts-of-faith/wp/2016/10/08/still-the-best -candidate-some-evangelicals-still-back-trump-despite-lewd-video/.

Balmer, Randall. *Bad Faith: Race and the Rise of the Religious Right*. Grand Rapids, MI: William B. Eerdmans, 2021.

Bass, Diana Butler. *A People's History of Christianity: The Other Side of the Story*. New York: HarperOne, 2010.

Beaujon, Andrew. *Body Piercing Saved My Life: Inside the Phenomenon of Christian Rock*. Cambridge, MA: Da Capo Press, 2006.

Berry, Wendell. *The Art of the Commonplace: The Agrarian Essays of Wendell Berry*. Edited by Norman Wirzba. Berkeley, CA: Counterpoint, 2002.

Boorstein, Michelle. "Trump on God: 'Hopefully I Won't Have to Be Asking for Much Forgiveness.'" *Washington Post*, June 8, 2016. https:// www.washingtonpost.com/news/acts-of-faith/wp/2016/06/08/trump-on -god-hopefully-i-wont-have-to-be-asking-for-much-forgiveness/.

Boorstein, Michelle, Sarah Pulliam Bailey, and Julie Zauzmer. "Would Billy Graham Be Disgusted by Evangelicals Today?" *Washington Post*, February 21, 2018. https://www.washingtonpost.com/news/acts-of-faith /wp/2018/02/21/what-would-billy-graham-think-of-evangelicals -today/.

Bote, Joshua. "He Wrote the Christian Case Against Dating. Now He's Splitting from His Wife and Faith." *USA Today*, July 29, 2019. https:// www.usatoday.com/story/news/nation/2019/07/29/joshua-harris-i-kissed -dating-goodbye-i-am-not-christian/1857934001/.

boyd, danah. *It's Complicated: The Social Lives of Networked Teens*. New Haven, CT: Yale University Press, 2014.

————. "Social Network Sites as Networked Publics." In *A Networked Self:*

Identity, Community, and Culture on Social Network Sites, edited by Zizi
Papacharissi. New York: Routledge, 2011.

Burgess, Matt. "Elijah Wood and Mike Tyson Cameo Videos Were Used in
a Russian Disinformation Campaign." *Wired*, December 7, 2023. https://
www.wired.com/story/elijah-wood-mike-tyson-russia-ukraine-disinfor
mation/.

Butler, Anthea D. *White Evangelical Racism: The Politics of Morality in
America*. Chapel Hill: University of North Carolina Press, 2021.

Butler, Josh. "4 Causes of Deconstruction." The Gospel Coalition,
November 9, 2021. https://www.thegospelcoalition.org/article/4-causes
-deconstruction/.

Carr, Nicholas. *The Shallows: What the Internet Is Doing to Our Brains*. New
York: W. W. Norton & Company, 2011.

CBE International. "About CBE: Our Mission and Values." Accessed
October 27, 2023. https://www.cbeinternational.org/primary_page
/about-cbe/.

Chastain, Blake. "Exvangelical TikTokkers Aren't a Sign of the End Times,
but Here's What Evangelicals Need to Understand About 'The Falling
Away.'" *Religion Dispatches*, July 22, 2021. https://religiondispatches.org
/exvangelical-tiktokkers-arent-a-sign-of-the-end-times-but-heres-what
-evangelicals-need-to-understand-about-the-falling-away/.

Christian Broadcasting Network. "Brody File Exclusive: Evangelical Leader
Says It's 'Still to Be Determined' Whether Evangelicals Will Show Up
Strongly in November." CBN.com, September 15, 2016. https://www2
.cbn.com/video/brody-file-exclusive-evangelical-leader-says-its-still-be
-determined-whether-evangelicals.

Christianity Today. "Our History." ChristianityToday.org, accessed
December 18, 2023. https://www.christianitytoday.org/who-we-are
/our-history/.

———. "The TNIV Debate." *Christianity Today*, October 7, 2002. https://
christianitytoday.com/ct/2002/october7/1.36.html.

Cloud, Richard C. "Bob Jones University v. United States." In the
Encyclopedia Britannica Online. Article published January 10, 2018; last
modified May 17, 2023. https://www.britannica.com/event/Bob-Jones
-University-v-United-States.

CNN. "You Are Either with Us or Against Us." CNN.com, November 6,
2001. https://edition.cnn.com/2001/US/11/06/gen.attack.on.terror/.

Cochran, Pamela D. H. *Evangelical Feminism: A History.* New York: New York University Press, 2005.

Cole, Nicki Lisa. "What Is a Total Institution?" ThoughtCo., updated October 24, 2019. https://www.thoughtco.com/total-institution-3026718.

Council on Biblical Manhood and Womanhood. "The Danvers Statement." CBMW.org, accessed January 1, 2024. https://cbmw.org/about/danvers -statement/.

Crouch, Andy. "The Emergent Mystique." *Christianity Today,* November 1, 2004. https://www.christianitytoday.com/ct/2004/november/12.36 .html.

Cunningham, Malorie. "'A Few Bad Apples': Phrase Describing Rotten Police Officers Used to Have Different Meaning." ABC News, June 14, 2020. https://abcnews.go.com/US/bad-apples-phrase-describing-rotten -police-officers-meaning/story?id=71201096.

Curtis, Jesse. *The Myth of Colorblind Christians: Evangelicals and White Supremacy in the Civil Rights Era.* New York: New York University Press, 2021.

Cusic, Don. *The Sound of Light: A History of Gospel and Christian Music.* Milwaukee: Hal Leonard, 2002.

Daw, Stephen. "Meet Flamy Grant, the Drag Queen Carving Out Her Own Lane in Christian Music." *Country Everywhere,* August 3, 2023. https:// www.countryeverywhere.com/news/meet-flamy-grant-the-drag-queen -carving-out-her-own-lane-in-christian-music.

Dayton, Donald W. *Rediscovering an Evangelical Heritage: A Tradition and Trajectory of Integrating Piety and Justice.* 2nd ed. With an introduction by Douglas M. Strong. Grand Rapids, MI: Baker Academic, 2014.

Dias, Elizabeth. "Top Evangelical College Group to Dismiss Employees Who Support Gay Marriage." *Time,* October 6, 2016. https://time.com /4521944/intervarsity-fellowship-gay-marriage/.

———. "Watchmen on the Wall: Pastors Prepare to Take Back America." *Time,* May 30, 2014. https://time.com/138134/watchmen-on-the-wall -pastors-prepare-to-take-back-america/.

Downen, Robert, Lise Olsen, and John Tedesco. "20 Years, 700 Victims: Southern Baptist Sexual Abuse Spreads as Leaders Resist Reforms." *Houston Chronicle,* February 10, 2019. https://www.houstonchronicle.com /news/investigations/article/Southern-Baptist-sexual-abuse-spreads-as -leaders-13588038.php.

Driscoll, Mark, and Grace Driscoll. *Real Marriage: The Truth About Sex, Friendship, and Life Together.* Nashville, TN: Thomas Nelson, 2012.

Du Mez, Kristin Kobes. *Jesus and John Wayne: How White Evangelicals Corrupted a Faith and Fractured a Nation.* New York: Liveright, 2021.

Eisenstein, Elizabeth L. *The Printing Press as an Agent of Change: Communications and Cultural Transformations in Early-Modern Europe.* Cambridge, UK: Cambridge University Press, 1982.

Enberg, Jasmine. "Global Instagram Users 2019." Insider Intelligence, December 12, 2019. https://www.insiderintelligence.com/content /global-instagram-users-2019.

"Evangelicals on Justice: Socially Speaking . . ." *Christianity Today,* December 21, 1973. https://www.christianitytoday.com/ct/1973 /december-21/evangelicals-on-justice-socially-speaking.html.

Evans, Rachel Held. "Life After Evangelicalism." RachelHeldEvans.com, November 14, 2016. https://rachelheldevans.com/blog/life-after -evangelicalism.

Fea, John. "Wheaton College Study on Race: 'We Cannot Be Healed and Cannot Be Reconciled Unless and Until We Repent.' " *Current* (blog), September 15, 2023. https://currentpub.com/2023/09/14/wheaton -college-study-on-race-we-cannot-be-healed-and-cannot-be-reconciled -unless-and-until-we-repent/.

FitzGerald, Frances. *The Evangelicals: The Struggle to Shape America.* New York: Simon & Schuster Paperbacks, 2018.

Fraser, Nancy. "Rethinking the Public Sphere: A Contribution to the Critique of Actually Existing Democracy." *Social Text* 25/26 (1990): 56–80. https://doi.org/10.2307/466240.

Frykholm, Amy Johnson. *Rapture Culture: Left Behind in Evangelical America.* Oxford, UK: Oxford University Press, 2007.

Gardner, David. "An Evangelical Icon Finds Salvation in West Hollywood." *Los Angeles Magazine,* December 8, 2021. https://lamag.com/featured /fallen-fundamentalist-rob-bell-venice-beach.

Generation Joshua. "About." GenerationJoshua.org, accessed February 12, 2024. https://generationjoshua.org/about.

Gerson, Michael. "The Last Temptation." *Atlantic,* April 2018. https:// www.theatlantic.com/magazine/archive/2018/04/the-last-temptation /554066/.

Gilbreath, Edward. "A Prophet Out of Harlem." *Christianity Today,*

September 16, 1996. https://www.christianitytoday.com/ct/1996
/september16/6ta036.html.

Gilgoff, Dan. "Exclusive: Grover Norquist Gives Religious Conservatives Tough Love." *US News & World Report*, June 11, 2009. https://www .usnews.com/news/blogs/god-and-country/2009/06/11/exclusive-grover -norquist-gives-religious-conservatives-tough-love.

Gloege, Timothy. *Guaranteed Pure: The Moody Bible Institute, Business, and the Making of Modern Evangelicalism*. Chapel Hill: University of North Carolina Press, 2015.

Goel, Vindu. "Facebook Tinkers with Users' Emotions in News Feed Experiment, Stirring Outcry." *New York Times*, June 29, 2014. https:// www.nytimes.com/2014/06/30/technology/facebook-tinkers-with-users -emotions-in-news-feed-experiment-stirring-outcry.html.

Goodman, Megan. *Abusing Religion: Literary Persecution, Sex Scandals, and American Minority Religions*. New Brunswick, NJ: Rutgers University Press, 2020.

Gospel Coalition staff. "Beautiful Union Book." The Gospel Coalition, March 1, 2023. https://www.thegospelcoalition.org/article/sex-wont-save -you/.

"Grace Semler Baldridge| 'Preacher's Kid' Going #1 on iTunes Chart." *Flaunt*, accessed January 2, 2024. https://www.flaunt.com/blog/grace -semler-baldridge.

Graham, Ruth. "At the Evangelical #MeToo Summit, Christians Grappled with Just How Deep the Church's Sexual Misconduct Problems Go." *Slate*, December 14, 2018. https://slate.com/human-interest/2018/12 /evangelical-metoo-summit-churchtoo.html.

Grant, Melissa Gira. "The Mysterious Case of the Fake Gay Marriage Website, the Real Straight Man, and the Supreme Court." *New Republic*, June 29, 2023. https://newrepublic.com/article/173987 /mysterious-case-fake-gay-marriage-website-real-straight-man -supreme-court.

Grossman, Cathy Lynn. "Salvation Is Showing Up: PW Talks to Lenny Duncan." *Publishers Weekly*, December 14, 2022. https://www .publishersweekly.com/pw/by-topic/industry-news/religion/article/91116 -tag-you-re-it-salvation-is-in-your-hands.html.

Grudem, Wayne. "If You Don't Like Either Candidate, Then Vote for Trump's Policies." Townhall.com, October 19, 2016. https://townhall

.com/columnists/waynegrudem/2016/10/19/if-you-dont-like-either
-candidate-then-vote-for-trumps-policies-n2234187.

———. "Trump's Moral Character and the Election." Townhall.com,
October 9, 2016. https://townhall.com/columnists/waynegrudem
/2016/10/09/trumps-moral-character-and-the-election-n2229846.

Haag, Matthew. "Memphis Pastor Admits 'Sexual Incident' with High
School Student 20 Years Ago." *New York Times*, January 9, 2018. https://
www.nytimes.com/2018/01/09/us/memphis-megachurch-sex-assault.html.

Hannah-Jones, Nikole, Caitlin Roper, Ilena Silverman, and Jake Silverstein,
eds. *The 1619 Project: A New Origin Story*. New York: One World, 2021.

Hemmer, Nicole. *Messengers of the Right: Conservative Media and the
Transformation of American Politics*. Philadelphia: University of
Pennsylvania Press, 2016.

Hersey, Tricia. *Rest Is Resistance: A Manifesto*. New York: Little, Brown
Spark, 2022.

Hicks, John Mark. "How Churches of Christ Responded When the 1918
'Spanish Flu' Killed Millions." *The Christian Chronicle* (blog), March 17,
2020. https://christianchronicle.org/how-churches-of-christ-responded
-when-the-1918-spanish-flu-killed-millions/.

hooks, bell. *The Will to Change: Men, Masculinity, and Love*. New York:
Washington Square Press, 2004.

Ignatiev, Noel. *Treason to Whiteness Is Loyalty to Humanity*. Edited by Geert
Dhondt, Zhandarka Kurti, and Jarrod Shanahan. New York: Verso,
2022. Kindle.

Ingersoll, Julie. *Building God's Kingdom: Inside the World of
Christian Reconstruction*. New York: Oxford University Press,
2015.

———. *Evangelical Christian Women: War Stories in the Gender Battles*. New
York: New York University Press, 2003.

Jackson, Jesse T. "Matt Chandler Responds to Deconstruction
Controversy." *Church Leaders*, December 8, 2021. https://churchleaders
.com/news/412237-matt-chandler-responds-to-deconstruction-contro
versy.html.

Jackson, Sarah J., Moya Bailey, and Brooke Foucault Welles.
#HashtagActivism: Networks of Race and Gender Justice. Cambridge, MA:
MIT Press, 2020.

Jenkins, Henry, Mizuko Ito, and danah boyd. *Participatory Culture in a*

Networked Era: A Conversation on Youth, Learning, Commerce, and Politics. Malden, MA: Polity Press, 2016.

Jennings, Willie James. *The Christian Imagination: Theology and the Origins of Race.* New Haven, CT: Yale University Press, 2011.

Jewish Telegraphic Agency. "Los Angeles Minister Urged to Apologize for Broadcasting Anti-Semitic Falsehood." *JTA Daily News Bulletin,* July 27, 1951. https://www.jta.org/archive/los-angeles-minister-urged-to -apologize-for-broadcasting-anti-semitic-falsehood.

Johnson, Andre E. "#WhiteChurchQuiet: Anything but Outrage Is Complicity." *Religion Dispatches,* September 27, 2016. https:// religiondispatches.org/whitechurchquiet-anything-but-outrage-is -complicity/.

Jones, Robert P. *White Too Long: The Legacy of White Supremacy in American Christianity.* New York: Simon & Schuster, 2020.

Jurgenson, Nathan. *The Social Photo: On Photography and Social Media.* New York: Verso, 2019.

Keller, Timothy. "Can Evangelicalism Survive Donald Trump and Roy Moore?" *New Yorker,* December 19, 2017. https://www.newyorker.com /news/news-desk/can-evangelicalism-survive-donald-trump-and-roy -moore.

Kellogg, Carolyn. "Can Bestseller Lists Be Bought?" *Los Angeles Times,* March 6, 2014. https://www.latimes.com/books/jacketcopy/la-et-jc -pastor-contract-resultsource-bestseller-lists-20140305-story.html.

———. "Pastor Mark Driscoll's Books Withdrawn from 180 Christian Stores." *Los Angeles Times,* August 13, 2014. https://www.latimes.com /books/jacketcopy/la-et-jc-pastor-mark-driscoll-books-withdrawn-from -christian-stores-20140813-story.html.

Kendi, Ibram X. *Stamped from the Beginning: The Definitive History of Racist Ideas in America.* New York: Bold Type Books, 2016.

Klein, Linda Kay. *Pure: Inside the Evangelical Movement That Shamed a Generation of Young Women and How I Broke Free.* New York: Touchstone, 2018.

Klein, Rebecca. "The Rightwing US Textbooks That Teach Slavery as 'Black Immigration.'" *Guardian,* August 12, 2021. https://www .theguardian.com/education/2021/aug/12/right-wing-textbooks-teach -slavery-black-immigration.

Kraft, Dave. "Dave Kraft, Mars Hill Church and Mark Driscoll." DaveKraft.org, March 21, 2014. https://davekraft.org/2014/03/21/dave -kraft-mars-hill-church-and-mark-driscoll/.

Kruse, Kevin. *One Nation Under God: How Corporate America Invented Christian America*. New York: Basic Books, 2015.

Laats, Adam. *Fundamentalist U: Keeping the Faith in American Higher Education*. New York: Oxford University Press, 2018.

Lakoff, George, and Mark Johnson. *Metaphors We Live By*. Chicago: University of Chicago Press, 2003.

Laughlin, Corrina. *Redeem All: How Digital Life Is Changing Evangelical Culture*. Oakland: University of California Press, 2022.

Levin, Dan. "'Everyone Was Taught to Be Accepting.' Readers Share Stories of Their Christian Educations." *New York Times*, January 29, 2019. https://www.nytimes.com/2019/01/29/us/christian-schools-students .html.

Mars Hill Church. *It's All About Jesus* (2013 Annual Report). December 18, 2013. https://web.archive.org/web/20141019041114/http://marshill.com /files/2013/12/18/MHC_Annual_Report_2013_o_web.pdf.

Martin, Michel. "Slave Bible from the 1800s Omitted Key Passages That Could Incite Rebellion." NPR, December 9, 2018. https://www.npr .org/2018/12/09/674995075/slave-bible-from-the-1800s-omitted-key -passages-that-could-incite-rebellion.

Martin, Michel, and Will Jarvis. "Far-Right Misinformation Is Thriving on Facebook. A New Study Shows Just How Much." NPR, March 6, 2021. https://www.npr.org/2021/03/06/974394783/far-right-misinformation-is -thriving-on-facebook-a-new-study-shows-just-how-much.

Martínez, Jessica, and Gregory A. Smith. "How the Faithful Voted: A Preliminary 2016 Analysis." Pew Research Center, November 9, 2016. https://www.pewresearch.org/short-reads/2016/11/09/how-the-faithful -voted-a-preliminary-2016-analysis/.

Matzko, Paul. *The Radio Right: How a Band of Broadcasters Took on the Federal Government and Built the Modern Conservative Movement*. New York: Oxford University Press, 2020.

McAlister, Melani. *The Kingdom of God Has No Borders: A Global History of American Evangelicals*. New York: Oxford University Press, 2018.

McBride, Hillary L. *The Wisdom of Your Body: Finding Healing, Wholeness, and Connection Through Embodied Living.* Grand Rapids, MI: Brazos Press, 2021.

McCrummen, Stephanie, Beth Reinhard, and Alice Crites. "Woman Says Roy Moore Initiated Sexual Encounter When She Was 14, He Was 32." *Washington Post,* November 9, 2017. https://www.washingtonpost.com /investigations/woman-says-roy-moore-initiated-sexual-encounter-when -she-was-14-he-was-32/2017/11/09/1f495878-c293-11e7-afe9-4f60b5 a6c4a0_story.html.

McCulloch, Gretchen. *Because Internet: Understanding the New Rules of Language.* New York: Riverhead, 2019.

McKinney, Larry. "The Fundamentalist Bible School as an Outgrowth of the Changing Patterns of Protestant Revivalism, 1882–1920." *Religious Education* 84 (Winter 1989–Fall 1989): 589–605.

McLuhan, Marshall, and Quentin Fiore. *The Medium Is the Massage: An Inventory of Effects.* Berkeley, CA: Gingko Press, 2001.

McNiece, R. G. "Mormonism: Its Origin, Characteristics, and Doctrines." In vol. 8 of *The Fundamentals,* 110–27. Chicago: Testimony Publishing Company, 1910. https://babel.hathitrust.org/cgi/pt?id=coo.319240923297 74&seq=644.

Medhurst, T. W. "Is Romanism Christianity?" In vol. 11 of *The Fundamentals,* 100–12. Chicago: Testimony Publishing Company, 1910. https://archive.org/details/cu31924098504685/page/n103/mode/2up.

Meis, Morgan. "Timothy Morton's Hyper-Pandemic." *New Yorker,* June 8, 2021. https://www.newyorker.com/culture/persons-of-interest/timothy -mortons-hyper-pandemic.

Merritt, Jonathan. "Mark Driscoll Accused of Plagiarism by Radio Host." *Religion News,* November 22, 2013. http://religionnews.com/2013/11/22 /mark-driscoll-accused-plagiarism-radio-host/.

Miller, Christopher. "Hundreds of Far-Right Militias Are Still Organizing, Recruiting, and Promoting Violence on Facebook." *BuzzFeed News,* March 24, 2021. https://www.buzzfeednews.com/article/christopherm51 /far-right-militias-facebook-recruiting-report.

Miller, Emily McFarlan. "Women Bloggers Spark an Evangelical 'Crisis of Authority.'" *Sojourners,* May 16, 2017. https://sojo.net/articles/women -bloggers-spark-evangelical-crisis-authority.

Molina, Brett. "Twitter Overcounted Active Users Since 2014, Shares Surge on Profit Hopes." *USA Today,* October 26, 2017. https://www

.usatoday.com/story/tech/news/2017/10/26/twitter-overcounted-active
-users-since-2014-shares-surge/801968001/.

Moody, Chris. "Mark Driscoll's Safe Space: How the Embattled Pastor
Built a New Church." *Religion Unplugged*, October 2, 2023. https://
religionunplugged.com/news/2023/6/20/mark-driscolls-safe-space-in
-arizona-2zxze.

Moore, Russell. "Donald Trump Is Not the Moral Leader We Need."
National Review, January 22, 2016. https://www.nationalreview.com
/2016/01/donald-trump-russell-moore-not-moral-leader/.

———. "My Dad Taught Me How to Love the Exvangelical." *Christianity
Today*, October 21, 2021. https://www.christianitytoday.com/ct/2021
/october-web-only/russell-moore-dad-taught-love-exvangelical-pastor
-church.html.

Morone, James A. *Hellfire Nation: The Politics of Sin in American History*.
New Haven, CT: Yale University Press, 2004.

Morton, Timothy. *Hyperobjects: Philosophy and Ecology After the End of the
World*. Minneapolis: University of Minnesota Press, 2013.

Nelson, Anne. *Shadow Network: Media, Money, and the Secret Hub of the
Radical Right*. New York: Bloomsbury, 2021.

Nhat Hanh, Thich. *Living Buddha, Living Christ*. New York: Riverhead,
2007.

Noll, Mark A. *The Scandal of the Evangelical Mind*. Grand Rapids, MI:
William B. Eerdmans, 1994.

O'Donnell, Paul. "Russell Moore to ERLC Trustees: 'They Want Me to
Live in Psychological Terror.' " *Religion News*, June 2, 2021. https://
religionnews.com/2021/06/02/russell-moore-to-erlc-trustees-they-want
-me-to-live-in-psychological-terror/.

O'Gieblyn, Meghan. *God, Human, Animal, Machine: Technology, Metaphor,
and the Search for Meaning*. New York: Anchor Books, 2022.

Onishi, Bradley. *Preparing for War: The Extremist History of White Christian
Nationalism—and What Comes Next*. Minneapolis: Broadleaf Books, 2023.

———. "Trump's New Civil Religion." *New York Times*, January 19, 2021.
https://www.nytimes.com/2021/01/19/opinion/trump-lost-cause.html.

Pashman, Manya Brachear. "Willow Creek Elders Apologize for Casting
Doubt on Women's Allegations Against Founder Hybels." *Chicago
Tribune*, May 10, 2018. https://www.chicagotribune.com/news/breaking
/ct-met-willow-creek-hybels-conduct-20180509-story.html.

Pashman, Manya Brachear, and Jeff Coen. "After Years of Inquiries, Willow Creek Pastor Denies Misconduct Allegations." *Chicago Tribune*, March 23, 2018. https://www.chicagotribune.com/news/breaking/ct-met -willow-creek-pastor-20171220-story.html.

Pew Research Center. "Growing Number of Americans Say Obama is a Muslim." PewResearch.org, August 18, 2010. https://www.pewresearch .org/religion/2010/08/18/growing-number-of-americans-say-obama-is-a -muslim/.

———. "In U.S., Decline of Christianity Continues at Rapid Pace." PewResearch.org, October 17, 2019. https://www.pewresearch.org/religion /2019/10/17/in-u-s-decline-of-christianity-continues-at-rapid-pace/.

Piper, Andrew. *Book Was There: Reading in Electronic Times*. Chicago: University of Chicago Press, 2013.

Posner, Sarah. *Unholy: Why White Evangelicals Worship at the Altar of Donald Trump*. New York: Random House, 2020.

r/Exvangelical (subreddit). Reddit. Accessed December 5, 2023. https:// www.reddit.com/r/Exvangelical/.

Reagan, Ronald. "James Robison: National Affairs Briefing." LIFE Today, filmed August 22, 1980, in Dallas. YouTube video, 12:57. https://www. youtube.com/watch?v=lH1e0xxRRbk.

Rhodan, Maya. "Christian Group That Flip-Flopped on Gay Marriage Loses Donors." *Time*, March 28, 2014. https://time.com/41918/christian -group-that-flip-flopped-on-gay-marriage-loses-donors/.

Rich, Spencer. "Carter Opens Conference on Families." *Washington Post*, June 6, 1980. https://www.washingtonpost.com/archive/politics /1980/06/06/carter-opens-conference-on-families/c9a4d872-0ea5-46e9 -ba52-0140d4ac2046/.

Riley, Naomi Schaefer. "Russell Moore: From Moral Majority to 'Prophetic Minority.'" *Wall Street Journal*, August 16, 2013. https://www.wsj.com /articles/SB10001424127887324769704579010743654111328.

Robertson, Campbell. "A Quiet Exodus: Why Black Worshipers Are Leaving White Evangelical Churches." *New York Times*, March 9, 2018. https://www.nytimes.com/2018/03/09/us/blacks-evangelical-churches .html.

Rood, Paul. "The Untold Story of *The Fundamentals*." *Biola Magazine*, September 2, 2014. https://www.biola.edu/blogs/biola-magazine/2014 /the-untold-story-of-the-fundamentals.

Sanders, Kirsten. "Wait, You're Not Deconstructing?" *Christianity Today,* February 14, 2022. https://www.christianitytoday.com/ct/2022/march /exvangelical-theology-wait-youre-not-deconstructing.html.

Sedensky, Matt. "Rush Limbaugh, 'Voice of American Conservatism,' Has Died." *Salt Lake Tribune,* February 17, 2021. https://www.sltrib.com /news/2021/02/17/rush-limbaugh-voice/.

Seidel, Andrew. "Attack on the Capitol: Evidence of the Role of White Christian Nationalism." In *Christian Nationalism and the January 6, 2021, Insurrection,* edited by Andrew Seidel and Amanda Tyler. Report from the Freedom from Religion Foundation and the Baptist Joint Committee for Religious Freedom, February 9, 2022. https://bjconline.org /jan6report/.

Seligman, Scott D. "The Franklin Prophecy." *Tablet,* August 4, 2021. https://www.tabletmag.com/sections/news/articles/franklin-prophecy -seligman.

Sharp, Isaac B. *The Other Evangelicals: A Story of Liberal, Black, Progressive, Feminist, and Gay Christians—and the Movement That Pushed Them Out.* Grand Rapids, MI: William B. Eerdmans, 2023.

Shellnutt, Kate. "Jen Hatmaker Brings Her 'Super-Christian' Family onto Reality TV." *Christianity Today,* March 19, 2014. https://www .christianitytoday.com/ct/2014/march/jen-hatmaker-brings-her-super -christian-family-onto-reality.html.

———. "Paige Patterson Fired by Southwestern, Stripped of Retirement Benefits." *Christianity Today,* May 30, 2018. https://www.christianity today.com/news/2018/may/paige-patterson-fired-southwestern-baptist -seminary-sbc.html.

Sider, Ron. "New Name, Same Mission." *Christians for Social Action,* September 13, 2020. https://christiansforsocialaction.org/resource/new -name-same-mission/.

Small, Mario Luis. *Someone to Talk To: How Networks Matter in Practice.* New York: Oxford University Press, 2019.

Smietana, Bob. "At the Other Mars Hill Church, New Co-pastors Hope to Build a Faithful Future." Religion News Service, December 16, 2021. https://religionnews.com/2021/12/16/at-the-other-mars-hill-church-a -new-co-pastors-hope-to-build-a-faithful-future/.

———. "Josh Butler Resigns as Pastor Following TGC Article Backlash." *Christianity Today,* May 4, 2023. https://www.christianitytoday.com

/news/2023/may/joshua-butler-resign-tgc-beautiful-union-redemption
-tempe-c.html.

Smietana, Bob, and Emily McFarlan Miller. "How the Battle over
Christian Nationalism Often Starts with Homeschooling," Pulitzer
Center, December 23, 2022. https://pulitzercenter.org/stories/how-battle
-over-christian-nationalism-often-starts-homeschooling.

Smith, Gregory A. "More White Americans Adopted Than Shed
Evangelical Label During Trump Presidency, Especially His Supporters."
Pew Research Center, September 15, 2021. https://www.pewresearch.org
/short-reads/2021/09/15/more-white-americans-adopted-than-shed
-evangelical-label-during-trump-presidency-especially-his-supporters/.

Smith, Warren Cole. "Mars Hill Church to Dissolve." *World*, November 3,
2014. https://wng.org/sift/mars-hill-church-to-dissolve-1617419517.

Stedman, Chris. *IRL: Finding Realness, Meaning, and Belonging in Our
Digital Lives*. Minneapolis: Broadleaf Books, 2020.

Stephens, Randall J. "The Klan, White Christianity, and the Past and
Present." Religion & Culture Forum, June 26, 2017. https://voices
.uchicago.edu/religionculture/2017/06/26/the-klan-white-christianity-and
-the-past-and-present-a-response-to-kelly-j-baker-by-randall-j-stephens/.

Stewart, Katherine. *The Power Worshippers: Inside the Dangerous Rise of
Religious Nationalism*. New York: Bloomsbury, 2022.

Stowe, David W. *No Sympathy for the Devil: Christian Pop Music and the
Transformation of American Evangelicalism*. Chapel Hill: University of
North Carolina Press, 2011.

Strand, Sophie. *The Flowering Wand: Rewilding the Sacred Masculine*.
Rochester, VT: Inner Traditions, 2022.

Stroop, Chrissy. "I Created the Hashtag #EmptythePews Because It's Time
for Evangelicals to Walk Out of Toxic Churches." Religion Dispatches,
August 17, 2017. https://religiondispatches.org/i-created-the-hashtag
-emptythepews-because-its-time-for-evangelicals-to-walk-out-of-toxic
-churches/.

———. "If you left Evangelicalism over bigotry and intolerance or this
election specifically, please share your story w/ the hashtag
#EmptyThePews." Tweet (@C_Stroop). Twitter, August 16, 2017. https://
twitter.com/C_Stroop/status/897967493800656896.

———. "Setting the Record Straight on #ExposeChristianSchools: Why
the Media Must Not Cede Coverage of Ex-Evangelicals to the Right."

Not Your Mission Field (blog), February 4, 2019. https://cstroop.com
/2019/02/04/setting-the-record-straight-on-exposechristianschools
-why-the-media-must-not-cede-coverage-of-ex-evangelicals-to
-the-right/.

Sutton, Matthew Avery. *American Apocalypse: A History of Modern Evangelicalism.* Cambridge, MA: Belknap Press, 2017.

———. "Preparing for Doomsday." In *Faith in the New Millennium: The Future of Religion and American Politics,* edited by Matthew Avery Sutton and Darren Dochuk. New York: Oxford University Press, 2015.

Swartz, Angela. "Menlo Church Leadership Acknowledges Abuse from Decades Ago." *Palo Alto Online,* March 29, 2023. https://paloaltoonline
.com/news/2023/03/29/menlo-church-leadership-acknowledges-abuse
-going-back-decades.

Táíwò, Olúfẹ́mi O. *Elite Capture: How the Powerful Took Over Identity Politics (and Everything Else).* Chicago: Haymarket Books, 2022.

Tarnoff, Ben. *Internet for the People: The Fight for Our Digital Future.* New York: Verso, 2022. Kindle.

Throckmorton, Warren. "On The Allegations of Plagiarism Against Mark Driscoll." Patheos, December 2, 2013. https://web.archive.org
/web/20141106132646/http://www.patheos.com/blogs/warrenthrock
morton/2013/12/02/on-the-allegations-of-plagiarism-against-mark
-driscoll/.

Tillich, Paul. *Systematic Theology.* Vol. 1, *Reason and Revelation, Being and God.* Chicago: University of Chicago Press, 1973.

Tisby, Jemar. "Leave LOUD: Jemar Tisby's Story." *Footnotes by Jemar Tisby* (blog), March 8, 2021. https://jemartisby.substack.com/p/leave-loud
-jemar-tisbys-story.

Tufekci, Zeynep. "YouTube, the Great Radicalizer." *New York Times,* March 10, 2018. https://www.nytimes.com/2018/03/10/opinion/sunday
/youtube-politics-radical.html.

Vaca, Daniel. *Evangelicals Incorporated: Books and the Business of Religion in America.* Cambridge, MA: Harvard University Press, 2019.

Vallor, Shannon. *Technology and the Virtues: A Philosophical Guide to a Future Worth Wanting.* New York: Oxford University Press, 2018.

Warner, Michael. *Publics and Counterpublics.* New York: Zone Books, 2002.

Warren, Tish Harrison. "The Church Needs Reformation, Not Deconstruction." *Christianity Today,* October 19, 2021..https://www

.christianitytoday.com/ct/2021/november/exvangelical-warren-guide-to
-deconstruction-church.html.

Wax, Trevin. "World Vision and Why We Grieve for the Children." The
Gospel Coalition, March 25, 2014. https://www.thegospelcoalition.org
/blogs/trevin-wax/grieving-for-the-children/.

Weaver, David, Lars Willnat, and G. Cleveland Wilhoit. "The American
Journalist in the Digital Age: Another Look at U.S. News People."
Journalism & Mass Communication Quarterly 96, no. 1 (July 4, 2018).
https://journals.sagepub.com/doi/10.1177/1077699018778242.

Wellman, Kathleen. *Hijacking History: How the Christian Right Teaches
History and Why It Matters*. New York: Oxford University Press, 2021.

Wheaton Archives and Special Collections. "'World Evangelism: Why?
How? Who?' A Backward Look at Urbana '70." *From the Vault* (blog),
December 1, 2020. https://fromthevault.wheaton.edu/2020/12/01
/world-evangelism-why-how-who-a-backward-look-at-urbana-70/.

Wheaton College Board of Trustees. "Historical Review Task Force Final
Report." September 14, 2023. https://www.wheaton.edu/historical
-review-task-force-final-report/.

Wingfield, Mark. "Russell Moore Leaves ERLC for *Christianity Today*,
Highlighting the New Schism Within SBC." *Baptist News Global*, May 19,
2021. https://baptistnews.com/article/russell-moore-leaves-erlc-for
-christianity-today-highlighting-the-new-schism-within-sbc/.

Worthen, Molly. *Apostles of Reason: The Crisis of Authority in American
Evangelicalism*. New York: Oxford University Press, 2014.

WTHR-TV, Channel 13. "Indiana's Corporate Leaders Call for Action on
RFRA." WTHR.com, March 30, 2015. https://web.archive.org/web
/20150331012131/http://www.wthr.com/story/28653210/indianas
-corporate-leaders-call-for-action-on-rfra.

Wu, Tim. *The Master Switch: The Rise and Fall of Information Empires*. New
York: Vintage Books, 2011.

INDEX

ABOUT THE AUTHOR

Blake Chastain is the host of the podcast *Exvangelical*, writer of the newsletter *The Post-Evangelical Post*, and cofounder of the Irreverent Media Group, a podcast collective and content network that highlights diverse voices doing work for ex- and postevangelical audiences. In 2016, he started the hashtag #Exvangelical, coining what would become a common term for a person who has left evangelical Christianity. Chastain's work and advocacy have been featured in publications such as *The New York Times, Newsweek, VICE,* and *The New Republic.* He lives in Illinois with his wife and daughter.